JAPANESE
FLOWER ARRANGEMENT

JAPANESE FLOWER ARRANGEMENT

A
Complete
Primer

by Ellen G. Allen

CHARLES E. TUTTLE COMPANY

Rutland, Vermont & Tokyo Japan

Representatives
Continental Europe. BOXERBOOKS, INC., Zurich
British Isles: PRENTICE-HALL INTERNATIONAL, INC., London
Australasia: PAUL FLESCH & Co., PTY. LTD., Melbourne
Canada: M. G. HURTIG, LTD., Edmonton

*Published by the Charles E. Tuttle Company, Inc.,
of Rutland, Vermont & Tokyo, Japan
with editorial offices at
Suido 1-chome, 2-6, Bunkyo-ku, Tokyo, Japan*

*Copyright in Japan, 1962, by
Charles E. Tuttle Co., Inc.*

Library of Congress Catalog Card No. 62-21731

International Standard Book No. 0-8048-0293-9

*1st edition published 1952 by National Council Books, Inc., Philadelphia
First Tuttle edition, 1963
Tenth printing, 1971*

PRINTED IN JAPAN

This book is humbly dedicated to
The Creator
in thanksgiving for
"the wonderful works of God." *Acts* II, 2

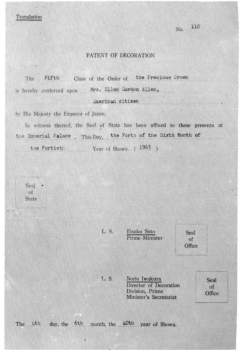

Translation

No. 110

PATENT OF DECORATION

The   Fifth   Class of the Order of   the Precious Crown
is hereby conferred upon   Mrs. Ellen Gordon Allen,
American citizen

by His Majesty the Emperor of Japan.

In witness thereof, the Seal of State has been affixed to these presents at
the Imperial Palace . This Day, the Forth of the Sixth Month of
the Fortieth   Year of Showa. (1965)

Seal
of
State

L. S.   Eisaku Sato
Prime-Minister

Seal
of
Office

J. S.   Norio Iwakura
Director of Decoration
Division, Prime
Minister's Secretariat

Seal
of
Office

The 4th day, the 6th month, the 40th year of Showa.

The citation which accompanied the Medal of the Precious Crown Fifth Order which Ellen Gordon Allen was awarded for her work as Founder of Ikebana International.

Mrs. Allen first studied Japanese flower arrangement, and earned her teacher's certificate, when her husband was Assistant Division Commander of the First Cavalry Division in Korea. It was only when she taught Japanese flower arrangement to foreign friends in Rome that she realized the international appeal of this art, and from this idea grew Ikebana International, which now has more than 5,000 members in 87 chapters all over the world.

CONTENTS

FOREWORD

It is with great pleasure that I learn that the unique art of Japanese Flower Arrangement has been introduced and warmly received in the United States.

In Mrs. Ellen G. Allen is found a most suitable interpreter of flower arrangement to the American public. While in Japan, Mrs. Allen studied with diligence and enthusiasm the principles of both the classic and the modern schools.

Unfortunately, some students of flower arrangement believe that once they have studied but one out of all the various schools, they have mastered all the secrets of Japanese Flower Arrangement. In contrast, the thorough training which Mrs. Allen has received leads me to lend my whole-hearted endorsement to this book with its wide and objective treatment of the subject matter.

It was my pride and pleasure to have taught Mrs. Allen and to have awarded her the diploma of my school, thus making her the first qualified teacher of the Ohara School in the United States since I became Founder and Headmaster.

I congratulate Mrs. Allen on her success in compiling this excellent outline of Japanese Flower Arrangement in general. I particularly recommend it to those in America who wish to know the correct fundam ntals of the Ohara School.

Kobe, Japan

February 14, 1955

Houn Ohara
Founder of
the Ohara School
of Japanese
Flower
Arrangement

8

INTRODUCTION

There is something of the artist in each of us. Some of us find expression in painting, poetry or sculpture, some in landscape gardening. With talent, and facility, expression in these art forms is satisfying. And this is true also of flower arranging, an ancient art that can express a thought or mood and in a sense combine the expressiveness of several other media. Yet special talent for flower arranging is not essential. The "feeling" for it is engendered by the practice of it.

Japanese Flower Arrangement at first seems very foreign, particularly to those who have never visited Japan. Living outside Japan where we are not exposed daily to its beauty and fascination, it is impossible to automatically appreciate it. Japanese Flower Arrangement is a cultivated taste.

Before commencing the lessons, let us examine the background of our subject. Then you will have a broader knowledge of the art and a clearer picture of the important position flower arrangement occupies in the life of the Japanese people.

Since Japanese Flower Arrangement is a form of art, it is based on certain principles which have been crystallized into rules and techniques. Perhaps the most difficult thing to understand in the beginning is how free-growing flowers may be arranged according to age-old precepts and still remain essentially free. Actually the principles of design which form the basis of this art are evident in all natural growth. They are not arbitrary rules but principles revealed by nature herself. The techniques ultimately developed were tailored to fit the material to be arranged as readily as a proper-sized glove fits the hand. The truth of this will be more easily understood as you progress in Japanese Flower Arrangement.

SHOWS AND EXHIBITIONS

Throughout the year in Japan numerous flower arrangement shows and exhibitions are held in public buildings and department stores—wherever ample space is available to accommodate the large crowds who come to admire them. Unlike our flower shows, niches are not used. The displays are set out on broad counters or tiers against a background of plain wall. The arrangements vary in size from small displays to those which reach the ceiling or cover an entire wall. There is one continuous unfolding of beauty with creative conceptions of breath-taking magnificence.

The exhibitions are not competitive. They are sponsored by the great masters and teachers and may be compared to an artist's one-man show in this country.

SCHOOLS OF FLOWER ARRANGEMENT

Japanese men and women of all backgrounds and professions attend flower arrangement schools. Training in the art is practically a requirement—if not obligatory—and often employers make it possible for their employees to attend classes. It is rare to encounter a Japanese without some knowledge of arrangement and it is unusual to find a house or a shop, humble or luxurious, without its flower arrangement.

There are hundreds of excellent flower arrangement schools in Japan, some modern, others conservative. Each school reflects the individuality, the artistic beliefs and trends of its master. Though all teach the fundamentals in the elementary phase of the art, their methods differ as to rules, techniques and nomenclature.

Loyalty to the headmaster and his school is very strong, and so there is rivalry. Consequently, the art is never dormant. Indeed this intense spirit of competition has resulted in continual progress.

Unless you journey to Japan to study Japanese Flower Arrangement in a definite school, the selection of your school may be a matter of chance or convenience. Groups often organize their own small classes with sessions being held in the various homes. If the group is larger, requiring more space, the lessons may take place in a club or large building. The teacher is selected usually because she comes to the neighborhood, irrespective of the school she represents.

For the ambitious student it is wise to study the teachings of various flower arrangement schools to obtain a more complete understanding of the art.

JAPANESE FLOWER SHOPS

Exquisite little flower shops are sprinkled all over Japan, each filled to overflowing with color and beauty. A remarkable variety of material is always on display. To aid in the selection, flowers and branches are placed loosely in bamboo vases. Almost every piece of plant material is sold separately, only a few being offered in bunches. You first choose a branch, then the flowers, always keeping in mind the suitability of the material to be combined.

THE TOKONOMA

The Tokonoma is an alcove, and is the most important feature in a Japanese home. It looks like an oversized bookcase without shelves, and usually measures about five feet high, six feet wide, and three feet deep, the base being about six inches above the floor. As a rule, the Tokonoma faces the garden. Its origin is vague, but it is probable that centuries ago it was used for the household altar or as a shrine.

Hanging against the back wall is a beautiful Kakemono, a scenic or floral scroll. Sometimes the scroll features the wise sayings of Buddha and his disciples, written, of course, in Chinese characters. Placed on one side of the Tokonoma is the flower arrangement. Opposite, on the other side, is an incense burner or small objet d'art.

Since the flower arrangement is placed so that it is viewed only from the front and sides it is natural for Japanese arrangements to have one unfinished or blank side. In our Western homes, however, where flower arrangements are used throughout the house, it is often necessary to complete the arrangement on all sides. This may easily be done by adding a few small shrub branches, flowers or leaves.

Etiquette of Admiring a Japanese Flower Arrangement

Etiquette requires that a guest, upon entering the Japanese home, admire the flower arrangement which has been made by the hostess for his enjoyment. This is the proper way to proceed; Approach to within three feet of the Tokonoma, look first at the dominant stem, then at the secondary stem and finally at the third stem. After viewing the arrangement, study the container or vase. This custom of admiring arrangements and commenting favorably on them is good. We never fail to admire exquisite works of art, and, when a flower arrangement falls within that category, it seems appropriate to speak of its beauty.

SYMBOLISM IN GENERAL

A knowledge of the symbolism which is an integral part of Japanese Flower Arrangement is not essential for the beginner. However, it is well to possess some information so that you will have a more complete background of the art. This knowledge will also serve to lessen the mystery which symbolism has focused on the art, thus producing an unnecessary hindrance to its study in our country.

Symbolism in Japanese Flower Arrangement attributes to trees, shrubs, flowers, and certain combinations of these, descriptive adjectives which are actual characteristics of the plant material. Thus, the pine, which is strong and sturdy, represents these traits of human character. The bamboo, also strong and enduring, stands for faithfulness. The peach, with its delicate blossoms, denotes feminine qualities of mildness and gentleness which make for a happy marriage. Certain types of iris leaves, because of their swordlike appearance, represent masculine traits of boldness and power. When used together at New Year's, pine and bamboo symbolize propriety, in addition to the individual characteristics, and with plum, good fortune. Many other appropriate combinations are made up for special occasions.

In addition, symbolism may also be present in additional features of a composition. In a summer flower arrangement a broad expanse of water is visible in the container, thus creating a cool effect so desirable during the warm months. Fall arrangements may include small dried leaves, forecasting the approach of winter.

FURYU (*Flowing Wind*)

This famous word is difficult to understand in its free interpretation, but when applied to flower arrangement it is easy to appreciate. It means a specific love of nature with all its imperfections, and a strong appreciation of their use and the place they fill. To be specific, it means the exact opposite of elaborate.

The Japanese will prefer a gnarled or moss-covered branch to a more perfect specimen. A few dead leaves, torn or ragged, will be "furyu" or appropriate in a flower arrangement. When a flower arrangement combines such imperfections with perfect material, the Japanese believe that it reproduces a more faithful reflection of nature in its entirety—it is "furyu." The arrangement may be said to have a feeling of serene maturity.

Japanese Flower Arrangement is truly a creative art. All of the long-established patterns, diagrams and rules are for instruction only and not intended to restrict. Let the principles guide you toward skill in this art. As you perfect your techniques and increase your knowledge, you will create many beautiful arrangements.

Moribana Style Form A with three pink roses combined with pittosporum leaves.

Heika Style Form A combining magnolia branches and chrysanthemums in a blue vase.

Part I

BASIC INFORMATION and EQUIPMENT
Moribana and Heika Styles

Before you begin these elementary lessons in Japanese Flower Arrangement, it is necessary for you to become familiar with the terminology and basic mechanics of arrangement. Ikebana, which is the Japanese word for flower arrangement, cannot be translated into one English word. Our interpretation, Japanese Flower Arrangement, is therefore misleading since it only includes flowers. Ikebana has other meanings, and includes everything that grows— flowers, shrubs, tree branches, even lifeless branches, driftwood, rocks and seashells. Any or all of these materials may form a part of a Japanese Flower Arrangement.

Ikebana also refers to flowers arranged according to rule so that they appear as living or growing flowers. Mr. Koshi Tsujii, one of the great masters under whom I studied, aptly expressed it thus: "The flower-vessel represents the good earth, and we should arrange the flowers to make them appear as if they had sprung from the earth and were still growing."

If these interpretations of Ikebana are borne in mind, they will not only give you a fuller understanding of the art in its entirety, but also a clearer and more correct approach to it. Moribana and Heika (Nagiere) are two fundamental styles taught in Japan today. They are ideally suited to our Western homes.

MORIBANA STYLE

The Moribana Style, literally translated as "piled-up or clustered flowers," uses the low open-mouth bowl or horizontal container. (The Japanese name for this is Suiban, meaning basin.) The best free translation of the word Moribana seems to be "flowers arranged in a horizontal container or bowl in which is placed a holder set in a fixed position."

HEIKA (Nagiere) STYLE

The Heika Style, literally translated as "thrown in," uses a perpendicular vase. Heika and Nagiere have the same meaning, when used in connection with flower arrangement. (Heika means in this instance "vase" and Nagiere means "thrown-in flowers.") For the lessons the word Heika will be used. No metal holder is employed in this style which is informal and natural. Although correct, the literal translation is somewhat misleading, since the flowers, branches or shrubs which appear to be "thrown-in" the vase are actually placed with the greatest care, and according to rules for this type of arrangement.

Additional styles developed from these two will be presented in the lessons which follow. Although a Form D is included by the Ohara School for a Moribana Style, it will not be developed in this Primer since it is not practical for Western homes. Instead, we will designate the Water-Reflecting Style as Form D, Natural Scenery as Form E and the lesson on the Iris Arrangement as Form F—all Moribana arrangements. In the Heika arrangements, Form D will be devoted to the "Cascade."

PRINCIPAL STEMS AND FILLERS

Since Japanese Flower Arrangement is basically concerned with the three principal flowers or stems, regardless of style or form used, it is up to the beginner to learn their correct positions. Additional flowers may be added to each arrangement, but *the correct positions of the principal stems are of utmost importance.*

These three principal stems are the Subject Stem, the Secondary Stem, and the Object Stem and are always so designated. Other materials will be called fillers. According to the Ohara School, intermediaries is the official name for fillers. In a number of other schools they are referred to as harmonizers, auxiliaries or supports. I prefer the term fillers. In the diagrams, solid black lines denote principal stems, dotted lines, the fillers.

COMBINATIONS OF MATERIALS

In connection with the Moribana and Heika styles, the most difficult problem confronting the American arranger—and this frequently proves a stumbling block for beginners—is the combination of materials that may be used. If you remember the meaning of Ikebana as related to the materials that may be used, it will be easier. For instance, one arrangement may have:

1. A flower or flowers for the Subject and Secondary stems, and a small shrub or branch for the Object Stem.
2. A branch or shrub for the Subject and Secondary stems, with a flower or flowers for the Object Stem.
3. A flower or flowers for the Subject Stem, and shrubs or branches for the Secondary and Object stems.

As you can see, there are many variations. All materials, however, are cut according to rule, and the same materials used for principal stems may be repeated as fillers.

Regardless of the combinations you select, *do not use more than three different materials in any one arrangement.* This is a tradition rather than a rule, since there seems to be nothing written about it. The idea is to prevent the arrangement from becoming fancy and elaborate, the antithesis of a pure Japanese Flower Arrangement.

HOLDERS

Two types of holders—open and needle-point—are used in the Moribana-Style lessons. The Japanese name for the open-type holder is Shippo, meaning "treasury opening." The three main divisions will be called *sections;* the smaller openings, *partitions.*

The Japanese refer to the needle-point holder as Kensan, meaning "needle mountain." This is commonly used throughout the United States. We will think of it as divided into four numbered parts—1, 2, 3 and 4. In explaining the use of the needle-point holder, these numbered divisions are important.

STEM LENGTHS

Before attempting the first lesson, be sure you have a firm grasp of the rules which follow. These are basic to all Japanese flower arrangements. Measurement rules for lengths of principal stems and fillers have been developed for both the Moribana and Heika styles. These rules will be exactly followed in the Primer:

Rule I (Moribana Style):

> Measure the Subject Stem the length of the container plus the depth.
> Measure the Secondary Stem ⅔ of the Subject Stem.
> Measure the Object Stem ½ the length of Subject Stem.

For example, if a round container is used, measure the diameter of the container, then add depth in inches for the Subject Stem. Thus, if the container is 10 inches in diameter and 2 inches deep, the Subject Stem should measure 12 inches. The Secondary Stem measures ⅔ of the Subject Stem, so if the Subject Stem measures 12 inches, the Secondary Stem should be 8 inches. The Object Stem measures ½ the length of the Subject Stem, making the Object Stem 6 inches long if a 12-inch Subject Stem is used. The same rules for length apply when oblong or rectangular containers are used.

Rule II (Moribana Style):

> Measure the Subject Stem 1½ times the length of the container.
> Measure the Secondary Stem ⅔ of the Subject Stem.
> Measure the Object Stem ½ of the Subject Stem.

Thus, if a container 10 inches long is used, the Subject Stem should measure 15 inches. The Secondary Stem is ⅔ the length of the Subject Stem, or, in this case, 10 inches. The Object Stem is ½ the length of the Subject Stem, or, in this case, 7½ inches.

Sometimes, depending upon the container and the materials used, Rule II is modified and depth of container is included in measuring the length of the three principal stems. Thus, for the Subject Stem the length would be 1½ times the length of the container plus the depth. If the container is 10 inches long and 2 inches deep, the Subject Stem would be 17 inches and the Secondary and Object stems would maintain the same relationship to the Subject Stem as in Rule I.

Rule III (Heika Style):

> Measure the Subject Stem 1½ times the height of the vase.
> Measure the Secondary Stem ⅔ of Subject Stem.
> Measure the Object Stem ½ of Subject Stem.

With this rule, if the vase is 10 inches high, the Subject Stem measures 15 inches. The Secondary Stem is ⅔ the length of the Subject Stem of 10 inches. The Object Stem is ½ the length of the Subject Stem or 7½ inches.

(All measurements are from *rim* of vase, consequently before cutting stems, be sure to allow sufficient additional length of stem to reach the water in the vase.)

These three basic rules of measurement are rarely varied. However, it should be noted that occasionally the opening of the vase is measured as well as the height. This adds additional length to the Subject Stem and a corresponding length to the other stems. This measurement is particularly desirable when a very long branch is to be arranged and it would impair the beauty of its line to cut it. On the other hand, it may be necessary to adjust the length of the Subject Stem if the flower or branch to be used is not long enough. After selecting a Subject Stem which comes closest to the proper length, measure Secondary and Object Stems accordingly.

This problem of a too-short Subject Stem occurred in preparing the arrangement for Lesson 2. To offset this shorter measurement, the holder was placed close to the front of the container to give an illusion of greater length. In Lesson 3, the rose stems selected were not long enough so the holder was placed just off center, thus giving the appearance of a longer stem.

It is practically impossible to add length to stems of flowers, shrubs and branches used in Moribana-Style arrangements, but in the Heika Style stems may easily be made longer by utilizing any of the artificial methods presented in Lesson 7, and the measurement for the Heika arrangements may be followed accurately. Common sense will guide you when problems of stem length arise. Remember as you progress that a flower arrangement is supposed to look beautiful as well as to follow the rules.

FILLER LENGTHS

No foolproof measurement rule can be laid down for fillers since flowers, branches, shrubs and other materials vary widely in shape and also in number of leaves on stems. These factors influence the use of fillers. To help you, a basic guide has been devised for fillers which will apply to all arrangements depicted in this Primer.

Rule IV (Fillers):

Measure Filler No. 1—$\frac{2}{3}$ the length of Secondary Stem.
Measure Filler No. 2—$\frac{1}{2}$ the length of Filler No. 1.
Measure Filler No. 3—either shorter or longer than Filler No. 2, depending upon the length best suited to the completed arrangement.

The *position* of fillers is left to your discretion. They are intended to make the completed arrangement beautiful, filled out and finished in appearance. Good taste and judgment are the best guides.

Most of the illustrations are of arrangements of one kind of material, usually of flowers sold by local florists or frequently grown in gardens, and so easy to obtain. Some arrangements, however, while following identical basic principles, include a variety of materials. These are more typically Japanese and should inspire you to greater effort. However, lack of variety in plant material need never discourage you since the Japanese consider it a challenge to arrange simple material well.

FREE-STYLE ARRANGEMENTS

A few pictures of free-style or advanced Japanese Flower Arrangement have been included in this book to train you for advanced work. Since I am stressing as strongly as possible the design in Japanese Flower Arrangement and the various combinations of materials which may be used, these additional photographs will show what can be accomplished once preliminary instructions have been mastered. Free-style arrangements will develop automatically as a result of training plus practice. The aim and goal of all instruction in Japanese Flower Arrangement is free-style or creative work. When this is reached, both teacher and student reap their rewards.

A definite design is strongly evident in all the illustrations, whether the examples are of fundamental, advanced or free-style arrangements. As Japanese Flower Arrangement is always concerned with line, no matter what the materials, a quotation from *Design in Flower Arrangement* by the late John Taylor Arms, distinguished artist and author, is appropriate here: "Take an arrangement which has only beautiful color, reduce it to black and white and you have nothing but unrelated mass; take another which is well designed, eliminate the color and you have a fine design .... It is not the materials you have selected that matter, but the way in which you put them together; design first, last and always."

Before you start the first lesson, let me assure you that the fundamentals of Japanese Flower Arrangement are easy to learn. At first they seem contrary to our way of thinking, but the basic concepts are easy when understood. Many students have remarked, "How sensible to arrange flowers according to their characteristics!" Once this concept is accepted, Japanese Flower Arrangement is the reward. Therefore be patient, stick to it, work hard and a new field of beauty will unfold under your accomplished hands and before your delighted eyes.

Equipment

The arrangements in this Primer will require only a few items, but these are essential and are principally for use in the Moribana and Heika styles:

- Horizontal container or low bowl
- Perpendicular container or vase, preferably tall, of round, tubelike or cylindrical shape
- Holders, both metal open-type and needle-point
- Clippers
- Wire and string
- Basket or tin box

Moribana Low Bowl

CONTAINERS

In flower arranging the term "container" is often used. It applies to two types; the horizontal, open-mouthed low bowl, and the perpendicular or upright container, referred to from now on as a vase.

Since both the low bowl and the vase may be of any size, shape, material and color, the important factor is the adaptability of the container to its use in the arrangements. Beginners should have one medium-sized low bowl and one medium-sized vase. For variety, I recommend a low white bowl and a green, yellow or gray vase, since these colors blend more successfully with flowers. The Japanese seem to prefer the darker shades because they are less conspicuous and suggest the "good earth" with the flowers growing from it. When purchasing containers, choose one with sides not more than two and one-half to three inches high and a vase with lip or rim.

Heika Vase

HOLDERS

The metal open-type holder or frog is most important in Japanese flower arrangements. It is a molded form, made of lead, with open sections designed to hold stems securely in position.

The Ohara School, like many other Japanese schools prefers this open-type to the common pin-type or needle-point holder popular in this country. Its advantage is that it is so designed that main flower stems, branch, or fillers remain firm where placed since stems can be cut to fit sections of the holder. Also, stems are always submerged because the base of this type holder is also open and rests directly on the bottom of the container. The needle-point holder is not open on the bottom and frequently, if a container is shallow, stems are held above the water level.

Besides preventing stems and fillers from wobbling or falling, once they have been correctly cut and placed in proper position, the open-type holder makes it possible to

Metal Holder

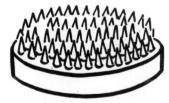

Needle-Point Holder

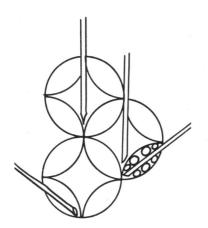

Method of wedging
and cutting stems
for holder.

Clippers

secure a flower stem that is too small to fit tightly in an opening. It can be securely wedged with small sticks or cuttings of leftover material. The open-type holder is also very practical for use with driftwood. The wood is easily whittled down to fit in one section of the holder, then flowers or foliage are placed in the other sections to complete the arrangement.

The needle-point holder is a heavy, round or oblong metal block from which sharp needlelike points extend. The flower stems are speared on the needles to hold them in proper positions. This type of holder is practical when thick, soft stems are arranged, but it is not easy to use with heavy branches or shrubs.

When the needle-point holder is used, cut heavy stems on an angle so that they fit into the holder without breaking the points. If the stems are not cut in this manner, the points will bend. Another method is to cut the stem end crosswise with clippers to soften it. Then press down on stem, bending it in whatever direction the style of arrangement requires.

CLIPPERS

The clippers you use may be either ordinary garden shears, strong, sharp scissors or the Japanese type which is designed for flower arranging. Obtain the Japanese type of clippers, if possible.

WIRE AND STRING

Wire and string are used to elongate stems. Often a stick may be added to a stem so that it is literally grafted. Wire is preferred for this Artificial Method as described in Lesson 7, but string may be used quite satisfactorily. (The Japanese use wet straw for this purpose.)

BASKET OR TIN BOX

Use a basket or tin box for storage of holders, shears, wire, string, extra sticks and various other equipment. In this way you have everything conveniently available in one place.

Moribana Style Form A using peach-colored gladioli.

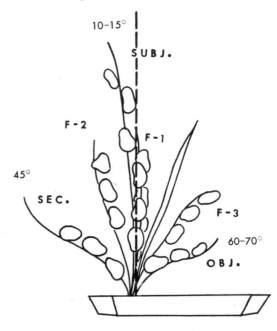

LESSON 1

MORIBANA FORM A
(UPRIGHT STYLE)

The flowers chosen for this first lesson are six gladioli. Their growing characteristic is strongly upright and so they are perfect for the Moribana Form A arrangement. Study carefully the picture on the opposite page and the sketch below it. They illustrate the position of each stem and filler to assist you in preparing this arrangement. Diagrams which accompany the major steps also clearly illustrate the appearance of the flower arrangement as it progresses toward completion.

For this lesson I have selected a low bowl, measuring 10 inches in length, and 2 inches in depth. Always follow the basic measurement rule, according to the dimensions of the container you use. Also at hand are an open-type holder, string and clippers.

Prepare your material carefully, cutting away all dead and discolored leaves or faded blossoms and other superfluous material. When using gladioli, you may want to break off the weak tips of the flower stalk, especially if they are very long and ungainly. Measure your material after the flower tips are broken off. As each flower is prepared, replace in water to preserve its freshness for the finished arrangement.

Select the finest blossom, having the longest and strongest stem. Measure the length of your container plus the depth according to Rule I, Moribana Style, and cut flower stem at this point—12 inches for the bowl I have used. This is the Subject Stem.

Select the next stem and cut it according to the basic measurement rule which is two-thirds the length of the Subject Stem—or 8 inches in this case. This is the Secondary Stem.

Select the third stem, cut it one-half the length of the Subject Stem—6 inches—and replace in water. This is the Object Stem.

The three remaining flowers are used as fillers. Cut filler 1 two-thirds length of the Secondary Stem. Cut filler 2 one-half length of Secondary Stem. Filler 3 is held in reserve until arrangement nears completion when it may be used to fill in any gap in the arrangement. The gladioli leaves may also be used in the arrangement.

In Japan, flowers are sold singly and six flowers would not be used in an arrangement. Instead, an uneven number would be arranged because the Japanese consider the uneven number more artistic and also odd numbers indicate good-luck. However, in other countries it is necessary to abide by the prevailing selling methods so in these lessons an even number of flowers or branches will frequently be used.

Place the open-type holder to the left rear in container as in the form of an L. With preliminary preparations and cutting of stems completed, we are now ready to arrange the flowers.

In this and all following diagrams, degrees of angles of the three principal stems made by intersection of Imaginary Vertical Line (heavy broken line) are correct degrees of these angles for basic Moribana styles.

Step 1. Place Subject Stem in an upright position in rear partition of back section of the holder. Make certain that the stem is secure. Wedge it with short sticks or pieces of stem if necessary.

Step 2. Place Secondary Stem in partition of second section, slanting the flower at an angle of about 45 degrees to the left.

Step 3. Place Object Stem securely in third section of holder at about an angle of 60 degrees from vertical. Slant stem to right front with blossom lower than Secondary Stem. Turn the Secondary and Object stems slightly to center so that the blossoms will show. Correct placement of these three principal stems is of paramount importance since they form the design and framework for the completed arrangement.

Step 4. Place filler No. 1 adjacent to Subject Stem to strengthen upright line. Place filler No. 2 in rear section, slanting it to the left to complement the Secondary Stem. Place filler No. 3 to right of Subject Stem, slanting it to the right or wherever a bare spot needs to be filled in. The length of filler No. 3 can be either longer or shorter than filler No. 1, depending upon where it is used.

Place longest leaves of gladioli in back of flower stems, using the shorter leaves in the center of your arrangement. It may be necessary to remove one of the principal stems or a filler to fit in the leaves. If so, remove stems and supporting wedges, fit in leaves and then replace stems firmly in proper positions.

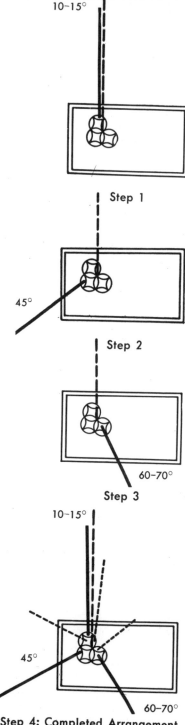

10–15°

Step 1

45°

Step 2

60–70°

Step 3

10–15°

45°

60–70°

Step 4: Completed Arrangement

Finally, cover the holder with small leaves, flowers or rocks. Covering the holder is comparatively new in Japanese Flower Arrangement and is the result of Western influence. In viewing the arrangement in a Tokonoma, the Japanese are in the usual ceremonial kneeling position, and about three feet from the arrangement, so the holder is not easily seen. In Western homes, however, the problem is different and the holders are in constant view. When covering the holders, be careful not to interfere with the lines of the arrangement or draw undue attention to the base of your flower arrangement.

USE OF NEEDLE-POINT HOLDER

With the flowers already prepared and measured for proper length, place the needle-point holder in position in left rear of your container. Divide the needle-point holder hypothetically into four numbered divisions as shown in the sketch below. Then proceed as follows:

Step 1. Place Subject Stem in division 1 in an upright position.

Step 2. Place Secondary Stem in division 2, slanting it to the left front.

Step 3. Place Object Stem in division 4, slanting it to the right front.

Step 4. Place filler No. 1 in upright position to cover Subject Stem. Place filler No. 2 between Subject and Secondary stems, slanting slightly to the left. Place filler No. 3 between Subject and Object stems, slanting slightly to the right. Use the leaves to fill out arrangement.

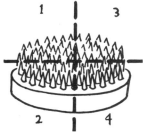

Numbered divisions of
needle-point holder

Moribana Style Form A
using Liatris branches with
loquat.

Moribana Style Form B combining yellow chrysanthemums with pompoms.

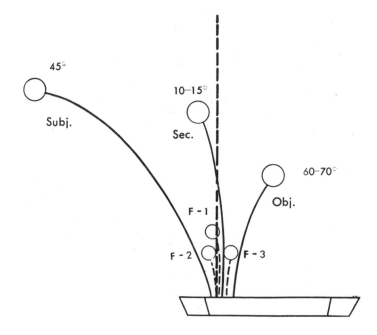

LESSON 2

MORIBANA FORM B
(SLANTING FORWARD STYLE)

The second basic form in the Moribana-Style arrangement differs fundamentally from Form A in two respects. The holder is now placed off center to the front and on the left side of the container. Notice that the holder is also turned in a slightly different position. Secondly, the slant or curve of the Subject Stem is the major point of interest.

Three medium-sized chrysanthemums and a few pompoms have been chosen for this arrangement. When using chrysanthemums you should break the stems instead of cutting them, and when placing the flowers in an arrangement always have the blossom facing upwards. Prepare the flowers by removing dead and discolored leaves. Select the flower which has the best curve for Subject Stem and measure it according to Rule I, Moribana Style. Select Secondary and Object stems, measure according to same rule, and return to water. In this lesson a few small pompom buds have been selected as fillers. Although these arrangements are strictly devoid of any bunching of flowers, when the flowers are small with weak and fragile stems, they are tied together to appear as one cluster.

Place the holder on left side of container as described above.

I will mention here that although the left-hand side of the container has been used exclusively in these lessons, all arrangements may be made using the right-hand side of the container if desired. Whether the left- or right-hand side of the container is used depends upon where you will place the finished arrangement. Always bear this in mind before deciding upon any arrangement! There are three important factors to be considered before arranging flowers:

1. Where the arrangement will be placed when finished.
2. What container or vase will be used.
3. What flowers, branches or shrubs are most appropriate to use, considering both the type of container and final location of completed arrangement.

With preliminary preparations out of the way, we are now ready to place the flowers in the container.

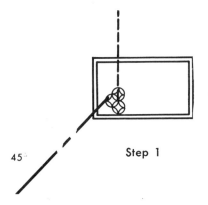

Step 1. Place Subject Stem in small partition of middle section of holder, slanting it to the left front. If stem is too large, trim it to fit partition. If too small, wedge securely with small sticks.

45

Step 1

Step 2. Place Secondary Stem in small partition of rear section, slanting slightly to the right rear.

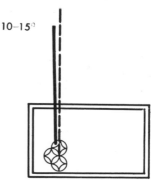

Step 2

Step 3. Place the Object Stem in front section of holder, slanting low to the right front. With this third stem in proper position, the arrangement resembles a framework.

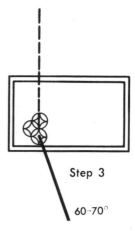

Step 3

Step 4. Using the string you have at hand, tie the pompom buds together and use them as fillers. Place this cluster in center section of holder, between Subject and Object stems. Cover holder, if necessary, with leaves or other material.

After an arrangement has been completed, it may appear too dense. If so, cut out the excess leaves, being careful not to trim out too much. In this respect, it will be helpful to cover that particular spot with your hand to visualize the final effect before cutting anything away. Do not group flowers, branches or shrubs too closely. Keep the arrangement airy and let it "breathe."

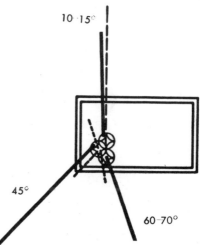

Step 4: Completed Arrangement

USE OF NEEDLE-POINT HOLDER

With flowers already prepared, place needle-point holder in position at left side of container, towards the front, and begin to arrange the flowers.

Step 1. Place Subject Stem in division 2, slanting or curving the stem to left front.

Step 2. Place Secondary Stem in division 1, slanting to right rear.

Step 3. Place Object Stem in division 4, slanting to the right in a low position.

Step 4. Buds which have been tied together are placed as fillers between the Subject and Object stems.

Moribana Style Form B with chrysanthemums.

Moribana Style Form C combining Tritoma with tube roses and loquat leaves.

29

Moribana Style Form C composed of pink roses.

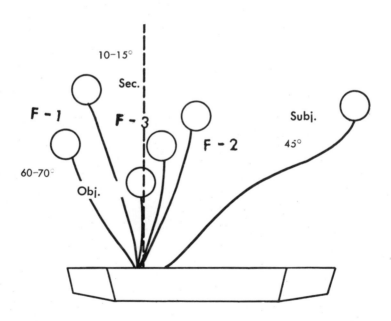

LESSON 3

MORIBANA FORM C
(SLANTING SIDEWAYS STYLE)

This is the final basic form in the Moribana-Style arrangement and it differs from the first two forms in two respects. The holder is now placed to the left of center in the container. The Subject Stem should have a strong slant or pronounced curve so that the length of the stem will slant over the container. Because of the position of the holder, you will find that the stem will slant slightly to the front. By comparing the picture on opposite page with those in the other lessons you will clearly see the pronounced curve of the Subject Stem.

In this lesson I have selected six roses for the arrangement. The equipment will be the same as previously used. Prepare flowers and select one which will form a strong slant, or has a natural curve, for the Subject Stem. Measure according to Rule I, Moribana Style, cut and replace in water. Prepare the Secondary and Object stems, as well as fillers, in the same way.

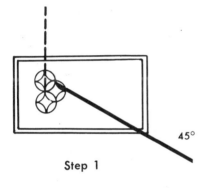

Step 1

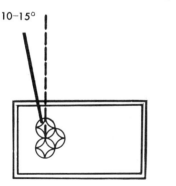

Step 2

Place holder in proper position as described above.

Step 1. Place Subject Stem in small rear partition of holder's middle section, allowing the stem to curve toward right front.

Step 2. Place Secondary Stem in small left partition of rear section, slanting this stem slightly to the left.

Step 3. Place Object Stem in small partition of front section, curving stem toward left front.

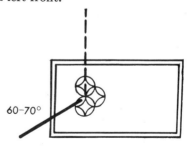

Step 3

Step 4. Place filler No. 1 to left of Secondary Stem, bending slightly to the left. Place filler No. 2 between Secondary and Subject stems, slanting to the right. Place filler No. 3 in center in low position to fill in arrangement. Add additional leaves, or ferns, wherever necessary and cover holder. Sometimes small rocks make an attractive cover for holders, serving also as a weight to steady the holder should the arrangement become top-heavy.

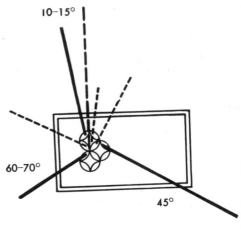

Step 4: Completed Arrangement

USE OF NEEDLE-POINT HOLDER

Since the flowers are already prepared and cut to proper lengths, all that is necessary is to place the needle-point holder in proper position in the container.

Step 1. Place Subject Stem in division 4, slanting to right front.

Step 2. Place Secondary Stem in division 1, slanting to left rear.

Step 3. Place Object Stem in division 2, slanting to the left front.

Step 4. Place filler No. 1 to left of Secondary Stem, bending it slightly to the left. Place filler No. 2 between Secondary and Subject stems, slanting to the right. Place filler No. 3 in the center in a low position, and cover holder with foliage.

You now have the essentials of the three basic forms of low-bowl arrangements. Remember that Form A used the Subject Stem in an upright position, Form B used the Subject Stem in a slanting forward position, and Form C used the Subject Stem with a pronounced sideways slant or natural curve. The dominant point in a Japanese Flower Arrangement is the subject flower or branch which is of paramount importance. The position of the Subject Stem is the key to and foundation of the style or design of the arrangement.

Always place the principal stems in the special partitions or sections, as designated in the lessons. Then use any of the openings for the fillers. In all Japanese arrangements, place the flowers in the holder in such a position that they appear to be growing from a single stem or root. This is a basic idea, both in the Moribana and the Heika styles. (Identical positions are used in the divisions of a needle-point holder.)

Three additional diagrams are presented here to impress upon your mind the orthodox positions of the three principal stems. It will be clear, by studying them, that although the flowers may be more vertical or horizontal, the ends of the stems must be placed in the correct partitions or sections of the holder at all times.

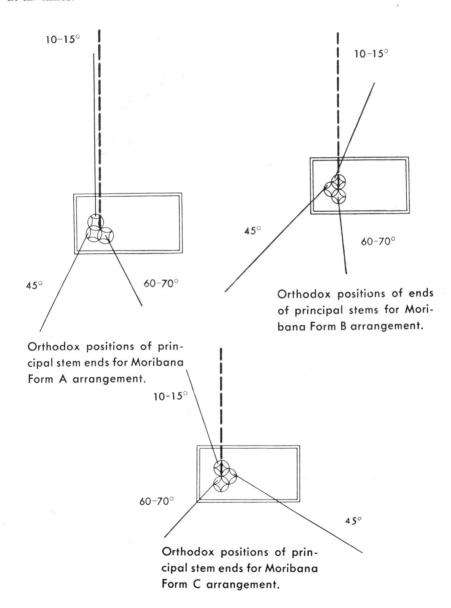

Orthodox positions of principal stem ends for Moribana Form A arrangement.

Orthodox positions of ends of principal stems for Moribana Form B arrangement.

Orthodox positions of principal stem ends for Moribana Form C arrangement.

Water-Reflecting Style combining china-berry branch with small white daisy-type wild flowers and galax leaves in a yellow container.

LESSON 4

MORIBANA FORM D
(WATER-REFLECTING STYLE)

Strongly resembling, and based on the principles of the Moribana Form C, is the Water-Reflecting Style arrangement. It is charming and very easy to make.

The object of the Water-Reflecting Style is to depict a little scene beside a lake or stream. Care must be given to the Subject Stem or branch. It must have a decided curve or slant so that it will be reflected over the expanse of water in the container.

Measure the Subject Stem in accordance with Rule II, Moribana Style. The Secondary and Object stems are upright in position and should be cut shorter than the measurement rule calls for so that they will in no way interfere with the dominance of the Subject Stem.

Before commencing the arrangement turn back to Moribana Form C (Lesson 3) and study carefully the diagram for Step 1. In this lesson the holder will be placed as indicated in Lesson 3. If desired, however, the holder may be turned slightly to the rear so that the Subject Stem or branch is extended completely over the water.

Step 1. Place the Subject Stem securely in the partition or adjacent section of the holder as indicated in the diagram, slanting it over the container to the right front. When placing the stems in the partitions or sections of open-type holder, hold the stem firmly in one hand and have small sticks prepared and available for use as wedges. With the free hand, place sticks around the base of the stem until it remains securely in the proper position. Since the Subject Stem in the Water-Reflecting Style is to curve out over the water, it will need to be properly wedged.

Step 2. As the Secondary and Object stems are of minor importance and are used only to complete the arrangement, no accurate measurement need be followed. Cut in appropriate lengths, keeping stems short—be guided by common sense in this. The Secondary and Object stems may be placed in any section or partition of the holder where they will be secure. They should be close together to give the appearance of "growing" beside the tree.

Step 3. Cover the holder with small rocks or pebbles.

USE OF THE NEEDLE-POINT HOLDER

With the material prepared, place the needle-point holder in the same position as shown in Lesson 3.

Step 1. Place Subject Stem in division 4, close to the center of holder, and extending over the container in a strong right front direction.

Step 2. The Secondary and Object stems are of minor importance and are used only to complete the arrangement. Place in appropriate positions in the needle-point holder.

Step 3. Cover the holder with small rocks or pebbles.

Moribana Style Form E, Natural Scenery, using nandina branch with small cedar shrub and daisy-type wild flowers in a cream container.

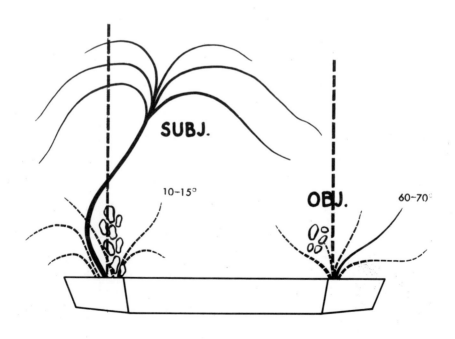

LESSON 5

MORIBANA FORM E
(NATURAL SCENERY STYLE)

This style, like the Water-Reflecting Style, is a most attractive and original form of Japanese Flower Arrangement. It draws vividly upon the imagination and skill of the arranger, but at the same time it is easy to make.

The main object of the Natural Scenery is to depict a miniature version of a woodland scene beside a stream or small pond. A great variety of branches and shrubs may be used as materials. Old gnarled, moss-covered, or leafless branches may be arranged very effectively.

The principal differences between the Natural Scenery and the Water-Reflecting styles are as follows: Either Moribana Form A or B may be used; two holders may be used. This is not obligatory but we will use two holders in this lesson. Whenever two holders are placed in the container, the Subject Stem will be placed in holder No. 1, and the Object Stem will be placed in holder No. 2.

Study closely both the picture and sketch of the arrangement before beginning the lesson. The material I have selected is Nandina which is upright in its nature so we will use Rule I, Moribana Style, for our measurements. Pine, laurel and azalea lend themselves admirably to both Water-Reflecting and Natural Scenery arrangements. However, in either style, keep the Subject branch dominant.

In preparing your material, select the longest and strongest branch for the Subject Stem. Measure it according to Rule 1, Moribana Style, and cut. Omit the Secondary Stem entirely. Measure the Object Stem slightly shorter than the rule calls for so that it will not in any way interfere with the dominant lines of the Subject Stem.

Place holder No. 1 in container to the left rear; place holder No. 2 diagonally opposite at the right front.

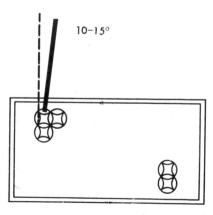

10–15°

Step 1. Place Subject Stem in rear partition of the rear section of holder No. 1, and wedge securely in an upright position.

Step 1

Step 2. Place Object Stem in any partition or section of holder No. 2— just so it remains secure. Allow this stem to slant a little toward the right front.

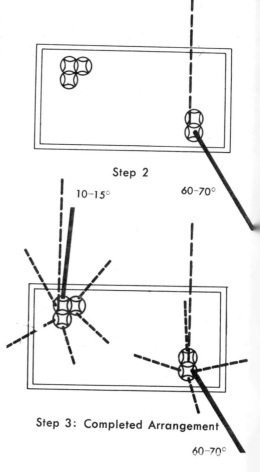

Step 2

10–15°   60–70°

Step 3. Cover the base of both holders with small pieces of shrub and little flowers, or small rocks may also be used, to create a small scene of embankments with a stream running between them.

Step 3: Completed Arrangement

60–70°

USE OF NEEDLE-POINT HOLDER

With the material already prepared, place the two holders as indicated in the diagram.

Step 1. Place the Subject Stem in holder No. 1, division 1, close to the center and slanting slightly to the right.

Step 2. Place Object Stem in holder No. 2, division 3, slanting to the right and a bit toward the rear.

Step 3. Cover the base of both holders with small pieces of shrub and little flowers. Rocks may also be added.

Moribana Style Form A, using two holders, Dutch Iris with leaves, in a deep blue container.

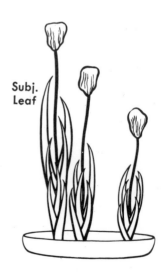

Subj. Leaf

LESSON 6

MORIBANA FORM F
(IRIS UPRIGHT STYLE)

The iris which is closely identified with Japan, growing there in great abundance, is equally prevalent in this country. In iris arrangements, as in all Japanese Flower Arrangement, the natural characteristics of the material are of great importance. However, it is the purpose of the Primer to acquaint you with the simple and easily made arrangements of this lovely flower, and not to provide advanced instruction.

This lesson, selected because it is particularly suited to the beginner, will not only acquaint you with the technique of the arrangement and with the beauty and dignity of the flowers, but also with certain features of the plant which are considered of great importance. The principal characteristics of this plant are that the leaves and flowers grow upright, and that the leaves grow in greater abundance than the flowers. You will also note that the flowers always grow above the leaves. Each leaf has a smooth side which is called the concave side; the other is rough and lined and is called the convex side. At the tip of each leaf is a small "hook."

Since the materials you will arrange are upright and two holders will be used, this lesson is actually a combination of Moribana Form A and Natural Scenery styles.

This lesson will be divided into three parts:

Part I (a) Preparation of leaves for Groups 1, 2 and 3
      (b) Placement of leaves for Groups 1, 2 and 3
      (c) Preparation of leaves for Groups 4, 5, 6, 7 and 8
Part II Placement of leaves—Groups 4, 5, 6, 7 and 8
Part III Preparation and placement of the flowers.

Study the picture, sketch and diagrams. You will note that all sets of leaves have been designated as Groups. In preparing these groups you will use three leaves each in Groups 3, 5 and 8. In each of the other groups you will use two leaves. Nineteen leaves and three flowers will be used in all, but you should have more leaves on hand to permit a proper selection.

Place two holders in your container according to the diagram illustrating their positions. The straight lines in this diagram indicate the position of the groups of leaves. The dots illustrate the placement of the three flowers. Now we are ready to proceed—

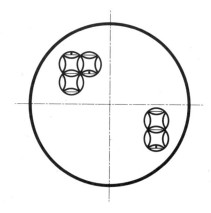

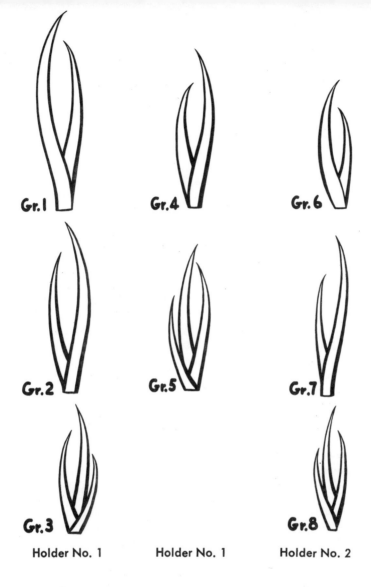

Gr.1 Gr.4 Gr.6

Gr.2 Gr.5 Gr.7

Gr.3 Gr.8

Holder No. 1   Holder No. 1   Holder No. 2

Part I (a) PREPARATION OF LEAVES

Group 1. Select the longest and strongest leaf for the Subject. (This is the only leaf to be identified by name.) With the hook of this leaf facing right, measure it according to Rule 1, Moribana Style, and cut. Select another leaf about 1½ inches shorter and place in back of Subject leaf with hook facing left. Cut the second leaf even at bottom with first leaf and lay them aside.

Group 2. Select the leaf for this group about 2 inches shorter than the Subject leaf, with hook facing left. Pair it with a slightly shorter leaf, hook facing right, cut them even at bottom and lay aside.

Group 3. In this group we use three leaves and they are shorter than the first two groups since they are placed in front. Place the longest in the center with hook facing left. Select a slightly shorter leaf and place it in front with hook facing right. The third leaf will be the shortest with hook facing left. Hold them together, cut even at bottom and lay aside.

(b) Placement of leaves for Groups 1, 2 and 3:

Place Group 1 in rear partition of Holder No. 1
Place Group 2 in middle partition of Holder No. 1
Place Group 3 in front partition of Holder No. 1

When fitting the leaves into the open-type holder, wedge them in with the small pieces of cut-off leaves. This will hold them securely in position. With these three groups in position you can easily visualize how the remaining groups of leaves are to be prepared and placed.

(c) Preparation of leaves for Groups 4, 5, 6, 7 and 8:

Follow the same procedure in regard to the preparation of the leaves for the remaining groups. Note, however, that the longest leaf in Group 4 is shorter than the Subject leaf and has the hook facing the Subject leaf.

Part II PLACEMENT OF LEAVES—Groups 4, 5, 6, 7 and 8:

Place Group 4 in rear partition on right of Holder No. 1
Place Group 5 in front partition on right of Holder No. 1
Place Group 6 in rear partition of Holder No. 2
Place Group 7 in middle partition of Holder No. 2
Place Group 8 in front partition of Holder No. 2

After all the leaves are securely placed in the proper positions in the holders, check to see that they are graduated in heights and with the hook of each leaf facing the correct way. Should any leaves be out of proportion or incorrectly arranged, now is the time to adjust them before preparing and placing the flowers.

Part III PREPARATION AND PLACEMENT OF THE FLOWERS

Measure the three flower stems so that one is two or three inches longer than the Subject leaf. The second, preferably a bud, should be longer than the longest leaf in Group 5. The third and last flower should be longer than the leaves in Group 8.

Place the flowers behind each group of leaves already identified as indicated in the diagram of the holders. If the stems do not fit tight enough, wedge the stem with cut-off bits of leaves.

When the arrangement is completed, cover the holders with rocks, stones, small pieces of driftwood or any material that is pleasing, but do not detract from the lines of the arrangement.

This lesson of necessity must be detailed. Nevertheless it should inspire you to try many other combinations of material. Whatever type is used, remember that the principal object is to have the flowers appear as though they were growing out of the container.

Moribana Free-Style in a Natural Scenery using a moss-covered branch with orange-colored pompoms with wild huckleberry leaves in a deep blue container.

Moribana Free-Style of driftwood combined with green shrub leaves and crushed white shells on a black lacquer base.

LESSON 7

NATURAL VERSUS ARTIFICIAL METHODS OF SUPPORTING FLOWERS

Japanese Flower Arrangement dates back as far as the 6th Century but many centuries passed before they invented the holder for low-bowl type of arrangement. Until the holder was invented, flowers were arranged in vases and various natural methods were used to keep them in a fixed position. In addition, the Japanese devised various props and wedges for this purpose and these are known as artificial methods of supporting flowers.

NATURAL METHODS

Flowers can be placed in a vase and the stems will hold the arrangement in place. This is designated as Natural Method 1.

Stems of varying lengths may be placed in a vase at an angle so that the stems remain in secure position. Leaves and small flowers used to cover the mouth of the vase when arrangement is completed also keep flower stems in fixed positions. This is Natural Method 2.

The alternation of stems in the vase will interlock them securely in proper position. This is Natural Method 3.

Stems may also be securely held in place by the rim of the vase. This is Natural Method 4.

In both natural and artificial methods of supporting flowers, the stems are always cut slantwise to insure a more secure fit against the wall of the vase.

ARTIFICIAL METHODS

Despite the various natural methods, you may still experience difficulty in arranging stems so that they remain in a certain position in the vase. Then artificial methods must be used. A brief description and diagram of each method is outlined and you should practice them so that you are thoroughly versed in what each method accomplishes for you. In addition, you may devise your own variations. Make certain, however, that they also accomplish the job and hold stems in the required positions.

ART. METH. 1

Artificial Method 1: First measure the diameter of the vase on the outside and cut a stick to this measurement so that it fits snugly inside the vase. If the stick is too long, snip small pieces from either end until it fits properly. Bind this stick to the stem, branch or shrub you wish to arrange and wedge stick down into the vase as far as possible so that it holds the stem firmly in desired position.

Artificial Method 2: Measure the stick in the same way as outlined in Artificial Method 1. Slit the bottom of the stem and insert the stick into the slit stem, binding them together. If the stem is weak, then split the stick instead, and insert the stem into the stick, binding them together. Wedge stick into the vase in desired position.

ART. METH. 2

Artificial Method 3: This method differs from the foregoing methods in that the flower or shrub stem is much longer. Therefore, for proper balance, the stick you prepare is placed in a slanting position low in the vase.

ART. METH. 3

Artificial Method 4: In this method a short stem is lengthened for proper balance. First bind an additional stick to bottom of stem to lengthen the stem. Then cut a second stick to proper measurement and bind securely to elongated stem.

ART. METH. 4

Artificial Method 5: Here we use a two-pronged stick to hold main stem securely in the vase.

46

ART. METH. 5

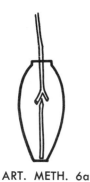

ART. METH. 6a

ART. METH. 6c

Artificial Method 6: (a) If the stem you wish to arrange must remain upright in the vase and is too short, an additional stick can be bound or spliced to the stem so that it is the required length. Measure distance from bottom of vase to end of the stem and cut stick accordingly. Sharpen one end of stick and insert this point into stem which has been split. Bind them together.

(b) If the stem still does not remain in upright position it may be anchored by an additional stick fastened crosswise at bottom of elongated stem. Cut this stick the same length as diameter at bottom of the vase.

ART. METH. 6b

(c) Split the end of elongated stem and fasten to cross stick securely. Wedge cross stick firmly in bottom of vase.

ART. METH. 7a

ART. METH. 7b

Artificial Method 7: Two simple methods of using sticks to anchor stems in proper positions are constantly employed by all schools of Japanese flower arranging:

(a) Wedge a stick directly across the inside of vase from one side to the other. The stick must fit tightly, otherwise it will float when water is poured into the vase.

(b) Bind two sticks together in the form of a cross, and fit them tightly into the vase.

Heika Style Form A using yellow chrysanthemums with water oak leaves in a deep blue vase.

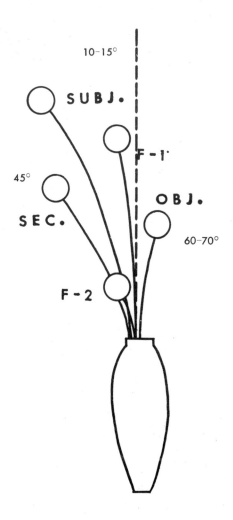

10-15°

SUBJ.

F-1

45°

SEC.

OBJ.

60-70°

F-2

LESSON 8

HEIKA FORM A
(UPRIGHT STYLE)

Now we arrive at the second major division of Japanese Flower Arrangement—the Heika Style—in which a perpendicular container or upright vase is used. Although the type of container differs, the same basic principles we applied in the Moribana-Style arrangements are used here.

In measuring principal stems for the Heika arrangement, you will remember that the Subject Stem measures one and one-half times the height of the vase. As in the Moribana Style, the Secondary Stem measures two-thirds the length of the Subject Stem while the Object Stem is one-half the length of the Subject Stem. (See Rule III on page 15.) In the Heika style, however, all the measurements are from the *rim* of the vase, so allow sufficient additional length of stem so that it will reach the water in the vase.

Five chrysanthemums are used for this arrangement. Study the picture on the opposite page and the sketch below the picture before beginning your arrangement.

Equipment used earlier will be utilized again, except that the container will be an upright vase instead of a low horizontal bowl, and holders will be omitted. Otherwise, we use clippers, wire, string and extra sticks so that artificial methods may be employed to secure stems in proper positions in vase.

Following preliminary removal of dead and discolored leaves, and unnecessary twigs and branches, we are ready to select and measure the flowers. Select the longest and strongest chrysanthemum, and measure it against the height of vase. In this lesson we will assume that the vase is 10 inches high so add one-half this height or 5 inches for a total length of 15 inches for Subject Stem. The stem is marked, *but not cut* at this point since additional length is needed to reach the water, and also to be securely fastened in position in the vase.

Measure the Secondary and Object stems according to Rule III, Heika Style. Mark stems at proper length and return them to water to retain freshness until ready for use.

In this lesson, water oak branches are used as fillers for the arrangement. Measure filler No. 1 two-thirds length of Secondary Stem. Filler No. 2 is one-half the length of Secondary Stem and filler No. 3 will be either longer or shorter than filler No. 2, depending upon where it is best-suited in the final arrangement.

Step 1. Place Subject Stem in an upright position in the left rear part of the vase. It must remain firmly in position. If not, then artificial means must be utilized to hold it in place.

In this lesson, let us assume that the stem requires Artificial Method 1, as described in Lesson 7. Measure the diameter of the vase and cut a stick to this measurement so that it fits snugly inside the vase. Fasten Subject Stem to this stick and insert into vase so that its position is tight. The Subject Stem should be long enough to reach the lower inside wall of the vase and be certain that the stem is cut slantwise so that it will rest firmly against the inside wall. The Subject Stem will extend 15 inches above lip of vase toward the left rear.

Step 2. Place Secondary Stem in left front section of vase, slanting it to the left front.

Step 3. Object Stem is now placed in right front of vase, slanting forward. This stem catches under the principal stem and its stick, or is placed wherever it is most secure. What happens to the stems below the rim of the vase is of no importance. The main thing is to be certain that stems will remain in proper position above the rim of the vase.

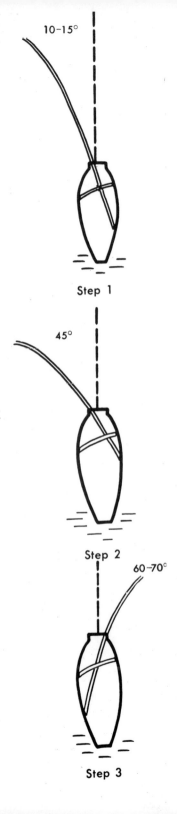

10–15°

Step 1

45°

Step 2

60–70°

Step 3

LESSON 9

HEIKA FORM B
(SLANTING FORWARD STYLE)

As we discovered earlier when planning a Moribana Form B arrangement, the Subject Stem either slants or curves forward and is arranged to bring out these characteristics. Heika Form B follows the same style.

In this lesson we use six asters and the Nandina shrub. Study carefully the picture and sketch on the opposite page. (A slanting forward style arrangement is very difficult to present properly in a photograph, so the vase in this picture has been turned slightly to the left to clearly show the positions of the flowers.) We will duplicate this arrangement in the instructions which follow.

Measure the three principal stems according to Rule III, and also measure the fillers in accordance with the basic rule. It is important to remember, however, that the fillers must be cut shorter than the principal stems. The principal stems must remain the dominant feature in any arrangement.

If the curve of a stem is slight and must be bent more, take the stem in both hands, bending it slightly a little at a time until the desired curve has been made. If the stem or branch is too thick to bend easily, cut a small nick in it to aid the bending process. Work gently and carefully so that the stem does not break.

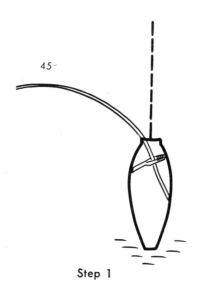

45°

Step 1

Step 1. Place Subject Stem in vase, slanting stem to left front. If stem will not remain securely in position, an artificial aid must be used. In this lesson we will use Artificial Method 2. Measure the diameter of the vase and cut a stick to this measurement. Since we are arranging asters which have rather weak stems, we will make a slit in the stick and insert the flower stem into the slit, binding them securely together.

Step 2. Place Secondary Stem in vase, slanting to the left rear. Again it may be necessary to use some artificial means of support to hold stem securely in place.

10–15°

Step 2

60–70°

Step 3. Place Object Stem low in vase, slanting slightly to the left front. Make certain it remains in proper position.

10–15°

Step 3

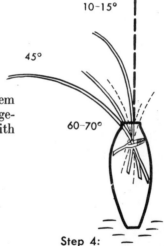

45°

Step 4. Cut fillers and place them where needed to complete the arrangement. Cover mouth of vase with leaves.

60–70°

Step 4:
Completed Arrangement

So far we have been using three fillers. As we progress and gain experience in flower arranging, we will find that additional fillers may be added with charming results. In this lesson, one Nandina branch has been used to cover the mouth of the vase and to add softness to the arrangement. You may find that additional blossoms, branches and shrubs may add beauty to the arrangement you make.

Heika Style Form C using
pine branches with sumac
in a brown vase.

Heika Free-Style with loquat
branches in a bronze vase.

Heika Style Form B combining persimmon branch with
lavender chrysanthemums in a
white vase.

Heika Style Form C using yellow chrysanthemums with water oak in pale green vase.

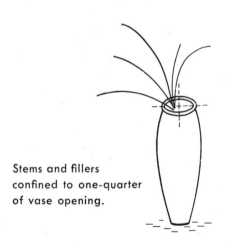

Stems and fillers
confined to one-quarter
of vase opening.

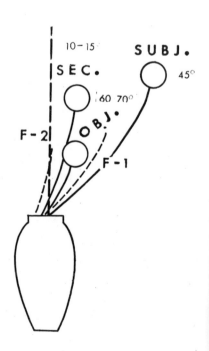

LESSON 10

HEIKA FORM C
(SLANTING SIDEWAYS STYLE)

The sixth basic division of Japanese Flower Arrangement is the Heika Form C. You will remember that this form employs as its Subject Stem a flower which forms a strong slant or broad sweep. If a straight stem is used, as was necessary in the arrangement on the opposite page, place stem in a slanting position. As we progress with this lesson, you will see how we accomplish the curve or slant of the Subject Stem when using a perpendicular vase.

Study the picture carefully before proceeding with the arrangement. The sketch and diagram below the picture clearly illustrate the location of all stems and fillers. All stems must appear to come from one section of the vase, no matter how spread out they may be in the final arrangement. This gives the arrangement a very neat appearance and can be accomplished even though heavy stems practically fill the mouth of the vase. As a test, divide the top of the vase into four sections by placing two sticks together in the form of a cross, and holding them over the vase. If all the stems do not appear to be within one of the four sections, you must continue to work. The finished arrangement may at first appear lop-sided to you but nevertheless this is truly Japanese in design.

Three chrysanthemums and water oak foliage are used in this arrangement. Measure principal stems and fillers as in previous Heika lessons, but do not cut them until you actually begin the arrangement. If stems need artificial support, experiment to determine which method will be best. In this lesson, we will use Artificial Method 5 in which a pronged stick is used to support the Subject Stem. However, you may substitute whichever artificial method you think most suitable.

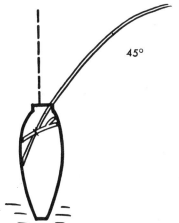

45°

Step 1. Place Subject Stem in vase, slanting it to the right of the vase. Use artificial method, if necessary, for adequate support.

In this and all following diagrams, degrees of angles of the three principal stems made by intersection of Imaginary Vertical Line (heavy broken line) are correct degrees of these angles for basic Heika styles.

Step 2. Place Secondary Stem in vase to the left rear and slanting right.

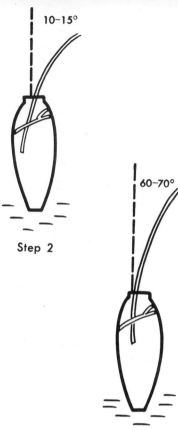

Step 3. Place Object Stem in vase at front, slanting to the right front.

Step 4. Cut fillers, placing them where needed. Cover the mouth of the vase with leaves to complete arrangement.

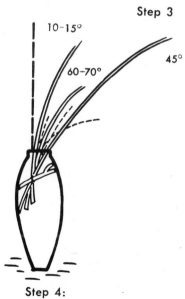

Step 4:
Completed Arrangement

Seika Style, Upright. Japanese iris, and iris leaves, in a Usubata.

Natural Scenery, Form A, Moribana, with Haw Shrub, small pompoms and a piece of old wood, in a bronze Sunabachi.

Heika Style Form D using pyracantha branch with bay leaves in blue vase.

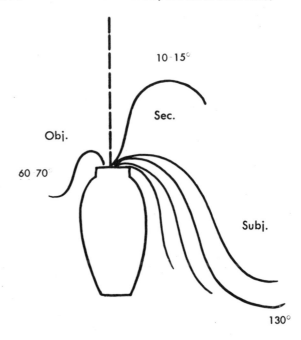

10-15°

Sec.

Obj.

60-70°

Subj.

130°

LESSON 11

HEIKA FORM D
(CASCADE STYLE)

The last basic form of Japanese Flower Arrangement is the Cascade Style, Form D. The object of this style, as its name depicts, is to have the principal stem or branch appear to fall from the vase in the form of a cascade. This arrangement should be placed in a high position, such as on a mantel, for the best effect.

Select material appropriate for this type of arrangement. In this lesson we use a branch of pyracantha and two bay leaves. Great care must be taken in the selection of this principal stem since it must be long enough for the measurements in Rule III and also have an additional small branch at its base which serves as a hook.

Artificial Method 7a will be used to secure the principal stems in this cascade arrangement. This method utilizes a stick extending across the rim of the vase, just below the lip, under which the Subject Stem will be hooked in proper position. This cross stick must be cut so that it fits tightly in the vase.

Prepare the material, discarding dead and discolored leaves, berries and extra branches. Also prune the Subject Stem to eliminate small branches which interfere with the cascade appearance of the branch.

Measure the principal stems according to Rule III. In this arrangement, however, the Secondary and Object stems are shorter than usual so that they will not detract from the Subject branch.

130°

Step 1

Step 1. Place Subject Stem under stick in vase, hooking it securely to this support.

61

Step 2. Place Secondary Stem in position so that it stands upright but slanting slightly to the right.

Step 3. Place Object Stem at left front of vase.

No fillers have been used in this lesson since the principal stems fill out the arrangment.

Another variation of the Heika Form D is the utilization of a container in place of a vase. With the cascade design firmly in mind, it is very easy to see how this arrangement may be adapted to the low container provided the material to be arranged is appropriate. The container is placed in a high position, of course, such as on a mantel, a high table or stand, or on a shelf.

Prepare the material and measure the Subject Stem according to Rule II. The Secondary and Object stems should be somewhat shorter than usual so they will not detract from the Subject branch.

The position of the open-type holder is indicated in the diagram. It is placed to the right and close to the front of the container.

Place the Subject Stem in the partition of middle section of holder with stem extending to the left and hanging down. Place Secondary and Object stems in partitions as indicated, and in a more upright position close to the Subject Stem. Add fillers when necessary to complete the arrangement.

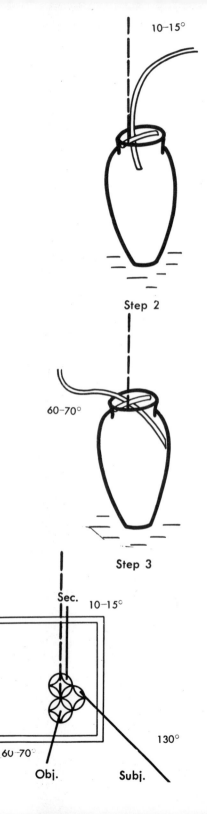

Step 2

Step 3

62

Part II

BASIC INFORMATION and EQUIPMENT
Seika Style

The Seika Style is the classical or formal style of Japanese Flower Arrangement. Devised about one thousand years ago by the Ikenobo School—the oldest flower arrangement school in Japan—this style changed the trend of the art. It provided a more practical form of flower arrangement for the home, as a substitute for the Rikka Style. The word Seika, also spelled Skokwa, Seikwa and Shoka, means "quiet flowers." The following translation gives a clear idea of it; "Simple in design, restrained, and though at times highly dramatic, always restful."

The basic elementary design of the Seika Style is upright. The arrangements are always made on three definite levels—the Upper, Middle, and Lower Levels—easily recognized in any Seika-Style arrangement. This style can be either a right- or left-hand arrangement in a vase or a low container. For a few inches above the container, before the branches curve outward, the stems must be absolutely bare. Regardless of the number of stems used in an arrangement, *they must appear as one when viewed from the front.* The bareness of the stems dramatizes the design and endows it with vitality and force. This is the most distinct characteristic of the Seika Style. The Japanese refer to it as "the strong center of growth" or "parent stem."

PRINCIPAL STEMS AND FILLERS

The three principal stems which form the framework of the arrangement are called Shin (principal), Soe (auxiliary) and Tai (opposite). Their symbolic interpretations are truth, deed, and meditation. Through the influence of Zen Buddhism and the Tea Ceremony, these original names have become known to us as Heaven, Man, and Earth. To unify instruction, however, we will continue to refer to these principal stems as Subject, Secondary and Object stems, and the additional material used to complete the arrangement will be called fillers.

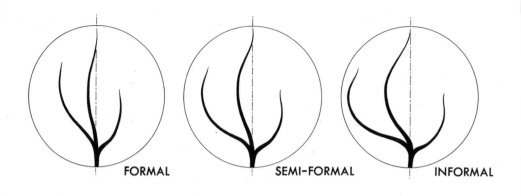

FORMAL | SEMI-FORMAL | INFORMAL

BASIC FORMS

The three basic forms are:

1. Formal—Shin, meaning "like a man standing"
2. Semi-formal — Gyo, meaning "like a man walking"
3. Informal—So, meaning "like a man running" against the wind.

COMBINATIONS OF MATERIALS

Many types of materials may be used although you must bear in mind that the basic design is always upright so your plant material must have this characteristic. The number of leaves or branches used may be 3, 5, 7, 9 or more. The Object Stem may be a flower or flowering shrub provided the material used in the balance of the arrangement is flowerless.

STEM LENGTHS

The natural line of the material, its length and growing characteristics are a guide to the measurement rule in all Japanese flower arrangements. This is particularly true of the Seika Style which is primarily a line arrangement. In this style no two branches, leaves or flowers are ever the same height in the finished arrangement—no matter how many are used. A general guide for measuring material, for either a vase or horizontal container, is as follows:

If you are arranging short material, consisting of only a few branches, leaves or flowers, follow Rule III (Heika Style) for the three principal stems and Rule IV for the fillers. Sometimes it is advisable to add the width of the vase to these measurements for proper proportions.

For long material, whose attractiveness would be destroyed by too much cutting, the following measurement rule is suggested:

Measure the Subject Stem 2½ to 4 times the height of vase.

Measure the Secondary Stem ⅔ the length of Subject Stem.

Measure the Object Stem ½ length of Subject Stem.

Each filler is measured in proper proportion to the principal stem it supports.

INSTRUCTIONS ON BENDING PLANT MATERIAL

In the Seika Style, the principal object is to bring out the rhythmic design of the branches and leaves, so select plant material which has curving and flowing lines. This is not always possible, however, so the following suggestions may be helpful:

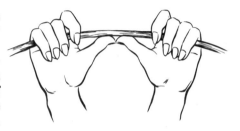

1. Do not attempt to bend stems at nodes, or joints, as they may break at these points.

2. Hold the branch or stem firmly in both hands with your thumbs close together along underside of stem. This gives support to the branch during the bending process.

3. Bend stem slowly and gently, with a slight twisting motion. This creates a more permanent curve so that the stem will not return to its original line.

In preparing your material for a Seika-Style arrangement, the Subject Stem must be bent to a bow shape, beginning its curve three to five inches above the container or vase. Then this principal stem curves back, and then up again. The tip of the Subject Stem should be directly above the spot where the stem emerges from the vase.

The extent which other leaves or branches may curve out for the Formal style is no further than the widest part of the tubular vase. This does not apply, however, to the Semi-formal and Informal styles.

EQUIPMENT

In addition to the equipment used in previous lessons you will need a pronged wooden fork and a wooden fastener. In Japan the metal holder is not used for the Seika-Style arrangement in a tubular vase. Instead a small pronged fork is used to keep the material in position. Then after the arrangement is completed the material is kept in position by the placement of a wooden fastener in the rim of the vase. You should endeavor to become skillful in the preparation and use of the pronged wooden fork so that a metal holder will not be needed.

PRONGED WOODEN FORK

Certain types of shrubs are ideal for use in making the 2-pronged fork. Privet, willow and Andromeda japonica are best but any type of material could be used, if necessary, provided it is fresh and strong. The natural fork, as the name implies, is one which you may be fortunate enough to find already fashioned by nature. The artificial fork is one you make by cutting a stick or twig as follows:

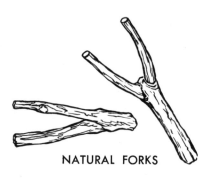

NATURAL FORKS

1. Make a slight groove about 1 or 2 inches from one end of stick, depending on size prong you will need for your arrangement. The stick should measure from $\frac{1}{2}$ to 1 inch in diameter.

2. Bind the groove with wire or string to prevent the stick from splitting when slit is made.

3. Slit the stick from other end to the place where groove is wired. Gently work the prongs apart with a slightly twisting motion of the clippers.

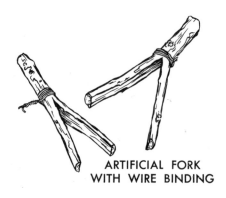

ARTIFICIAL FORK WITH WIRE BINDING

If the material to be arranged has thick stems, the opening between the prongs should be wide. If the stems are thin, the opening should be narrow. You may decide to make several pronged forks, of varying sizes, so that one will always be on hand for any size vase you wish to use. The pronged fork should fit tight in the vase. If too long, notch at either end of fork, measure and cut to proper size.

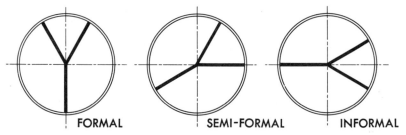

FORMAL   SEMI-FORMAL   INFORMAL

PLACEMENT OF PRONGED FORK

The position of the fork in the tubular vase determines the form of Seika Style arrangement so you must decide in advance which of the three forms you plan to make. Examine the diagram and note the position of the fork for each of the three forms.

FASTENER

**NATURAL FORK AND FASTENER
IN TOP OF CYLINDRICAL VASE**

Place the pronged end of the fork into the tubular vase first, about one inch below the top of the vase. Then press the solid end of the-fork into the vase. If the fork is difficult to fit into the vase, squeeze the prongs together. If it is too long you will have to snip off a little at a time until the fork fits snugly.

WOODEN FASTENER

This is a small stick made from leftover stems of material used in the arrangement. It is placed over the prongs of the wooden fork after the arrangement has been completed. It locks the material securely in place. Cut each end of the fastener slantwise so that it will fit against the inner walls of the vase. The sketch will give you a clear picture of how the fastener is used.

VASES AND CONTAINERS

Sketches of several vases and a container are presented here to acquaint the student with the traditional styles. These are usually made of bamboo or bronze, but earthenware is also used. Any tubular vase may be used for the Seika Style but the addition of a small shallow inset will greatly facilitate your work of arranging material.

Before beginning the actual lessons, it is important to keep the following two points in mind:

1. Regardless of the number of leaves or branches used, they must be placed closely together so that they appear as one stem when viewed from the front.

2. All stems must be absolutely bare for three to five inches from top of vase before the stems curve outward.

Bronze Sunabachi

Bamboo Tubular vase

Bronze Usubata

Basket

**Boar's head vase
with tray.**

**Shallow inset
for tubular vase.**

**Shallow tray inset
for the Usubata.**

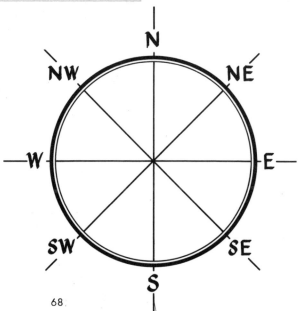

LESSON 12

SEIKA STYLE SEMI-FORMAL UPRIGHT ARRANGEMENT

(*Tubular Vase*)

Aspidistra leaves have been selected for this lesson because of their dignity and simplicity. Although only five leaves are required, you should have more available to assure a proper selection of material. We are going to make a semi-formal, right-hand form arrangement in a tubular vase. You will notice that a strong vein runs through the center of the leaf. If possible, select leaves that are identical in shape and appearance.

Place the pronged fork in the vase in the correct position for a semi-formal style arrangement. Prepare fastener and lay aside.

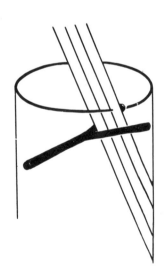

PREPARATION OF MATERIAL

Select the longest and strongest leaf for the Subject Stem. Measure it according to Rule III (Heika Style) plus the width of the vase inset. Cut and lay aside. Select the Secondary and Object stems, measure according to the rule, cut and lay aside. Select two smaller leaves, suitable for fillers, and measure them according to Rule IV. They will be called the front filler and back filler. The end of each stem should be cut slantwise so that they will fit closely against the inside wall of the vase.

PLACEMENT OF LEAVES

The placement of the leaves in the fork of the tubular vase is in an entirely different order than either the Moribana or Heika styles. Before actually placing the leaves, draw a diagram of the instructions for placement of leaves according to compass directions. Experience has proven that this is the best way to understand the placements—it also brings out the three-dimensional quality of the arrangement. Although it is not evident in a photograph, there is always a strong three-dimensional quality to all Japanese arrangements.

Study the picture and sketches, then proceed as follows:

Place the left hand directly over the fork with thumb and forefinger ready to hold material.

Step 1

Step 1. Place Secondary Stem in crotch of the pronged fork with leaf facing Southwest.

Step 2. Place the front filler leaf against stem of Secondary Stem—the stems should fit close together with the front side of the filler leaf facing due North, or almost upright. The front filler stem should rest between the right and left prong of the fork, but closer to the right side.

Step 2

Step 3

Step 3. Place the back filler leaf next to front filler leaf. The stem should rest against the left prong of the fork, and the leaf tip should point almost upright, slightly Northeast.

Step 4

Step 4. Place the Subject Stem next to the back filler, with back of leaf (or underside) facing Northeast. The stem should rest against the left side of the fork.

Step 5. Place the Object Stem beside the Subject, with stem resting against the right prong of the fork. The leaf should point Southeast. (In the picture of this arrangement, the Subject leaf is more to the east so that you may more easily observe the curl of the leaf, but ordinarily it curves out more to the front in a southeasterly direction.)

Step 5

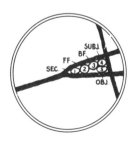

Step 6

Step 6. Place the fastener tightly against the stems just above the prongs of the fork.

Adjust the leaves if necessary. Take the Object leaf between your fingers, roll it up tightly, press gently, then release and a curl will result. If the leaves do not curl easily, wet them and then roll them again.

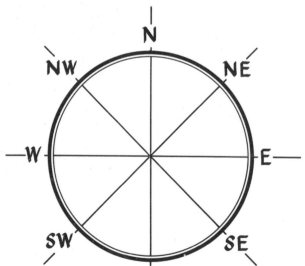

LESSON 13

SEIKA STYLE FORMAL UPRIGHT ARRANGEMENT

(Tubular Vase)

This is a formal, right-hand form arrangement in a tubular vase using nine pussy willows. The beautiful lines of this material will be stressed and, for emphasis, the stems are bare for five inches above the vase. It is particularly important with this material that the stems fit securely in the fork.

Study the picture and sketches carefully before beginning the arrangement. This will help you to understand the instructions as we progress.

Place the fork in the proper position for a formal style arrangement and prepare the fastener.

PREPARATION OF MATERIAL

Select three branches for principal stems and six for fillers. Each principal branch is supported by two fillers, graduated in height and measured according to the principal stem they support.

Select the longest and strongest pussy willow for the Subject Stem. Measure from two to two and one-half times the height of the vase and cut.

Select and measure the Secondary and Object branches according to the same measurement rule.

FILLERS

The Subject and Secondary branches each have two fillers which will be referred to as front and back fillers. The two fillers for the Object branch will be referred to as middle and back fillers.

Subject Fillers: Measure the front filler about four to five inches shorter than the Subject branch, and the back filler should be two to three inches shorter than the Subject branch.

Secondary Fillers: Follow the same measurement rule for the front and back fillers supporting the Secondary branch.

Object Fillers: The middle filler is about one-half the length of the Object branch. The back filler, however, is about one-half the length of the Subject branch.

BENDING OF BRANCHES

Subject Group: About five inches above the top of the vase, the Subject branch should have a slight curve to the left (toward the west), then curve back, with the last few inches of the tip in an upright position directly above the point where the branch emerged from the water. Bend the two fillers for Subject branch in the same way. (In the diagram, the Subject branch is No. 5, and the two broken lines, 4 and 6, are the fillers.)

Secondary Group: The Secondary branch should curve out, about five inches above the vase, in a strong flaring line to the left (toward the northwest) with the tip bent towards the Subject branch. Bend the two fillers for this branch in the same way. (In the diagram, the Secondary branch is No. 9 and the two broken lines, 7 and 8 are fillers.)

Object Group: The Object branch should curve out, about two inches above the vase, to the right (toward the southeast) in a slightly horizontal line. The back filler for the Object branch, however, follows the line of the Subject branch, and the middle filler follows the same line with the tip slightly forward. (In the diagram, the Object branch is No. 1, and the two broken lines, 2 and 3, are the fillers.)

PLACEMENT OF MATERIAL

Before arranging the material in the vase, remove all irregularities from lower portion of stems so that the stems fit together as closely as possible. The material will be arranged in a slightly different order than in Lesson 12 since we begin with the Object Group as follows:

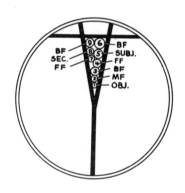

Step 1. Object Group: Place the Object branch in the crotch of the fork with the branch extending in a southeast direction. Place the middle filler next to the Object branch, and the back filler of this group next to the middle filler. The fillers are placed against the right-hand prong of the fork. Hold the stems in this position with your left hand so that they will not slip and become disarranged.

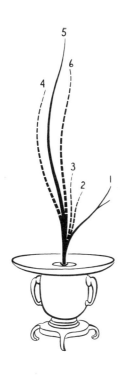

Step 2. Subject Group: Place the front filler, the Subject branch, and then the back filler behind the Object Group with stems against the right-hand prong of the fork. These branches curve out to the right with the tip of the Subject branch directly above the point where it emerged from the vase.

Step 3. Secondary Group: This group will be placed against the left-hand prong of the fork alongside the Subject Group. Place the front filler just back of the Object Group, as close as possible, then follow with the Secondary branch and back filler. These branches should curve to the left (toward the northwest) in a slightly vertical position with the tip of Secondary branch curving toward the Subject branch.

If there is any vacant space back of the stems, wedge a short piece of stem into this space to secure the branches in a tight position before using the fastener. These additional bits of stem, if used, should never be visible.

To complete the arrangement, place the fastener in a horizontal position, with the slanting ends against the wall of the vase, above the prongs of the fork.

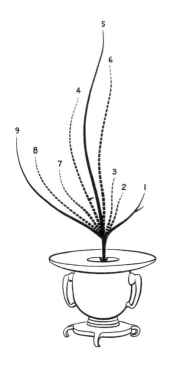

75

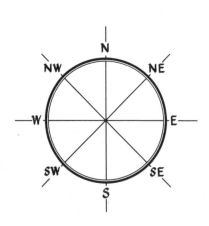

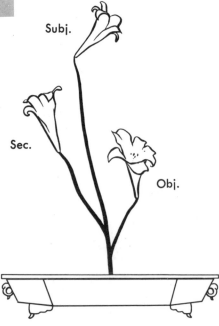

Subj.

Sec.

Obj.

LESSON 14

SEIKA STYLE FORMAL
UPRIGHT ARRANGEMENT

(Horizontal Container)

In this lesson we will arrange three Easter lilies in a Sunabachi. It is a formal, right-hand arrangement and, as in all Seika-Style arrangements, the stems must appear to be as one as they emerge from the container. We will use the directions of the compass in describing the placement of the material in the container to bring out the three-dimensional quality of this arrangement.

Place a needle-point holder in the center of your container.

Select the longest and strongest flower for the Subject Stem and measure it according to Rule II, Moribana Style, adding the depth of your container to this measurement. Follow the same measurement rule for the Secondary and Object stems.

Step 1. Place the Subject Stem in division 1 of the needle-point holder, close to the center. Bend the flower stem back and slightly to the left (between north and northwest) so that the flower head is facing upward.

Step 2. Place the Secondary Stem in division 2 of holder, close to the center. Bend the flower stalk toward the left front (southwest) with the flower head facing toward the right and upward.

Step 3. Place the Object Stem in division 4 of holder, close to the center. Bend the flower stem to the right front (southeast) with the flower head facing upward.

The picture of the magnolia leaves, arranged in a Sunabachi, is another example of the Seika Style. It is a formal left-hand arrangement.

Seika Style, Upright Formal, left hand arrangement, with magnolia branches.

77

THE MODERNISTIC STYLE

The modernistic style of Japanese Flower Arrangement is revolutionary compared to the usual conception of this art. Resembling present-day trends in modernistic art, it is considered *avant garde* by the Japanese. The association with flower arrangement seems to be that these modernistic styles are created by the great masters whose genius has evolved the new designs. Since Japanese Flower Arrangement is an art, it is flexible, with scope for broad development. The quality in common with Ikebana is the all-important element of design. Though called *avant garde*, it is more appropriately termed "advanced design."

Unusual combinations of material are arranged—sections of trees, driftwood, large rocks, stones, shells, iron or wire forms, plaster-of-Paris molds, along with living flowers, branches, and foliage. Materials are painted in bright or subdued colors. When a container or vase is used, this too is chosen with originality.

A few of the simple styles, mainly of driftwood and flowers, are presented in the Primer. Whether this modern trend will prevail remains to be seen.

RIKKA STYLE ARRANGEMENT

The Rikka Style (literally "standing flowers") is one of the most magnificent and elaborate ever developed. It was originated by the priest Ono-no-Imoko some years after the advent of Buddhism in Japan. It will be described in the Primer, but not in lesson form, since it requires a great deal of special material. However, the student should have knowledge of it in order to understand clearly the full development of Japanese Flower Arrangement.

The Rikka Style developed from temple offerings which suggest nature in its entirety. This conception is in accordance with Buddhist beliefs that the Shumi-sen Mountain represents the Universe. Rikka has three levels: Upper, Middle, and Lower, a concept also followed in the Seika Style, which developed from the Rikka.

Strong, artistic branches dominate the arrangement. Those are placed in the Upper Level representing growth at the top of the mountain. Middle and Lower levels of shrubs and flowers represent growth on the slopes and in the valley.

Sometimes nothing but bare branches are used for the basic design to which small bundles of pine needles and other appropriate materials are nailed. The same bare branches may be used time and time again. They are so expertly adorned they seem actually to be alive.

A simple bronze vase may be used with short twigs or bundles of straw placed inside to hold material securely. Or a horizontal container, called a Sunabachi, may be selected. In the early days, a board covered with sand was placed across the container, to give the appearance of outdoor growth, and also to keep material in position.

What gives the Rikka its dramatic appearance is the height of the Subject branch or stem, which is many times the height or width of vase or other container.

In this country the Rikka arrangement has great decorative value for use in large homes, churches, and public buildings.

In general, the Rikka Style is a floral offering that reflects the majesty of the Creator, interpreted through the skill and imagination of man.

82

A FINAL WORD

Imagination, coupled with patience and practice, is the principal attribute of the successful arranger. Beginners can best gain experience through working with a wide assortment of materials. Within the bounds of the basic principles outlined in this Primer, imagination is the guide to the selection and use of materials.

As in all forms of art, perfect results come with practice. In Japan the shortest course in flower arranging lasts for three months—even then, the student has barely commenced. I once asked my teacher what period of time constituted a "complete" course and was told one year was the minimum. It takes that long for the student to acquire dexterity in handling flowers *gently*. Also she must train her eyes to see the proper design and style for each arrangement. Furthermore, changing seasons produce new flowers, and the student must learn to use and combine them as they come into bloom.

Japanese Flower Arrangement is not an art to be learned overnight as we Westerners, in our impatience, are inclined to expect. Original arrangements only result from a good foundation in this art. So don't be discouraged if your first attempts at arranging in the Japanese style are not too successful. Practice will bring competence. Keep in mind that it took the Japanese centuries to develop their technique and skill.

Think about Japanese Flower Arrangement while you are learning. Observe Nature, and be guided by it. I remind my students constantly to "let the flowers and branches tell you how to arrange them."

Here it seems appropriate to remark that the Japanese word *Kado* means "the way of the flowers." Arrange flowers their way. This is the secret of Japanese Flower Arrangement. Above all, enjoy yourself while you are learning the art. The hours of learning should be hours of pleasure. As Mary Averill states so beautifully in *The Flower Art of Japan*, "We will discover by the constant study of flower arranging that we are beautifying all that touches our lives."

HISTORY

Japanese Flower Arrangement naturally reflects the character of the Japanese people. We all know that they are bold, strong, aggressive, and fearless, but few of us realize that they also possess gentler traits, and are imbued with a love of beauty and an interest in art and culture. The Japanese are descended from a union of migrant Tartars from the North and what apparently were Malayans from the South. The Tartars brought the strong. bold characteristics, while the Malayans are responsible for the love of beauty,

Historical sources for Japanese Flower Arrangement are very limited. We must largely rely on references in a few ancient books and poems, on accounts of exhibitions, on prints, designs on kimonos, and finally on legend and tradition. Since the information is not too accurate, there are many different versions of the history of arrangement in Japan.

Evidently the beginnings lie in the Buddhist religion which was brought to Japan from China by way of Korea about 540 A.D. It was the enthusiasm of Prince Shotoku which introduced it to the Japanese people. One of the early rites was to place floral offerings to Buddha in the temple.

A Buddhist priest, Ono-no-Imoko, was probably the originator of Japanese Flower Arrangement. Certainly he was responsible for the magnificent Rikka arrangements for the temple. Arrangement, according to rules, is generally credited to the Emperor Saga who originated them about 810 A.D. He probably devised the system of Ikebana, "flowers arranged effectively according to rule."

With the Buddhist religion from China came the rapid cultural advance of the people. Gradually the crude early arrangements developed into the magnificent creations for which Japan has become so renowned. The sponsorship of early emperors and their followers resulted in such mastery that arranging was raised to the level of an art. At the same time it retained a strong spiritual significance.

Improved living conditions were another influence. As the centuries passed crude huts gave way to elaborate and luxurious homes. Flowers were used for home decoration as well as in the temple. Floral displays were, and still are, placed in a Tokonoma, the place of honor in the Japanese home. From emperors, noblemen, and priests, the techniques of arrangement spread to other individuals. "Masters," or experts began to appear. From the Rikka a more practical, modified style developed for the home; this was called the Seika.

Through the centuries the formal style (Seika) gave way to the informal Heika. Contact with the West resulted in the Moribana. At one time, Japanese Flower Arrangement deteriorated considerably because of too numerous and too rigid rules.

Beauty of flowers was apparently forgotten. In the Golden Age of Flower Arrangement (1573-1868) the art was rescued and developed anew. About fifty years ago Mr. Ushin Ohara, founder of the Ohara School, broke with tradition and the formal style. He was the first master to do this. Today, the art follows the modern trend similar to what has developed in this country and abroad in the other arts.

The influence of Zen Buddhism and the Tea Ceremony, established even before the early sixteenth century, had a profound effect on the development of flower arrangement, particularly since the ritual required a floral display. In it religious sentiment and esthetic feeling are harmoniously combined.

Japanese Flower Arrangement was not practiced solely for the satisfaction of arranging flowers beautifully according to the rules, but because the art was imbued with deep philosophical and religious significance. It was a "new way of life." Even the principal stems were given the symbolic names of Heaven, Earth and Man. Heaven was interpreted as "the firm soul of all things"; Earth, "the source through which all things take form"; Man, "the fundamental way by which all things become active."

Today in the West, we are learning more than the techniques of the art. A well-made Japanese Flower Arrangement should present to the beholder much more than a clever piece of work. It should have subtlety, an esthetic and spiritual quality. It is no wonder that this beautiful art has permeated the life of the Japanese people for so many centuries. Japanese Flower Arrangement is one of the noblest and most fascinating pursuits.

INDEX

Artificial Methods of Supporting Flowers, 18, 45-47, 50, 53, 61

Bending of Stems, 53, 65

Combination of Materials, 16. 27, 37

Containers, 15, 19, 20, 27, 62, 67

Exhibitions, 11

Fillers, 16, 54, 63
measurement rule, 18, 64

Flower Arrangement Schools, 10, 11, 12, 20

Flower Shows, 11

Free-Style Arrangements, 19

Furyu, 13

Heika Style, 10, 15, 16, 17, 19, 48-62, 85
measurement rule 17, 18

Holders, 16, 19, 20, 21, 33, 65
covering of, 25, 32

Ikebana, 15

Japanese Flower Arrangement:
Etiquette of admiring, 13
history, 84, 85
schools, 10, 11, 12, 20
also see Styles

Japanese Words, Translations of
Furyu, 13
Gyo, 64
Heika, 15
Ikebana, 15
Kado, 83
Kensan, 16
Moribana, 15
Nagiere, 15
Rikka, 81
Seika, 63
Shin, 63, 64

So, 64

Soe, 63

Tai, 63

Kakemono, 12

Measurement Rules, 17, 18, 64

Modernistic Style, 79

Moribana Style, 10, 15-42, 85
measurement rule, 17

Nagiere (see Heika)

Natural Methods of Supporting Flowers, 45

Principal Stems, 16, 32, 33, 63
measurement rules, 17, 18, 64
wedging of, 21

Pronged Wooden Fork, 65-67

Rikka Style, 81, 84

Seika Style, 10, 63-77, 84
formal form, 64, 73, 77
informal form, 64
semi-formal form, 64, 69

Styles of Japanese Flower Arrangement
see Free-Style, 19
Heika Style, 48-62
Moribana Style, 15-42
Modernistic Style, 79
Rikka Style, 31, 81, 84
Seika Style, 63-77

Sunabachi, 67, 77, 81

Symbolism, 13, 63, 85

Tokonoma, 12, 13, 25, 84

Vases, 15, 19, 49, 67

Wooden Fastener, 65, 67

THE PLAY'S THE THING

by Lawrence Langner

FOR ANYONE WHO has ever been stage-struck, even in the slightest degree (for the affliction is incurable), this informative new book raises the curtain on the world behind the world of make-believe. On one level the book is an intimate, informal record of some of the most memorable productions of the past forty years. No one else in the theatre has worked with as many great men of the theatre as Mr. Langner. His book contains recollections of George Bernard Shaw, Eugene O'Neill, Robert Sherwood, Philip Barry, Maxwell Anderson and other memorable names—playwrights, actors, designers—and provides firsthand insights into the working methods, the quirks, the peculiar genius of each.

For the playwright, Mr. Langner's book is a professional guide to play construction, rewriting, adaptation, production, etc., with special chapters devoted to television. His observations are based on a career of unparalleled variety in the professional theatre, and, understandably, THE PLAY'S THE THING is also a book of great interest for everyone who knows and admires Lawrence Langner's work, for those who want to learn more about the craft of the theatre, and for all who love the theatre and respond to the magic of its great names.

Jacket Design by Ben Feder, Inc.

...book enabled to devote the necessary time to further his theatrical career, to which he now gives his entire effort.

THE PLAY'S THE THING

Books and Plays by Lawrence Langner

BOOKS

The Importance of Wearing Clothes
The Magic Curtain (an autobiography)

PLAYS (*published*)

The Pursuit of Happiness (with Armina Marshall)
Suzanna and the Elders (with Armina Marshall)
Five One Act Plays (Licensed, Pie, Another Way Out, Matinata, The Family Exit)
Moses
The Broken Image
The School for Husbands (adapted with Arthur Guiterman)
Patent Applied For
Accidents Will Happen (Bennet Cerf's Anthology of Best One Act Plays)

Lawrence Langner is also the author of or collaborator in the following plays produced in Westport, New York, and other cities: *These Modern Women, For Husbands Only, Lady Godiva, Holding Helen, Henry Behave, Tangerine, Champagne Sec, Once Married Twice Shy, The Life of the Party, The Compromisers, The Red Cloak*, and adaptations of *The Country Wife, Love for Love* and *Princess Turandot*.

The
Play's The Thing

LAWRENCE LANGNER

G. P. Putnam's Sons
New York

To

My Friend and Colleague
JOHN GASSNER

Sterling Professor of Playwriting and Dramatic
Literature at the Yale University School of Drama

and formerly head of the Play Department
Theatre Guild, New York City

> *This writing of plays is a great matter,*
> *forming as it does the minds and affections*
> *of men in such sort that whatsoever they*
> *see done in show on the stage, they will*
> *presently be doing in earnest in the world,*
> *which is but a larger stage.*
>
> Bernard Shaw in *The Dark*
> *Lady of the Sonnets*

Acknowledgments

I wish to express my gratitude for the help given me in writing this book and checking its many references by my friends and associates Worthington Miner, John Gassner, George Kondolf, Harold Sherman, Hobe Morrison, Arthur Heinemann, Harold Freedman, Mr. and Mrs. Mark Schoenberg, Mary Lou Allbright, and Armina Marshall.

Publisher's Note

Lawrence Langner is the founder of the Theatre Guild and of the American Shakespeare Festival Theatre and Academy. He has had a unique experience in the modern theatre, having with his partners, Theresa Helburn, Armina Marshall and other directors of the Theatre Guild, worked on the production of many of the most important plays of our era. He had been involved in the presentation of eighteen plays by Bernard Shaw, of which *Heartbreak House, Back to Methuselah, Saint Joan, Too True to Be Good, The Millionairess* and *The Simpleton of the Unexpected Isles* were world premières. He also worked day by day with Eugene O'Neill on the production of *Strange Interlude, Mourning Becomes Electra, The Iceman Cometh,* and six others of his later plays.

Among the other important American playwrights with whom he has had a working relationship during the writing (and rewriting) of their plays produced by the Theatre Guild, may be mentioned S. N. Behrman (8 plays), Robert Sherwood (3 plays), Maxwell Anderson (6 plays), Philip Barry (6 plays), Sidney Howard (4 plays), and one or more plays by William Saroyan, William Inge, Elmer Rice, Lynn Riggs, Ben Hecht, Tennessee Williams and Sophie Treadwell. Among these plays were some of America's modern masterpieces, including Sherwood's *Reunion in Vienna* and *There Shall Be No Night;* Maxwell Anderson's *Elizabeth the Queen* and *Mary of Scotland;* Sidney Howard's *They Knew What They Wanted* and *The Silver Cord;* S. N. Behrman's *The Second Man* and *Biography;* Philip Barry's *The Philadelphia Story;* William Inge's *Come Back Little Sheba* and *Picnic;* and William Saroyan's *The Time of Your Life.*

Notable plays by foreign authors include St. John Ervine's *John Ferguson* and *Jane Clegg;* Franz Werfel's *Goat Song, Juarez and Maximilian* and (with S. N. Behrman) *Jacobowsky and the Colonel;* Ferenc Molnar's *Liliom, The Guardsman* and *The Glass Slipper;* James Bridie's *The Sleeping Clergyman* and *Storm Over Patsy;* Chekhov's *The Seagull;* and Andreyev's *He Who Gets Slapped.*

Lawrence Langner has also been associated with the production of some of our most notable musical plays, including the Heyward's and the Gershwin's *Porgy and Bess;* and Rodgers and Hammerstein's *Oklahoma* and *Carousel,* as well as "The Theatre Guild on the Air" and the Theatre Guild productions for the United States Steel Hour on television.

With his wife, Armina Marshall, he opened the Westport Country Playhouse in 1931; and together they wrote the successful comedy *The Pursuit of Happiness,* which ran a season in New York and was also presented in London. He has written, either alone or in collaboration, over twenty plays which have been produced in New York and Westport; he also collaborated on the successful musicals *Tangerine* and *Champagne Sec.* He has also made and produced a number of adaptations of the classics, including *Princess Turandot, Love for Love, The Country Wife, The Inspector General,* etc. In the year 1915 he was one of the founders and leading spirits of the original Washington Square Players, which produced over fifty one-act plays.

Out of this vast experience, Langner has taken time out to write *The Play's The Thing*, by which he hopes to pass on to others interested in the theatre and television some of the knowledge he has gained in working over forty years in the production of some of the best plays of his generation. This book is also based in part on a series of lectures on "Playwriting for the Theatre and Television" delivered at Westport, Connecticut, under the auspices of the Academy of Television Arts and Sciences, 1958.

Since the writing of this book, Mr. Langner has been appointed by the Honorable Robert H. Thayer, Special Assistant to the Secretary of State, to establish an American Acting Company in a repertory of three outstanding American plays to tour in Europe and Latin America under the auspices of the President's Special International Program for Cultural Relations, in association with the American National Theatre and Academy.

Lawrence Langner was born in Swansea, South Wales, and educated in England; he passed the examination of the British Chartered Institute of Patent Agents and came to the United States early in 1911 where, after three years, he founded the firm of foreign patent and trade-mark specialists, Langner, Parry, Card and Langner. With the addition of a number of partners, Langner was soon enabled to devote the necessary time to further his theatrical career, to which he now devotes most of his time.

CONTENTS

CHAPTER I

The Joy of the Theatre

ALL the world's a stage—and most of the men and women living in it are stage-struck. Indeed the very word "stage-struck" implies a form of universal madness which does not exist in any other calling, for I know of no banker who is "bank-struck," nor any engineer or other professional man who carries his love for his vocation to a point of similar irrationality.

Explorers who push through the green walls of the jungles of Africa, South America and Melanesia find stage-struck aborigines performing plays for other stage-stuck aborigines. They take part in these with the same fervor with which their more civilized stage-struck brothers and sisters are presenting or witnessing plays, motion pictures or television performances from Maine to California, from Land's End to John o' Groats, and from the Atlantic coast of Western Europe to the Pacific coast of Eastern Asia. Indeed, wherever people live there is some form of theatre, and this is as characteristic of the world of communism as it is of the world of the democracies. Indeed, the leaders of the two systems now boast of the advantages of one system over the other, not merely in terms of economics, but also in terms of their support and accomplishments in the theatre, ballet, music and motion pictures.

A glance through a list of the fifty or more festivals which are being held throughout the world in the year 1960 will show that most civilized countries are increasingly engaged in showing off their performing arts as a mark of cultural superiority. Festivals for Shakespeare are presented annually at Stratford-on-Avon, Stratford, Canada, and Stratford, Connecticut, while theatre, dance and music festivals are held throughout Europe and include such world-renowned festivals as Salzburg, Bayreuth, Spoleto and Edinburgh. Moreover, crowds of motion picture devotees flock to the International Film Festivals of Venice, Cannes or Berlin. In addition, we in America have been transporting to Russia, at government expense, our native companies in musicals such as *Porgy and Bess* and *My Fair Lady,* and we send our ballet and theatre companies all over. The British are sending their Shakespearean and ballet companies to Europe, the United States and India, while the Russian Bolshoi Ballet and Moiseyev Dance Company periodically visit England, France, Canada and the United States. Verily, all governments are getting into show business, and the so-called road has now become an international thoroughfare. As Shakespeare remarked of the world, "This huge stage presents naught but shows, whereon the stars, in secret, influence comment."

With the invention of "dubbing," motion picture actors all over the world have been given "the gift of tongues" which makes them understandable in all languages, as does a new electronic system which enables the speech of actors playing on a stage in one language to be translated into that of their foreign audiences. As a result of "dubbing," playwrights and actors of all countries can now exchange their theatrical wares, which can be dispatched in the form of motion pictures to almost all parts of the world where stage-struck audiences are willing to part with their good money to watch these performances.

Why is it that from time immemorial, men and women have wanted to perform in plays, authors have wanted to write them, and audiences have wanted to attend them? Psychologists tell us that the actor, striving to be godlike, has enjoyed the ability to change his personality and to give expression to a character created by himself and the author, and has thus achieved a certain superiority by the exercise of his talents. He is rewarded not only by this personal satisfaction, but also by the plaudits of an admiring public, and in the case of great talent and popularity, with the highest financial remuneration. The author also participates in the godlike ability to create people and events, and to move his characters through the comedy or drama of their lives with considerably greater precision than Providence. Indeed, he can impart a pattern to the lives of his characters and a meaning to events which must make the gods themselves feel envious. As to the audiences, they too can partake of the godlike quality of observing the unfolding of these events, even as the gods might watch them, enjoying the joys and travails of others without actively participating in them. Thus mankind, well knowing that the theatre is a world of make-believe, nevertheless partakes of the pleasures and sorrows of this imaginary world as if it were better than the world of reality, which indeed it often is.

Assuming there are no psychologists lurking around the corner to give you Freudian explanations for anything and everything, you may well ask yourself the question why *you* enjoy the theatre, motion pictures or plays on television? There will be almost as many answers as there are different kinds of people. The Puritan may reply that plays are the most successful manifestations of the devil's handiwork, and that is why so many of us sinners enjoy them. Others will say that they prefer football or baseball. But the majority will find simple reasons, such as "they make me forget my troubles"; "they open up vistas of the past or the future"; "they enable me to experience the joys and sorrows of others"; "they make me cry or they make me laugh." Or finally, you may find your greatest enjoyment in spending an evening now and again in the company of your favorite actors and actresses whose talents you admire, rather than with your friends or relatives. All of these, and many other reasons, explain why we enjoy the theatre, an enjoyment which I first experienced at the age of seven. And I have been stage-struck ever since.

The love of humanity for the theatre is deep and abiding. It goes back as far as we can trace man's history. The earliest cave paintings, believed to be over twenty thousand years of age, depict priests or medicine men wearing masks, and dressed as animals which they imitated in a dance-drama addressed to the spirits. These were the first actors, and they performed in shrines in the innermost depths of their caves. And from these humble beginnings have grown the players, the plays and playhouses of the centuries—the enormous open-air amphitheatres of Greece and Rome, the shapely playhouses of the Renaissance, the Elizabethan apron-stage theatres, and the Restoration and Victorian proscenium theatres which are still with us today. And the expenditures of billions of dollars on theatre buildings for motion pictures, studios and television equipment during the first half of the present century show that mankind's interest in the theatre in all its forms is increasing rapidly with the increasing populations of the world. Only in the building of new dramatic theatres is there any notable lag, but even this is being overcome as new auditoriums and playhouses are built, or old theatres are modernized throughout the country.

The kingpin in all these manifestations of humanity's love of the theatre is the playwright. Because of the esteem in which men and women have generally held the theatre through the ages, the position of the author has usually been recognized as of paramount importance, and his contributions have been rated amongst the highest attributes of civilization. I remember some years ago standing outside St. James Theatre in London with Bernard Shaw, who discussed with me the impressions of the play he had just seen. He was recognized, and a crowd began to gather around him which soon reached the proportions usually associated with the presence of royalty. There was a smattering of applause and a murmur of adulation as the great man bowed and made his way through the crowd, a twinkle in his eyes and his white beard waving in the wind. I thought, as I watched him go, that probably only a prime minister or a movie star could have attracted a similar gathering at eleven o'clock at night.

Because of the importance the world has usually ascribed to the theatre, it is not surprising that some of the greatest men in the world's history have achieved fame in this field. Reputations such as those of Euripides, Aristophanes and Sophocles, have lasted over two thousand five hundred years along with the marble-hewn works of Praxiteles and Phidias —reputations which have lasted over six times as long as the scant four-hundred-year-old reputations of the great artists of the Renaissance. And some of the greatest poets, writers and thinkers of all time have written for the theatre. Who compares among the world's poets, philosophers, novelists, or other writers with William Shakespeare? Who among comedy writers compares with William Congreve and Wil-

liam Wycherley? Who compares in wisdom or wit with
Molière, in gaiety with Sheridan, in character drawing and
social criticism with Ibsen, in tragedy with Strindberg and
O'Neill, in intellectual breadth with Bernard Shaw, in
humanity and pathos with Chekhov? And if there are modern
novelists in this country whose writings compare in stature
with the plays of Eugene O'Neill, Thornton Wilder, or
Robert E. Sherwood, they are few and far between.

Anyone who has decided to work in the theatre can begin
with the knowledge that the career he or she has chosen is
important enough for the greatest minds the world has
known. He need not apologize to the local banker, industrial-
ist, scientist, or his family for adopting this career. In it one
can rise to heights far beyond those which the banker, in-
dustrialist, or scientist can ever attain, for in this profession
he can elevate the human spirit, illuminate life and give
the generations of men and women who come after him a
meaning and understanding of the times we live in which
they might never attain but for his work.

The young writer who wishes to make a career of playwriting has selected an occupation which is probably one of
the most rewarding if he can master the art. Rewarding, I
mean, to the writer, for he may not always attain worldly
rewards or even recognition. And he may be relatively sure
that if he is not recognized during his own lifetime, there
is very little chance that he will be recognized after his
death. In literature and art we have the examples of Samuel
Butler, Paul Gauguin, Vincent Van Gogh and others who
won posthumous fame, but in the theatre we have none. But
that need not be a deterrent. The author should plan to be
recognized by his own age, and his recognition can be as
great, if not greater, than in any other art.

It is not possible, however, for every individual to

evaluate himself in the light of the greatest achievements of his profession. There comes a time when a man's ability to control his destiny comes to an end, and God steps in. I must assume anyone entering this field is ambitious to succeed in the profession he has chosen, and that he will try to rise to the top. If one is ambitious to succeed as a doctor, engineer or scientist, he would not be satisfied to be a poor doctor, engineer or scientist, or a mediocre one. He would aspire to be among the best, and the standards are high. There is an old Japanese proverb which states, "If you aim at a star, you will bring down a flower." And so it is in playwriting. If the writer aims at the highest standards of his art, he will achieve a far higher success than if he is satisfied with the commonplace and the mediocre. Indeed, things being what they are today, if the writer is satisfied with the commonplace and the mediocre, he should not write for the theatre at all, but for some of the auxiliary media, such as motion pictures and television.

For the fact is that with motion pictures and television in America attempting to fill the needs of mass audiences, the theatre audiences who must pay relatively high prices for this form of entertainment have become increasingly selective, and selective in the best sense. An examination of the most successful plays during the past thirty years will indicate that the majority of them were of high quality in the writing and production, no matter what their genre.

To write a great play, a writer must have within himself either the greatness which makes his play great, or an appreciation of greatness in others. He cannot borrow these qualities. They must flow from himself. The nobility of theme and character, the high level of heroic conflict which contributes to the greatness of a play, all must be part of and come out of the soul of the author. If his preoccupation is with trivia and frivolity, his plays will reflect this. They may enjoy commercial success and result in substantial monetary rewards; but the inner satisfaction, the inner reward, will be missing, especially if the writer is one who knows in his own heart that he is capable of better things.

"Some people are born great, some achieve greatness, and some have greatness thrust upon them," wrote Shakespeare. When a person is born great, we are apt to regard him as a "genius," believing that his creative talent was to a considerable extent inherited. This may be true of child prodigy chess players, mathematicians and musicians, but it is not true of dramatists. I know of no child dramatist, and while we have encountered brilliant writers of comedy in their early twenties, such as Richard Brinsley Sheridan and Noel Coward, we must believe from the evidence before us that most dramatists are neither born great nor have had greatness thrust upon them, but have achieved it by their own efforts. Assuming always that he begins with a creative talent, it is the writer himself who will determine the extent of his achievement. His first job is to furnish his own mind with all the knowledge and appreciation of beauty, philosophy, poetry and science he can acquire, first from life and living, and, second, from books—which are the condensed experiences of others. The amount of mental furniture a man can amass in his memory is prodigious, but mere universal knowledge is not sufficient. More important is the use to which his knowledge of life and living is put. A lately departed playwright whom I knew was a living encyclopaedia, yet the plays he wrote were almost all mediocre. Of what use is it for a writer to be a master of all the knowledge he can acquire, if this knowledge is not put to use in his writing in the form of wisdom?

But even this kind of knowledge is not sufficient. Beyond

the curiosity of the writer's eternally active mind which acquires its knowledge as far as possible firsthand by observation of people, the way they live and die, and the world they live in, their characters, customs, religions, hopes, dreams and ambitions—beyond all this is the "point of view" which the writer has acquired from life and its living. It is this "point of view" which makes a writer's plays unique, because it is the product of a person who not only knows life but has something to say about it which is worth listening to.

And to gain this "point of view" takes living. It cannot be gained in the library. The first job of a creative writer is to live in the workaday world and to observe firsthand what is going on around him. Eugene O'Neill, speaking to me of Professor George Pierce Baker's 47 English Workshop at Harvard, once observed, "You can take a playwriting course and learn all the techniques of playwriting as well as all the tricks of the trade, but the one thing you can't learn is the most important ingredient—life itself. They can't teach you that." And he went on to say that one of the most valuable periods in his life was when he went to sea as a sailor and learned its ways of life and met the seafaring men who inspired so many of his earlier sea plays. Yet O'Neill agreed that much could be learned about writing for the theatre by taking a playwriting course. Among others of our best writers, he attended the famous English 47 Workshop of Professor Baker at Harvard, and later on inscribed a volume of his plays *To Professor George P. Baker—with the hope that these plays may prove to him that at least some of his constructive advice and criticism of 1914-15 stuck midway between my ears.*

Among the students of Professor Baker's courses were such successful playwrights as Sidney Howard, Philip Barry, Edward Sheldon, Edward Knoblock and Robert Sherwood, while among other prominent theatre people may be mentioned Brooks Atkinson, George Abbott, Theresa Helburn, Kenneth Macgowan, Frederick Koch, Glenn Hughes, John Mason Brown and Walter Prichard Eaton. The fact that the techniques of playwriting can be taught is one of the prime reasons for college courses on the subject as well as the many books which have been written to assist the young writer.

It was fashionable a few years ago to bemoan the fact that there is no subsidy for young authors to enable them to learn their trade. (This has been partly remedied by subsidies to playwrights by the Ford Foundation and others.) However, the most useful apprenticeship such writers can have is to work for a living in varied fields, both during and after acquiring an education which can be gained with or without benefit of college or university. If a writer is discouraged with his inability to secure a college education, he should remember that Shakespeare, Sheridan and Shaw did very well without one. Education begins at birth and continues throughout life until death, and is not limited to spending certain hours in certain buildings on a certain campus.

Book learning is most important to the young writer for the stimulus he receives from meeting with other minds. And with the existence of public libraries and inexpensive editions of good books which are now available almost everywhere, there are no practical limits to what he may acquire in the way of self-education if he possesses the requisite intellectual curiosity.

But the young writer should beware of accepting all that he reads in books as gospel. Part of an individual's point of view is due to his ability to separate the true from the false as he reads, and to add new facts and what is true about them, to the sum of his knowledge. Charles F. Kettering, one of America's greatest practical scientists, stated that above the door of every library should be written the words ENTER AT YOUR PERIL. This is because every book tends to embalm thought or knowledge—to provide a terminal beyond which we feel we cannot pass. But in reality knowledge is ever-fluid, ever-flowing, and is varied or modified as we learn more and more about the world we live in. A fact which seemed to be true in the year 1890 may look very different in the light of the knowledge of today. Thus it is given to every generation of writers to illuminate all that has gone before with the knowledge of our own times, and to give new facets to old facts and make them to shine anew.

If, to my readers, I seem to be unduly emphasizing the importance to writers of acquiring knowledge by firsthand observation and experience of living, let me make it clear that I intend this to be so. Textbooks may help a writer after he has experienced some chapters of living, but he should never bemoan the fact that he is so busy earning a living that he has no time to write—unless he carries this to a point where he stops writing altogether. If he is gaining experience from his contacts with people in varying walks of life, he is finding something to write about, and is on his way to becoming a writer.

Today, as never before, young playwrights can learn some of the writing part of their trade while earning a living by writing plays for television. They will not learn from the medium itself to acquire the point of view which distinguishes the important playwright, and which can be gained only by profoundly deep thinking, and feeling and suffering over the phenomena of life itself. This cannot be learned either in theatre buildings or in television studios.

But what of the writer who does not wish to become "an

important playwright"; a man who is not ambitious to stand
in the top echelon—but will be satisfied to be a successful
writer of plays, light plays, frivolous plays, entertaining
plays, plays to make an evening pass gaily and happily?
Such a writer can also be an important figure in the field
he has chosen, to the extent to which he has achieved originality and the highest standards which apply to the particular kind of play he has chosen to write. For the theatre is as
large as life, if not larger, and almost any part of life can
find a place on the stage. It asks only of all writers that they
aspire to do the best work in the particular field they have
chosen, be it in the nature of comedy, farce or drama. It
offers no easy success, but the rewards for success are great
enough to compensate for the utmost effort on the part of
the writer.

In Chapter IX, I have listed over thirty categories of subjects for plays in most of which reputations have been made
in the past forty years. It is interesting to note that very few
writers have made an important reputation in more than
two of these fields. All the most important plays ever
written are found in the majority of these categories, and
less important, but financially successful, plays have been
written in the remaining few categories. It is also interesting
to note that whereas it was once correct to believe that the
great author worked in an attic and died in poverty, this
condition no longer exists. Bernard Shaw amassed a fortune
during his lifetime and his estate became even wealthier
after his death, partly because of the earnings of the musical
based on his play *Pygmalion*. Eugene O'Neill garnered his
largest earnings from his greatest plays, *Strange Interlude*
and *Mourning Becomes Electra*. Let any playwright write a
successful play today from which a motion picture or television play or series can be based, and he may unexpectedly

discover that he is a millionaire, as well as the unhappy victim of the tax collector.

Our greatest dramatists have been poets. This does not mean that they have written their plays in poetry or poetic dialogue—although the greatest of all dramatists have done so. It means that they have been poets because they have been blessed with an awareness of the beauty of life in all its phases, the beauty of love, of nobility, and of tragedy. Illuminated by the greatness of the human spirit and being moved by this awareness, they have been able to communicate their feelings to us, their audience, and we, too, have felt and been touched by their awareness. Consequently, many plays written in the vernacular are nevertheless works of poetry because of the poetry in their conception. Several of these stand out in my mind: Molnar's *Liliom* with its moving love scenes between Liliom and Julie, and its death scene which reaches such tragic heights; Andreyev's *He Who Gets Slapped* with its colorful clown trying to escape from the world; Sherwood's *There Shall Be No Night* singing a tragic melody of man's ever-continuing struggle for freedom; O'Neill's *Strange Interlude* with its unforgettable "My Three Men" scene; *Green Grow the Lilacs* with its joyous song of the early days of Oklahoma which inspired Richard Rodgers and Oscar Hammerstein to write their musical masterpiece; Philip Barry's *Hotel Universe* with its dreamlike quality of unreality. All these are poetic plays, and blank or rhymed verse is in none of them. It is a tragedy of our times that our authentic poets, such as Robert Frost and Edna St. Vincent Millay, did not write more for the theatre. England's Christopher Fry and our gift to England, T. S. Eliot, have done better, but still not enough. If I had my life to live over again, I would spend much of it in encouraging the poets to invade the theatre.

A young dramatist, reading these lines, may well exclaim, "All this is expected of me—and poetry too?" If a writer has a desire to write for the theatre, there is probably a poet lurking within him of whom he may not be too aware. When he is selecting a subject for a play, he should try to express his feeling about it in terms of a poem. It will help him to clarify what he wishes to convey to his audience. Ibsen is reputed to have done this, and there are extant copies of the poems he composed before he wrote A Doll's House, The Master Builder, and others. It is extraordinary how much poetry lurks in the soul of every writer, and even more extraordinary how often he is afraid to give voice to it.

With the rewards so great, why is it that we do not possess more important playwrights? With a population of over 170,000,000 in the United States, of which at least 60 per cent have reached maturity, why is it that not one in five million turns out to be a successful playwright? To state that one must be born with a special talent is too easy an explanation. The real facts lie elsewhere. The writer for the theatre who does not achieve immediate success tends to become discouraged after a while and leaves the field. This is because, until recently, there was no partial success possible for the young playwright. His first play either failed or succeeded, and if it failed, he starved. But the medium of television may now provide the dramatist with the means of earning a livelihood while he is concentrating on his more serious work. This is rapidly becoming a pattern which is already bringing a number of new and important writers into the theatre, since the art of constructing a television play is far closer to that of the art of the stage than the motion picture.

Furthermore, the budding playwright is urged not to overlook the fact that while he is waiting for his first play to be produced he has an equal possibility of earning a living by writing short stories or novels. This was well recognized by certain English playwrights who made themselves proficient in all fields of the storytelling art.

The field of playwriting is as open to women as it is to men, and some of our best writers in this medium have been women. I mention in passing Lillian Hellman, Rachel Crothers and Rose Franken in America and Clemence Dane and Dodie Smith in England. There seems to be no logical reason why there should not be many more women play-wrights, since in the field of the novel there are proportion-ately far more women writers than in the theatre. Moreover, women writers often have a special veiwpoint which is im-portant for the world, and should be represented on the stage as well as in the novel.

My own practical experience of working with many of the important authors of my day has taught me that no sex has any monopoly on artistic talent in the theatre, and that good plays can come from any creative source. Neither "normality" nor the lack of it is of any importance so long as the indi-vidual is creative. Good plays have been written by normals and abnormals, neurotics and psychotics, as well as hetero-sexuals and homosexuals.

It is usual in textbooks on playwriting to warn the aspir-ing writer not to enter this field lightly, because of the ob-stacles he will encounter and the difficulties with which he will be faced before he achieves success. As pointed out in the beginning of this chapter, playwriting is one of the most difficult of the arts; but the difficulty lies rather in the prac-ticing of the art than in training for it. I know too much about the world of business, science and the professions to subscribe to a general warning as regards these difficulties, without also pointing out some of the advantages on the other side of the ledger. When I compare the amount of training required for a talented writer to become an accomplished playwright, with the amount of training required to produce a successful engineer, scientist, or doctor, I believe the balance to be all in the favor of the playwright. I do not include as "training" the amount of time spent by the writer in gathering material from life itself, from which his plays will be fashioned, but the time spent in classrooms, examinations and apprenticeships which the professional man must undergo before practicing his profession.

Let us consider a story which lends itself to treatment either as a novel, a motion picture or a play. A writer who has already mastered the technique of the novel or the motion picture would not necessarily have to spend years learning the techniques of the theatre in order to use his material as the basis of a play instead of a novel. In England (but not in the United States), it was not unusual in the past to find novelists who passed from the form of the novel to that of the play with the greatest ease, and with but little training for the theatre. Among these may be mentioned John Galsworthy, Somerset Maugham, St. John Ervine, J. B. Priestley, Aldous Huxley and Arnold Bennett. Other novelists were never able to master the dramatic form. Most notable among these was Henry James, who made several unsuccessful attempts, and several of whose novels have since been dramatized successfully by lesser men.

A slight training in playwriting, or even no training at all, may result in a lucky break for a young author on a first play which would not be comparable with the obstacles and difficulties men in other professions (such as science, engineering or law) encounter before they are experienced enough to practice their professions successfully. In playwriting, as in almost every other walk of life, there is a shortage of men of talent, and the obstacles and difficulties encountered are no greater than those encountered in other professions, and in certain respects even less.

This does not mean that the playwright will not encounter many problems in the transfer of the play from the page of his manuscript to the boards of the stage. There he may well lose some of the good results of his work on paper, or he may greatly improve his play. The latter is more often true in practice, although the cases where the play is alleged to have been hurt in transit from the manuscript to the stage are usually far more widely advertised. This is because such cases generally come to light when there is a red-hot dispute between an author and a stage director or producer, the spicy details of which are reported in the newspapers.

In writing his play, the playwright functions as an individual artist; in producing it on the stage, he acts as a member of a team and, in the case of the first production of each play, his presence is usually essential. He then learns that the theatre is a co-operative art, and also that his work which seemed complete on paper is only partly finished. It is at this point that the playwright so often wishes he had written a novel, because the publisher usually makes some minor editorial comments and then prints the book, so that it reaches the public with the minimum effort on the part of the novelist once he has completed his writing. Not so with the playwright. Before his play reaches the stage, it must pass through the hands of a manager, a director, a group of actors, a scenic artist, a costume designer and others. What finally appears before the audience will be the result of their efforts as well as his, and if the collaboration is unsuccessful, it may bear only a distorted resemblance to what the playwright originally conceived in his study or his tower of ivory.

In order that the writer may imbue his collaborators with

what he intended by his play, he should always be present at rehearsals, where he is protected by his Dramatists Guild contract in insisting that the wording of his script be respected. He learns from watching his play in rehearsal whether changes are or are not necessary, whether scenes are too long and need cutting, or too short and need developing, or whether other or more drastic rewriting may be necessary. So that the attendance of the author at rehearsals is an essential part of the business of playwriting, and requires certain disciplines and attitudes which we will examine later. That such attendance at rehearsals is of extreme importance is demonstrated in the case of O'Neill's *Dynamo*, which was unsuccessfully produced by the Theatre Guild while O'Neill was on a tour around the world. Here is what O'Neill wrote me after he read the reactions of the critics to his play:

> I never should have let the play out of my hands so soon after completing it—contrary to my usual practice. Besides being in a distraught state of mind at the time I went over the script, I had no perspective on it. When I read it over—after settling here—too late—I was appalled by its raggedness and, in the third part, vagueness and complicatedness. It was in no shape for production. You will see what I mean when you read the book.
>
> I should have been there and all I'm doing now would have been done at rehearsals. Or, more to the point, I should have held over the play until next season when I could be there. This is no beef against Phil, of course [Philip Moeller, the director of the play]. I know he did a fine job with what was there, but he couldn't be expected to read my mind and rewrite from it!

Nine writers out of ten would have blamed someone else for the failure of his play; not so Eugene O'Neill, who was big enough to admit his mistakes, most of which could have been rectified had he been present at rehearsals.

It should be apparent from O'Neill's letter that the playwright's work is not completed merely because he has handed to the producer or director what he regards as a final script of a play. Most of the important writers in the past, as well as of today, made it their business to be present while the play was in rehearsal, and to make such changes as might be required in order to bring the play to life on the stage in the form in which the author conceived it. Among prominent playwrights who stood behind their plays while they were being produced and were ready to make changes when needed may be mentioned Shakespeare, Molière, Shaw and O'Neill. In fact, so necessary is this attention by the author to details of casting, rehearsal, and so forth, that when the author signs a contract with a manager in the United States, he agrees to be available for consultation and assistance during the rehearsal period. Because of these facts, I have decided that no practical book on playwriting can be regarded as complete unless it also includes, along with the technical aspects of writing, sufficient information to enable the playwright to function in all phases of the production of the play, including the selection of the cast, the director, the scenic artist, and all the others whose collaboration is essential to bring about a successful production.

Finally, I should like to leave my readers with the thought that as playwrights, they will not merely be holding the mirror up to nature with its reflection of what is seen by the artist's eye, but they will also be influencing the behavior and morals of the community in which the play is given. Hence, whatever subject the author is writing about successfully, what he has to say about it may be affecting his times irrespective of whether he wishes to do so or not. He may not be a moralist, but he cannot avoid the consequences if his play successfully promotes his own moral or immoral point of view, whichever it may be according to the mores of the day. Thus the proliferation of violence (as is current in television crime plays), nihilism, suicide, sadism, alcoholism, drug addiction, or sexual violence and perversion, will necessarily affect the thinking of those who witness them, and the playwright cannot escape the responsibility for the consequences merely because he is not interested in them. For, as Bernard Shaw has stated correctly, "This writing of plays is a great matter, forming as it does the minds and affections of men in such sort that whatsoever they see done in show on the stage, they will presently be doing in earnest in the world, which is but a larger stage."

CHAPTER II

The Subject—The Story—The Theme

IF the playwright is a truly creative person, no one can tell him the kind of subject to select for a play he wishes to write. He will be brimful of his own ideas, and they will keep beating at his brain until he puts them on paper. But it will be worth his while to consider which of his many ideas are most susceptible to treatment for the theatre. In general he should remember that the theatre is considerably larger than life as it is lived around him, and is capable of dealing with any kind of subject however fantastic, realistic, spiritual or political. It has room for the explanation of all kinds of religious phenomena, philosophical thought, and the vulgarities of humanity as well as its highest aspirations. The playwright will naturally choose the subject which is closest to his heart and about which he feels a compulsion to write. Curiously enough, there is a tendency to regard the theatre today as an escape from life, as well as a medium for immersion in its deepest waters. Writers of the "escape from life" school often tend to place the story back in the past, so that it carries the audience away from the present into what seems a fairer day when the world was younger, gayer and not suffused with the difficulties and anxieties of our present everyday life. This fact has often led authors to use stories of the past which illuminate the present, as for example,

Robert Sherwood's use of the story of Hannibal's march on Rome to create enjoyment for the audience while making a thematic point against war, in his comedy *The Road to Rome.*

It is, however, a mistake to assume that each and every subject can be written in play form. We can obviously rule out a subject which calls for enormous quantities of scenery, unless you decide that it can be written for a stage without using scenery at all, as is sometimes the case. Or you may decide to use scenery as in the Elizabethan theatre, in which the play moved swiftly from scene to scene with bare indications by properties or other objects to denote the locale.

An episode is seldom sufficient for a long play, although many one-act plays are based on episodes. An episode may be said to bear the same relation to a play as an anecdote bears to a story or novel; that is, it has insufficient body or content to support the larger form of writing. A number of episodes held together by a single character or group of characters or an interesting theme can make a desirable chronicle play, such as Laurence Housman's *Victoria Regina,* or Arthur Schnitzler's *Reigen (The Ring)* and *The Affairs of Aantol.*

In my opinion, the kind of subject for which the play form is best suited is one in which there is a major situation or situations involving conflict between characters or groups of characters, or between characters and their destiny, which build in conflict, interest or intensity throughout the play to some sort of conclusion. The majority of plays in the literature of the modern theatre are based on such conflicts between individuals. The same was also true of the Elizabethan theatre. A typical example is the conflict between Hamlet, his uncle and his mother, ending in tragic consequences for all three. An individual may also be in conflict with himself. This is true of Hamlet, whose irresolution in the first part of the play is an important part of his character. Many of the important Greek tragedies represent man's conflict with fate or destiny. This type of conflict is rarer in the modern theatre. *The Diary of Anne Frank*, by Frances Goodrich and Albert Hackett, a recent play about the fate of a small Jewish family which lived in hiding in Amsterdam during the period of the Nazi occupation, may be regarded as a modern example of the latter type of play. Here destiny takes the form of the Nazis who were tracking down these unfortunate people, and who ultimately discover their hiding place, so that fate in the form of capture and death finally overwhelms them.

Plays in which there is insufficient conflict between the characters, or in which the conflict is largely internal or introspective, do not usually play as well as those in which the conflict is dramatized between the characters. Mere mood, or poetry, or character drawing, is not enough in itself to constitute a play. Many attempts are being made by dramatists today to break away from the convention that plays should consist mainly of conflict. Among these should be mentioned such plays as *Waiting for Godot* and *Endgame* by Samuel Beckett and *The Chairs* by Eugene Ionesco.

However well these plays may excite contemporary interest, they have usually been conspicuously lacking in the kind of dramatic conflict which is found in the greatest achievements in drama, nor are they likely to achieve much popularity with audiences when written in this form. However, as in all art, everything is possible, and a play form may well be developed which is a combination of introspective writing with or without dramatic conflict. If such a dramatic form could be evolved, it would be an exception to the rule that a story which is placid, or moves along on an even keel of interest without any climax, is usually unsuited to the theatre.

Aristotle, the first teacher of playwriting, and hence the predecessor of all the others who have since taken pen in hand on the subject, has stated that a play must have a beginning, a middle, and an end. This seems obvious, but it is a rule which is often honored in the breach. I would prefer from my own experience to state that a play today must have a rapid beginning, a middle which builds in excitement, and an end which either completes or suggests the completion of the promise of the play.

The best kind of story for the theatre, in the case of a drama or tragedy, is one in which scene after scene of mounting interest build up tension until a point is reached when the play attains its highest moment of climactic excitement. Such plays are usually most interesting when the audience is able to perceive that the events which take place in one scene are responsible for the events which take place in the next, or later, scenes. Thus we note in the play itself, by direct action, how one dramatic episode leads or builds to the next. Somewhat similarly, comedic stories best suited for the theatre are those in which the mounting scenes of comedy are piled one on top of the other in succession until a hilarious climax is achieved. In both these cases, the resolution which arrives toward the end of the play constitutes an ending which satisfies the audience by reason of our greater understanding of the nobility of the human spirit in the case of high tragedy, or the solution, or suggestion of a solution, of the human problems involved in the case of comedy.

For a period of nearly fifty years, the "play of ideas" was an important part of the theatre of England, the Continent and this country. The leading writer of such plays in England was Bernard Shaw, and he was followed in this country by

Robert Sherwood, S. N. Behrman, Elmer Rice, Maxwell Anderson and others. Giraudoux and Lenormand led the parade in France, Pirandello in Italy, Ibsen in Norway, Sudermann, Kaiser and Brecht in Germany, and Werfel in Austria. The plays written by these men were based on their experiences and studies outside the theatre. They represented the impact of creative intellect on the problems of humanity, and they created a modern theatre which will long survive them. The present-day theatre cries for a similar resurgence of the playwrights with intellect who will apply this to living subjects.

It is because so many of our present-day American dramatists live in the parochial confines of present-day Broadway, that the plays of today seldom deal with the lively issues of our times, and even when they do, it is in terms of sophistication rather than intellect and intelligence. Today our theatre is ten years behind our novelists in dealing with the problems of humanity. We must either look to them, or to a new generation of playwrights with intellectual curiosity, to provide subjects for plays which will counteract the gradual loss of stature which has taken place among the playwrights of the past twenty-five years. There has seldom been a time when the world has abounded with more important subjects about which to write, and the field is wide open in the United States, England and France. And since audiences are always ready to follow intellectual leadership which actually leads somewhere, such writers would be warmly welcomed in the theatre of today and tomorrow.

Perhaps a negative approach to the present subject will assist the budding dramatist by giving some warning of what not to write about. This is not an easy task, since almost every subject is susceptible of dramatic treatment, even those which are strongly pitted against the mores of the community or audience of the day. Indeed, some of these subjects make the most exciting and controversial plays. It will be difficult, however, to write plays on subjects which lack any general audience interest, such as plays dealing with scientific concepts or formulas even if a dramatic form could be found for them. Plays based upon the burlesque of characters, that is, stretching the exaggeration of character beyond believability, are seldom acceptable in the American theatre of today. Burlesque is differentiated from satire in the same way that the clown who slaps his fellow clown with a bladder is differentiated from the fencer who attacks his adversary with a rapier. The burlesquing of characters is acceptable in short plays, in revue sketches, in the musical theatre, or as a minor accompaniment to a long play, but will seldom interest an audience for an entire evening when it is the sole ingredient of a play. Satire, which is a product of the sophisticated mind, is an entirely different matter, and is universally accepted, although it calls for an intelligent audience for its best appreciation. An American school of satire, led by George S. Kaufman and Moss Hart, has achieved considerable success in this difficult field. It is often contended that it is harder to achieve popularity in this medium in the United States than abroad. But this is belied by the success of plays and revues such as *Of Thee I Sing, Boy Meets Girl, Born Yesterday, State of the Union, The Thurber Carnival* and so forth.

Dramas or semitragic plays with stories of pathos which reach a depressing conclusion without any particular illumination of life seldom succeed in pleasing present-day audiences in the American theatre; for when a playwright delves into the material of misery, we usually prefer a conclusion which testifies to the courage or nobility of the human spirit in meeting disaster. However, many plays with depressing or down-beat endings are written and produced in our theatre;

but since we are inherently an optimistic people, plays which emphasize the hopelessness of life are usually less popular than those which do not.

We must be careful to define what we mean when we speak of plays with depressing endings. Most of the plays of Chekhov might be regarded as coming under this category, but this would be a superficial judgment. Chekhov's plays were concerned with the futility of life in Russia in the early part of this century, but in the writing of them Chekhov was holding the mirror up to nature and showing the tragic waste of human lives which resulted from false values. The spirit in which Mme. Ranevsky leaves her home in *The Cherry Orchard* is that of high tragedy, for while we are left realizing the hopelessness of her position, we also love and admire her, for we know that basically in her innermost soul, she will never be defeated by material things. The tragic ending with the old coachman, the symbol of the old order, left to die in the ancestral home is assuaged by the knowledge that the vigorous but vulgar newcomer, Lopahin, will build a new order on the ruins of the old.

Tragedy need not necessarily end in death. Indeed there can be a living death which is far worse. Thus the self-immolation of Lavinia in O'Neill's *Mourning Becomes Electra*, who locks herself up in her home in New England in expiation for the deaths of her mother and her mother's lover, compares with the cracking of Blanche's mind in *A Streetcar Named Desire* and her removal to an institution which comes as a tragic climax to her irrational behavior. Such tragic endings, which follow a succession of theatrically exciting scenes, are of the finest stuff of which dramas are made. Where the story is merely a transcript of human misery, however, the novel is usually a better place than the theatre for its telling, if only for the reason that should it become unbearable, we can close the book more readily than we can leave the theatre.

Plays written for propaganda purposes seldom succeed in the theatre unless they are also works of art. By this I mean that the author of such a play must have the same respect for all the attributes which make for a good play, such as character development, situation and suspense, as if he were writing a play without propaganda value. In other words, he must concern himself first with writing a good play, in which the propaganda is a secondary attribute. While a few of such plays have succeeded in the theatre of our time, they were good propaganda only because they were first and foremost good plays. Among these may be mentioned Galsworthy's *Justice*, which resulted in changing the English penal laws by drawing attention to the misery inflicted on a prisoner released from prison on parole under the so-called "ticket of leave" system which existed in England at the time. Brieux's *Damaged Goods*, which dealt with the subject of syphilis, was a well-written play which aroused public opinion to the necessity for dealing with the subject of venereal disease from the standpoint of public health rather than public morality. We must remember that at the time this play was written, the subject of venereal disease was a forbidden topic of conversation, and the play itself fulfilled a propaganda value in bringing the evils resulting from this disease into the open so that it could be dealt with on a civilized basis rather than treated as the punishment for immorality. A further example of a play on the same subject, which was a work of art first and only secondarily propaganda, was Ibsen's *Ghosts*.

Another play which comes to mind which had a propaganda value after it had first succeeded as a work of art was Robert Sherwood's *There Shall Be No Night*, which aroused the country to the dangers of dictatorship at a time when the American people were making up their minds regarding the menace of Hitlerism and fascism. We must be careful not to confuse propaganda with theme, as explained later in this chapter. Propaganda in a play may be defined as a theme expanded beyond artistic limits to promote a cause. Many propaganda plays have been written in Russia in the last twenty years to prove one political point or another, such as the importance of collective farming by the use of tractors, or the futility of capitalism as burlesqued by political writers of the day. Propaganda plays were also written in this country during the depression of the thirties in an attempt to influence current political thinking. Such plays, no matter how well written, were not usually effective propaganda, for the audiences attending them often resented the fact that the art of the dramatist was being harnessed to the cause of propaganda in order to persuade them to change their way of thinking.

While there are a number of examples in which the theatre has influenced the life of its time, such as those mentioned above, it will be realized that there are other means of propagandizing a cause which might enable the propagandist to reach a far greater audience, since the theatre audience is small as compared to the mass audiences which can be reached by radio, television, motion pictures or books. Therefore, if the playwright's prime motive for writing a play is to promote a cause, he should consider well whether he cannot achieve this purpose more effectively in some other medium.

Among other subjects to avoid in writing for the theatre, beware of the comedy which is based upon the repetition of the same joke in different forms. These are often referred to as "one-joke" plays and it is surprising how often such plays appear upon the stage, and how seldom they achieve popularity. This is because, in the realm of comedy, we are most pleased by the quality of invention, and when this runs out, the play runs down and the audience runs out.

The question of the extent to which the dramatist should use the present-day knowledge of abnormal psychology in depicting psychotic situations in plays, is a controversial one. The tendency of some modern writers to people the stage with homosexuals, drug addicts, and mentally sick neurotics may be only a phase due to the opening of the floodgates of knowledge on these hitherto dark areas of human nature. In this respect the theatre is usually about a decade or so behind the novel, which has attempted to deal honestly with these subjects for many years. However, honesty alone does not make a good play, and I question whether plays which are based on sexual abnormalities will be staple fare for the theatre in the years to come. This is because audiences are composed largely of normal men and women who, when they attend the theatre, participate vicariously in the emotional experiences of the actors on the stage, and are moved by their emotions. However much love scenes between two men or two women may be enjoyable to an audience of homosexuals, an audience of normal men and women either find this distasteful or, at best, their curiosity for sensationalism is aroused.

I remember seeing a play in London some years ago entitled *Prisoners of War* by J. R. Ackerly in which the love affairs between a group of male English officers in a prison camp in Switzerland provided the plot. The bewildered members of the audience were viewing the characters on the stage as through some strange distorting mirror. The more passionately the men made love to one another, the less the audience could understand or participate emotionally in what was going on, and such interest as was aroused by the play was solely that of the voyeur.

Plays dealing with the subject of homosexuality or other forms of sexual perversion have from time to time rung up a high score at the box office, but I doubt that such plays have contributed constructively to the growth of a healthy theatre. On the contrary, their success has acted as an invitation to the young dramatist to delve even deeper into the subject of sensational perversion, a subject which, while it sometimes produces immediate financial results, ultimately turns far more people away from the theatre than it brings into it. Forty years ago, the plays of Wedekind, such as *Pandora's Box* and *Earth Spirit,* which dealt with every form of sexual perversion and even outdid in sensationalism the efforts of some of our modern American writers, attracted only scanty audiences (largely made up of sexual perverts) to the Kleines Theatre in Berlin, while the large Deutches Theatre next door was filled to overflowing with devotees of Reinhardt's productions of the plays of Shakespeare, Goethe, Sudermann, Hauptmann and Shaw. The plays of Wedekind are as forgotten today as those of our own generation who fish in the same muddied waters will be forgotten tomorrow, for in art as in life, that which best serves the life-force of humanity ultimately survives.

Given a subject which has been selected, the next problem to be considered is the story. With the greater interest on the part of modern audiences in character development, the story or plot has been growing less important than it was in Victorian days, when plays often exhibited situations of labyrinthine complication which were usually solved in the last few minutes of the last act. Such plots still find a home in the modern theatre in the form of "murder mystery" plays, of which Agatha Christie is the leading exponent. The story on which the play is based, however, is equally as important as character development, and in the best modern plays they are almost indivisible, because the best stories proceed from the characters themselves and are not superimposed on them.

The most effective stories for the theatre are usually those which affect one or two characters who are in the central position of the story. The story line of a single character who moves along the play and is its central figure usually results in a fine acting role for an actor or actress, as well as a unified play. As onlookers, we share the experiences of this central or main character as we pass with him from scene to scene. Ideally, other characters should be introduced only as they affect our main character. The same unity of story line can also be achieved when we deal with two main characters, especially in the case of a man and woman and their involvement with one another. Equally good story lines are possible with three main characters which may be two women and a man, two men and a woman, or two couples, when we are dealing with stories based on love or sex. However, as soon as we divide our stories between a considerable number of main characters, we begin to make the story line more difficult to follow and to achieve cumulative build.

My use of the words "story line," as compared with the word "story," is important. A good story may involve the use of a main character who appears only in the first and last acts of a three-act play. A good story line would involve the appearance of this same main character in all three acts so that he follows, so to speak, a continuous line throughout the play. Where the main character is to be played by an important actor or star, the desirability of a strong story line is emphasized.

A good example of the development of a story line, and

how it was brought about, comes to mind in connection with S. N. Behrman's brilliant comedy *End of Summer*. This play included Behrman's usual young liberal, played by Van Heflin, and his challenging woman of affairs, played by Ina Claire. When the play was handed to us by Harold Freedman, Sam's play representative, it had not quite made up its mind whether it was to be a comedy or a melodrama, a point on which Behrman had also not quite made up his mind. However, it contained so many brilliant scenes that we were delighted to have it, and we urged Sam to get the play ready for rehearsal as soon as possible since Ina Claire was available for it and liked the part. I shall always remember a scene in the famous Theatre Guild rehearsal room 64, while the play was being rewritten in rehearsal. Miss Claire was standing in the center of the room, her part in her hand, while Sam Behrman and Philip Moeller, the director, were seated dejectedly on the ramshackle chairs which were placed against the walls. Ina Claire looked Sam squarely in the eyes and said, "Sam, this play is about me, isn't it, so what do I do next?" Philip Moeller remarked, "Why Ina, at this point you're supposed to walk out." "I don't understand this at all," Ina stated. "Here I am. This scene is mine, and I've got to say something here. In fact, I have to have some lines written for me at this point. What do you think, Sam?"

There was little left for Sam to do—indeed for any of us to do—except agree with her. Nor was this bad for the play, as it turned out, for in this manner she helped Behrman to keep herself in the center of the story line, as a result of which the play was transformed during rehearsal into a well-constructed play. I do not advise this procedure, however, for many reasons. First of all, there are very few writers with this author's ability to write this kind of dialogue during rehearsals, and secondly there are very few actresses like Ina

Claire who know how to keep scenes moving along logically in this way.

Plays which are composed of different scenes between entirely different characters, each telling the separate stories of these characters as the play progresses, and these stories being either unrelated or only loosely related to one another or to the main story, are to be avoided. However, every rule has its exceptions. A *Midsummer Night's Dream* with its four separate groups of lovers, fairies, low comedians, and nobles of the court, has satisfied audiences for three centuries. Nevertheless, this play suffers badly from diffusion, and its blending of stories is its weakest aspect.

The employment of a subsidiary story with subsidiary characters, or a subplot, is often extremely valuable in plays for the purpose of securing variety. Such subplots also give the actors who participate in the main story the opportunity to make costume changes or to rest. It also sometimes enables them to avoid wearing out their welcome from the audience by too long an unbroken occupancy of the center of the stage and story. Shakespeare, Sheridan, and Shaw all provide many examples of comedic subplots for comic relief. Indeed, Shakespeare's subplots are characteristic of most of his plays, and it is evident that he wrote for the comedians in his company just as importantly as for the leading actors. Thus a mixture of high tragedy and low comedy was the essential ingredient of the Shakespearian drama, and is found in many of the successful tragedies of today, although usually in a less obvious or low comedy form.

The ingredient of humor in a story or subplot, when tastefully applied, is gratefully appreciated in the modern theatre, even in the heaviest of dramas, but its use must be carefully rationed. Throughout the staging of *Strange Interlude*, O'Neill was constantly cutting the play. Philip Moeller often remarked to him, "But you are cutting out a big laugh." "That is exactly what I want to do," replied O'Neill. "A laugh relieves the tension. I want to build up as much tension as possible in the audience, and that is the reason for removing any tendency to laugh at this point."

Since the building of tension is one of the prime objectives of the dramatic playwright, the extent to which this is interrupted by a comedic subplot should therefore be carefully watched. An interesting exaggeration of the use of subplot is found in the plays of Dryden in which two separate stories, one dramatic and one comedic, are told in alternating scenes, so that the audience is moved alternately from the scene of drama belonging to one story to the scene of comedy belonging to another, as in *Marriage à la Mode.* Plays written in this manner are seldom or never given today, despite the excellent poetry which they contain, and this is undoubtedly due to the confusion created in the audience by telling two separate stories at the same time.

The theme of the play, in my opinion, is one of its most important components. The modern theatre did not achieve maturity until Ibsen added this ingredient to the plays of his time. *The Pillars of Society,* one of his earliest plays, followed the plot complications which were characteristic of the theatre of Sardou, but it differed from the plays which preceded it by the introduction of a theme—that of corruption in high places. As Ibsen matured as a writer, he relied more and more on character development and theme, to which he added his mastery of story and dramatic exposition. He achieved in his best works a combination of character development, plot and theme, all progressing through the play like three harmoniously intermingling melodies. These moved together until all three aspects of the play reached a common dramatic climax. So in *A Doll's House,* the theme of woman's dependence on men and her desire to win independence for herself is illustrated in the development of Nora's character, which clashes with her husband's conservatism, until in walking out of his house and slamming the door, Nora achieves simultaneously the beginning of her independence, the symbolic fulfillment of the theme, and the ending of the play.

It is fashionable in these days to deplore Ibsen's influence on the modern theatre. This is due to the fact that so many hundreds of plays have been written which follow his basic forms of construction, that these have become stereotyped. Since we have been so greatly influenced by this magnificent artist in the past, this attitude of prejudice against the pattern set by him is healthy, but only so long as we also appreciate his significant contributions. Because of Ibsen's great mastery of play construction, so many lesser writers followed his realism until a point was reached when it became important for the growth of the modern theatre to liberate writers from Ibsen's domination. O'Neill was a great believer in removing the shackles of Ibsen's realism from the modern theatre. He rejoiced in the use of asides, as in *Strange Interlude,* masks, as in *The Great God Brown* and *Lazarus Laughed,* and other devices which broke the Ibsen tradition, and he had no hesitation in stating that in this respect he was at heart anti-Ibsen. As a result he carried the modern theatre far beyond the artificially created realism of the great Norwegian, and indeed into realms where no other author has yet successfully followed him.

All important writers since the days of Ibsen have included in their plays a theme as well as plot and characters. By "theme" I mean here some illumination of life, so that the audience does not take away with them upon leaving the theatre merely the story of a group of characters, but also an important comment on them or their behavior, or a point of view or philosophy of living. When I speak of Ibsen as having been the first to introduce the theme into the theatre, I do an injustice to some of the earliest writers for the ancient Greek theatre. Aristophanes, in many of his comedies, dealt with themes in the same way as we do in the modern theatre today. For example, in *Lysistrata,* he showed by a comedic play which has lasted for nearly 2500 years that war was a futile way of settling disputes between peoples. That the theme of this play has not had much effect over the ages is an indication that our lowest form of human folly cannot be dissipated by mere ridicule.

The theme of protest against wars was also present in *The Trojan Women* by Euripides, which is still vitally affecting in its story of the sufferings of the women of Troy caused by the senseless Trojan wars. It is a sad comment on humanity that its tragic treatment of the theme has been no more effective than the ridicule of Aristophanes. In another play, *The Council of Women,* Aristophanes made fun of the communism or socialism which was preached by Plato in his plans for reorganizing society set forth in *The Republic.* Here Aristophanes was using satire in an attempt to demolish communism by ridicule, in much the same way that Shaw used satire to ridicule the marriage customs of his day in *Getting Married.*

From the days of the ancient Greeks to the days of Ibsen, the use of the theme fell into disrepute except in the so-called morality plays, or passion plays, put on in the churches on the general themes of Christian behavior or morality. One can examine the plays of Shakespeare in vain for a theme in the sense that we use it here; that is, as a comment or illumination on a way of life. It is true that many of Shakespeare's plays can be said to have a theme, such as *Othello,* which is obviously a play about jealousy, or *Romeo and Juliet,* which can be regarded as a play on the theme of the ill effects of family hatreds. However, such themes as exist in these plays are not social ones, and exist only as the result of reflection away from the theatre after the play is over.

In the plays of Molière, the follies of individual human beings were held up to ridicule, and to this extent the plays may also be said to have themes, such as the folly of the neurotic in *The Imaginary Invalid,* who created a series of psychosomatic illnesses; or in *The Would-Be Gentleman,* the folly of the social climber. Most of his plays, however, were directed against the follies of individuals, rather than against the follies of the social life of the day. This latter is the direction in which Ibsen led the modern theatre in the development of social themes such as in *A Doll's House,* where he dealt with the position of women; in *The Pillars of Society,* where he pointed a finger of scorn against the rapacity of businessmen; and in *An Enemy of the People,* in which he showed the dishonesty of politicians in hushing up the unhealthiness of a health resort.

Once Ibsen had led the modern theatre into a trend toward themes, the matter was taken in hand by Bernard Shaw, who had plenty he wished to say about the society of his day, and he used the play form as part of his way of saying it. Thus in *John Bull's Other Island* he attacked the position of the English in Ireland, as well as the position of the Irish who attacked the position of the English. In play after play he attacked the Victorian morality which he actively despised, but by which he lived to the point of utter respectability in his own private life. By the time of Shaw's death the use of a theme was finally established as a desirable ingredient of a good play.

The question of whether or not a play appears to have something to say to its audience beyond its mere story depends to some extent on the manner in which the author introduces the theme. It is desirable, in my opinion, at the very beginning of the play, or somewhere close to the beginning, to introduce the theme in a direct or indirect manner, as may best serve the purposes of the play. This is so that after the theme has been established, the audience can follow it as it unfolds in the play along with the development of the characters and the story. A faulty method of writing such a play is to proceed as though there were no theme present at all, and then suddenly confront us with it in the second or last act. Indeed, in some instances of clumsy playwriting, we may notice that toward the end of the play a speech is introduced telling the audience what the play is trying to say. While this may sometimes succeed in its purpose, more often than not it fails to be either good playwriting or a good presentation of the theme. The use of theme in the modern theatre, and the extent to which our modern playwrights are influenced to write plays with themes, may be gathered by an examination of the plays which in the last forty-three years have won Pulitzer Prizes. The following table gives the year and the title of the play, and an examination of these indicates that, with few exceptions, they included important themes. Those which seem to me to have had the greatest thematic impact on the audiences of their day, I have marked with an asterisk.

PULITZER PRIZE PLAYS

1917 to 1959

* *Why Marry?* Jesse Lynch Williams	1917–18
* *Beyond the Horizon* Eugene O'Neill	1919–20
Miss Lulu Bett Zona Gale	1920–21
* *Anna Christie* Eugene O'Neill	1921–22

PULITZER PRIZE PLAYS (*cont.*)

* *Icebound* Owen Davis	1922–23
* *Hell-Bent fer Heaven* Hatcher Hughes	1923–24
* *They Knew What They Wanted* Sidney Howard	1924–25
* *Craig's Wife* George Kelly	1925–26
* *In Abraham's Bosom* Paul Green	1926–27
* *Strange Interlude* Eugene O'Neill	1927–28
* *Street Scene* Elmer Rice	1928–29
* *Green Pastures* Marc Connelly	1929–30
Alison's House Susan Glaspell	1930–31
* *Of Thee I Sing* George S. Kaufman, Morrie Rys- kind, Ira and George Gershwin	1931–32
* *Both Your Houses* Maxwell Anderson	1932–33
* *Men in White* Sidney Kingsley	1933–34
The Old Maid Zoë Akins	1934–35
* *Idiot's Delight* Robert E. Sherwood	1935–36
* *You Can't Take It With You* Moss Hart and George S. Kaufman	1936–37
* *Our Town* Thornton Wilder	1937–38
* *Abe Lincoln in Illinois* Robert E. Sherwood	1938–39
* *The Time of Your Life* William Saroyan	1939–40
* *There Shall Be No Night* Robert E. Sherwood	1940–41
* *The Skin of Our Teeth* Thornton Wilder	1942–43
* *Harvey* Mary Coyle Chase	1944–45
* *State of the Union* Howard Lindsay and Russel Crouse	1945–46
* *A Streetcar Named Desire* Tennessee Williams	1947–48
* *South Pacific* Richard Rodgers, Oscar Hammer- stein II, Joshua Logan and James Michener	1949–50
The Shrike Joseph Kramm	1951–52
Picnic William Inge	1952–53
* *The Teahouse of the August Moon* John Patrick and Vern Sneider	1953–54
Cat on a Hot Tin Roof Tennessee Williams	1954–55
* *The Diary of Anne Frank* Frances Goodrich and Albert Hackett	1955–56
* *Long Day's Journey into Night* Eugene O'Neill	1956–57
* *J.B.* Archibald MacLeish	1958–59

It is a complaint against the present-day American theatre that our authors do not deal with important themes which come to grips with modern life, or when they do, deal mainly with small people living in a small world, as though viewing life through the wrong end of a telescope. Authors who are dealing with contemporary life have it in their power either to enlarge the subject by including an important theme, or to bring it down to the level of the commonplace or mediocre by omitting one. Our present theatre cries for the first treatment, the enlargement of the life of our era in dealing with these problems seriously in the theatre—as seriously as Galsworthy, Shaw, Behrman, Sherwood, and Anderson dealt with them twenty-five years ago. In the seasons of 1958–59, only three plays appeared in the New York theatre (other than off-Broadway) which may be said to have an important theme. One of these was *Sunrise at Campobello* by Dore Schary, which relates to the life of Franklin D. Roosevelt and presents the theme of a man's ability to overcome physical incapacitation by will power and imagination. In *J.B.* by Archibald MacLeish, a religious theme underlies the retelling in modern terms of the Book of Job. In *A Majority of One* by Leonard Spigelgass, the theme of racial and other national prejudices being overcome by a woman of good common sense lifts this play from the superficial level of a light comedy to an illumination of the prejudices about different races which seem to be a continuing part of life in the twentieth century.

Many of our recent playwrights are more interested in the subject of sex and sexual aberrations than they are in the larger aspects of life. We too often tend to praise a writer today for his mastery of character and situation rather than his point of view. One of the most important of modern-day writers, William Inge, shows a certain amount of preoccupation with sexual problems, but seldom goes out of his way to explore perversion as is the tendency with some American writers today. Inge's main fault in my opinion is that his characters are limited in size. They need to come off the front porch and pass into the great crossways of life, as they would actually do in life itself. Abilene, Kansas, childhood home of President Eisenhower, was the doorstep to all the great capitals of the world for a man with the requisite Kansan character.

The suggestion has been made in some quarters that many of our present-day playwrights are too much interested in the doings of the theatre itself, and that they tend to insulate themselves from real life, and to lead the artificial life of the theatre people. This is why some authors today, after having had their first play or motion picture produced, then write a play about the production, such as *Say Darling* written about *The Pajama Game*. While these plays are sometimes successful, they represent a hothouse use of the theatre, and too much living in this hothouse may eventually blunt the observation and intelligence of the author in his selection of his subjects.

Of course, it may well be argued in reply that both Shakespeare and Molière spent their lives in the theatre. However, they peopled their plays with characters who did not live in the theatre. We have no accurate knowledge of the company kept by either of these famous writers, or their contacts with life outside the theatre, but it is hard to believe that such great characters as King Lear, Hamlet, Shylock, and so forth, or Molière's Misanthrope, Would-Be Gentleman or Imaginary Invalid, were garnered while hanging around the theatres and hobnobbing with theatrical folk whose lives are generally as parochial as any other coterie which shuts itself off from the rest of the world.

In modern times Shaw, O'Neill, Robert Sherwood, Maxwell Anderson, Sidney Howard, Elmer Rice, Philip Barry, and S. N. Behrman were imbued with the spirit of their era and spent little time in the hothouse atmosphere of the theatre. Indeed, Robert Sherwood spent so much of his life working with Franklin D. Roosevelt and Harry Hopkins that undoubtedly his output as a playwright was considerably reduced as a result. Perhaps the best rule on this point would be for the young playwright to be aware of the dangers which may arise by being too greatly enamored of the glamour of backstage life.

It is well to remember that while the best plays of the last fifty years have included themes, it is also true that magnificent plays have been written without them. The historical plays of Shakespeare may be given as examples of plays in which, through the characterization of individuals, we can learn a great deal about human beings and life itself, although none of them shows Shakespeare's point of view toward the social problems of his day.

The Characters

"WHAT a piece of work is a man! How noble in reason! How infinite in faculty! In form and movement, how express and admirable! In action, how like an angel! In apprehension, how like a god!" Thus Shakespeare exuberantly pictures the variety of man's characteristics (*Hamlet,* Act II—Scene 2), to which we can add an infinity of other qualities ranging from saintliness to infamy.

It is the exciting fact that due to the never-ending adding and dividing of the genes, no two human beings are born exactly alike in character. Moreover, even if this were almost possible, as in the case of identical twins, environment and other factors will produce important variations. With all the world to choose from, a writer may easily people his plays with characters drawn from the many hundreds of persons he has encountered in day-by-day living without drawing at all on his imagination, and the results may be excellent. On the other hand, many writers find it easier to imagine their characters rather than draw them from living originals. Some writers, and by far the largest group, combine both drawing from imagination and drawing to some extent from life, thus creating a new character suggested by some living person, but endowed with additional characteristics and mental attitudes by the imagination of the author. But more important and rarer than all the other methods is that of "inspiration" when the writer possesses it. There the characters are not only drawn from imagination, but also from some part of the writer's unconscious which mysteriously endows the imagination with the godlike attribute of creating entirely new people.

The imaginative writer for the theatre is under no obligation to use any particular method of creating characters. He may use all four described above. It is argued by some psychologists that there is no such thing as "imagining" or "creating" a character; that the writer always draws from memory, and that when he draws on his subconscious, he takes out of his mind only what has been put in as the result of experience. I think this explanation is too pat, and certainly does not take into account the phenomenon of inspiration, when the writer may draw on both his subconscious and what Jung calls the racial unconscious. Psychological analysis of the process of creation is beyond the range of this book, but the process of inspiration has often been described. The creation of the character may proceed by leaps and bounds, seemingly beyond the control of the author.

When I visited Shaw on the occasion of his seventieth birthday, he described to me the writing of *Saint Joan:* "Although I was writing in shorthand," he said, "the words came rushing out at such a speed that I could barely write fast enough to put them down. I verily believe that the Saint herself was guiding my hand." In quoting Shaw I am not quoting a religious mystic who might be expected to give a supernatural explanation of a natural fact. What Shaw was actually describing was the surge of inspiration, a force the existence of which we cannot doubt, and the hidden sources of which cannot be taught.

When a character is created by the imagination or inspiration of the author, it often happens that it gets out of control. This may sound absurd, but many writers have said to me: "I had thought out clearly how to write my play a certain way, but the leading character took possession of me, and I couldn't stop it; and before I knew it, the character wouldn't do what I wanted him to do but did what *he* wanted to do."

On the other hand, one of the most talented writers of comedies in America, S. N. Behrman, is an assiduous student of life, and keeps notebooks in which he writes meticulous descriptions of persons he encounters in the course of living, together with notes of their conversation and thoughts, to which he adds his own inspired sense of sharp comedy in delineating his characters.

O'Neill drew heavily on his own life. *Ah, Wilderness* is the story of his own childhood. He told me he was having difficulties in writing a metaphysical play, *Days Without End*, when he actually dreamed the idea and feelings of *Ah, Wilderness*. He dropped the other work, and the play literally "wrote itself" in three weeks, so ardent were the words to leap from his mind onto the paper. Later on, O'Neill wrote another play about his childhood, *Long Day's Journey Into Night*, the same childhood which was so enchanting in *Ah, Wilderness!* The same characters were depicted as grim and unhappy. Thus, in drawing characters from childhood memories or other sources, these may vary according to the way you happen to feel about them at the moment. We may find a character that amuses us or charms us when we look at him through rosy-hued glasses, or we may at another time feel very grim about him; and the way he will be depicted in the play will depend upon the kind of glasses through which we are looking at him.

The scene of O'Neill's *The Iceman Cometh* was the famous "Hell Hole" saloon in Greenwich Village, and some of the

actual characters in it were known by both O'Neill and myself in the early Greenwich Village days. But O'Neill in writing about them endowed them with a third dimension, the
fact that each and every one of them could exist only by
dreaming what O'Neill called "a pipe dream." It was this
dimension that lifted these characters from creatures of pho-
tographic realism to creative art. Most of the characters of
O'Neill's early sea plays were persons he had met in his seafaring days, and were usually depicted by him in a mood of
romanticism. Nevertheless, even in his early days, he was
concerned with the social problems of mankind, as evidenced
by his plays *Gold, The Emperor Jones,* and *The Hairy Ape.*

In writing historical plays where the author draws on
books for information about his characters, imagination is
essential to give such characters flesh and blood. Research on
original source material can be the basis for the best results,
but without creative inspiration, research can produce only
cardboard figures. In the case of *Saint Joan,* already mentioned, Shaw studied the written accounts of the trial, and
used some of the actual words spoken by the Maid. In the
case of Shakespeare's historical plays, unfamiliar characters, such as Falstaff, seem to have a more vivid life than
the actual historical characters. Yet in Prince Hal, Hotspur,
Henry V, and many others, he also created through his
genius characters who were probably far more vivid than
the originals on which they were based. For this reason, the
scholars of today who are so busily trying to prove that
Richard III was maligned by Shakespeare and was actually
a gentle bore, will never remove the breath of life from the
character of the extraordinary scoundrel Richard created by
Shakespeare.

In considering the works of the giants, we may seem to be
straying somewhat from the workaday world of the theatre,

yet not so far as one might imagine. We no longer people our plays with the so-called "great" of the world, and the theatre may have taken a step forward in recognizing that there may be as large a tragedy in the life of a salesman as in the life of a king—though I doubt it. For it has not been proven by the efflux of time that you can interest an audience in the tragedy of a salesman to the same degree as in that of a king. Indeed, the death of a salesman, no matter how important his little world is to him, will never seem as important as the death of Hamlet, Prince of Denmark. And it is the rank or position of the characters themselves, as well as the power of the dramatist, which imparts this kind of importance. Historical characters take on an aura which pre-exists with the audience long before they enter the theatre, as did the gods and legendary figures in the plays of ancient Greece.

In a recent play about a man who overcame, by his personal courage, the handicap of infantile paralysis, it was the fact that this man was Franklin D. Roosevelt, and not just anybody, which gave an additional theatrical interest to *Sunrise at Campobello*. And as we move toward a world in which the so-called "common man" is now king, we must rely on our authors to select for the stage those characters whose personalities are vivid and exciting enough to place them above the herd. Indeed, since we are pursuing excitement in the theatre, we cannot expect to succeed in this merely by asking our audience to become interested in the ordinary, everyday doings of mediocre people. This was possible forty years ago, when it was a novelty to find on the stage any milieu lower in the social scale than a drawing room. Now that the novelty of this has passed, we find this phase of realism has been largely taken over by the so-called "soap operas" in television, which may be snobbishly described as plays of the domestic problems of mediocre people designed to distract the mediocre viewer's mind from his or her own domestic problems.

Fortunately there is no such thing as an ordinary man or an average man, so that a sensitive writer may be able to make any man or woman interesting to the audience so long as there is some underlying facet of interesting character present to be revealed. We can even make mediocrity interesting if we can throw new light onto the mediocre character to ascertain "how he ticks." But we are starting with a handicap which was never overcome in depicting such "average" persons as Mr. Zero in Elmer Rice's *The Adding Machine*.

The case is different, however, when the writer's work is suffused with the compassion and understanding which can make ordinary people appear extraordinary. One such writer is William Inge, who while writing generally about the man and woman in the street or sitting on a front porch, usually manages to give them a dimension of interest by making their unconscious motivations apparent to the onlooker. When we first produced Inge's *Come Back Little Sheba* at Westport, we had considerable difficulty in persuading the brilliant actress Shirley Booth to play the part of the slovenly woman, Lola, whose commonplace life seemed dull and mediocre. Yet so tenderly and revealingly was the character written, that the audience wept with sympathy over her loneliness. The combination of this with Shirley Booth's great acting talents conspired to make her portrayal of Lola the most interesting moment in her career. Equally inspired was the character of the husband, played so movingly by Sidney Blackmer. Of a truth, the writers of such characters can say, as O'Neill once said to me, "I don't need stars, I create them."

In selecting characters, it is sometimes desirable for the writer to select or create the unusual in terms of the universal. By this, I mean that the writer may do well to use characters who, unusual in themselves, have traits which enable us to recognize them because we have often seen some of these traits in others. Thus George Kelly's *The Show-Off*, a character whose showing off was so far beyond normal as to make him unusual, was universally recognizable, as was the leading character in *Craig's Wife*, a woman whose instinct for meticulous housekeeping was raised to such unusual proportions as to constitute a destructive force, yet whose basic characteristics exist to a lesser extent in many people and are universally recognizable.

The modern playwright faced with the problem of making the common man interesting to an audience has often attempted to solve the problem by peopling his play with one or more so-called "offbeat" characters; that is, characters with some extraordinary quirk or exaggerated quality which leads us to refer to him as an "eccentric" in real life. The present vogue for offbeat characters probably came into the theatre in Moss Hart's and George S. Kaufman's comedy *You Can't Take It With You*. Offbeat characters have since been used in the modern theatre in such quantity and quality as to take the place of true characterizations, as though the author had said to himself, "I'm going to people my play with everyone who is slightly crazy or eccentric." The result is that plays with offbeat characters have now become stereotyped and almost as conventional as plays with conventional characters. How many times have we seen in the theatre the sharp-tongued wealthy old lady who rudely speaks her mind with telling comic effect? She was an original character when she first appeared in the person of Lady Bracknell in Oscar Wilde's *The Importance of Being Earnest*, and she will probably continue to be popular as long as we have sharp-tongued elderly actresses to play her. She was seen on the stage recently again, in the character of Mrs. St. Maugham, played by Gladys Cooper, in *The Chalk Garden*, by Enid Bagnold.

One of the pitfalls for an author lies in writing "types" instead of individuals. It is easy for an author who is lazy or incapable of creative thinking to reach into an old theatrical trunk and pull out recognizable "types" with which he peoples his play, but the breath of life will usually be absent, especially if the manager or director foolishly follows the author's lead and casts the parts with actors who are also "typed" in the same way. Where it may not be possible for the author always to create distinct individuals, he can at least cover his own deficiency by giving his "type" some characteristics which will make him less obviously a carbon copy of a person we have all met on the stage many times before.

Many authors find it useful to combine some of the qualities of the character they create with those of a particular star or stars. "What is the secret of your success?" someone is once reported to have asked the late Robert Sherwood. "I write plays for the Lunts," was the reply. And there is no doubt that it often helps an author to write a play with a particular actor in mind (as well as help to sell the play for that same actor if it turns out well). Shakespeare, I feel sure, was greatly helped in creating characters by the fact that he wrote for an Acting Company, and that he could imagine the way his actors would play their roles even as he wrote them. So while it is not always possible, I recommend that the author bear this practical rule in mind, remembering, however, that he must go to life itself and not to the theatre in order to create the role which the actor will play.

The number of characters used in a play is a prime consideration today, not only for economic reasons, which are quite potent, but also because the talking picture is a far better medium for pageantry or plays requiring large casts and sweeping scale. How many characters are best for a play? The answer, "as few as possible," is too obvious to be true. Each story calls for its own quota in order to make the play acceptable. Better not select a subject which calls for a great number of characters, or the writer will have difficulty in getting a production in the professional theatre; although the very numbers may be a factor in making the play successful in community or college theatres where a large number of actors are available. Plays with two or three characters are difficult to sustain, for the actors who are capable of holding the interest of an audience for an entire evening without respite are few and far between.

What is more important—from a practical playwriting viewpoint—is not the number of characters so much as the number of good parts or leading parts. Write the play with a single "star" part, and if the author can find the actor to play it, and sustain it, he will be lucky. Most of the great plays of the past contained one or more "star" parts, and conditions of the American theatre today are such that the production of a play with one or two "star" parts is more readily obtainable than is the case where the leading roles are more or less equally divided among several characters. If his play has two star parts, a male and a female, the author is in a better position than with three or more.

Some very amusing remarks on this subject will be found in Shaw's correspondence with Mrs. Patrick Campbell, who wished to be the sole star of the original *Pygmalion*. Shaw wrote her that he insisted on two stars, one male and the other female, as each would have a following and thus double

the length of the run. Shaw's rule was at least partially correct, but there are many exceptions to it in the present-day
theatre, in which long runs are longer, and are often achieved
by plays with only one star or, on rare occasions, with no
star at all.

Let us face one practical fact. Whether authors like it or
not, the "star" system has been in the theatre ever since the
theatre existed and ever since playwrights wrote parts calling
for unusual talents or personality on the part of the actor.
For twenty-one years the Theatre Guild was dedicated to
the proposition that "the play's the thing" and refused to
star anyone, but it was one of America's most important
playwrights, Robert Sherwood, who caused us to change our
policy. This policy was correct in the Guild's early days
(circa 1920), for at that time it was customary in the commercial theatre to produce plays whose main merit was to
provide a vehicle for a star, and to surround the star with
inferior actors. As a result the star system ultimately brought
the theatre into disrepute. This was particularly true of the
actor-manager star who, by surrounding himself with con-
genial friends of inferior talents, gained by comparison, as
well as saving on the salaries he paid. Fortunately our few
remaining actor-managers usually realize that their own efforts are enhanced by engaging the best actors available for
the supporting parts.

When we use the word "star" today, what do we really
mean? The usual connotation is an actor or actress of such
great ability and personal quality that he or she stands head
and shoulders above other actors. But this represents the use
of the word in the best sense. Often it is used to signify any
person who, irrespective of acting ability, attracts masses of
people to the box office. As a result, men and women with
very little acting talent, but with a genius for attracting at-

tention, are often referred to as "stars." However, when I refer here to writing for a "star," I do not intend to include the ladies and gentlemen whose talents do not go beyond an attractive appearance and a flair for publicity.

The most severe limitation on the number of important parts in a play is that imposed by the playing time. The modern theatre usually calls for a period of from two hours to two and a quarter hours, with two intermissions of about ten additional minutes each, or a single intermission of about fifteen minutes. The more characters we meet during this time, the less we will be able to learn about them. This time limit imposes upon the dramatist the necessity, as to his minor characters, of giving them flesh and blood with a few bold strokes.

To indicate the number of characters, it was customary in former days to list on the play manuscript the names of the characters, as well as their businesses or professions, and their relationship to one another. On reading the play, the list of characters and scenes indicated to the manager the size of the cast and the amount of the acting cost. Bernard Shaw originated the custom of omitting the names of the characters, in order that his plays in book form might command a sale among members of the reading public who would come upon his characters, with their appropriate descriptions, in the same way as in a novel, where the characters are not listed at the beginning of the story. This has unfortunately been copied by some playwrights today for an entirely different reason.

Play agents know that if a play requires a large (and necessarily expensive) cast of characters, it will be difficult to secure a reading of the play, so they advise their clients to omit the names, except where these are only a few. The net result is that where a manager today is given a play to read with no list of characters, he assumes there are so many that the author is afraid to list them!

A compromise between the two extremes is sometimes used by authors who list five or six main characters with full descriptions of their occupations and relationships, but follow this list with a statement that there are "Additional characters, including ——"

Since the playwright will in most cases draw his characters either wholly or partly from life, the extent and quality of his observation is of particular importance. Advances made in modern psychology since the days of Freud, Adler, and Jung, however, have supplied many writers with short cuts to character by making us especially conscious of the part played by the parents and the position of the child in the family. As a result, the tendency of the young writer today is to provide his characters with a ready-made past derived from the textbooks. Here a little knowledge is a dangerous thing, for the writing of a character from case histories alone will not give it the breath of life, though it may simulate life. It is the dramatist's business to know all there is to know about his people from firsthand observation or the exercise of his imagination, but he may use the knowledge derived from the textbooks in helping him to understand the behavior of the people about whom he is writing. However, he should be careful not to use this knowledge to create synthetic characters who are explained to the audience in psychoanalytical terms.

I must utter a strong word of warning against selecting characters simply because their medical case histories supply interesting neuroses. While we live in a world in which many people are neurotic, the use of too many such characters is apt to result in a turgid, introverted documentation rather than an exciting play. The textbooks on psychiatry are best regarded as a group of new tools by which we can implement our understanding of people, but tools which cannot take the place of observation or imagination. Perhaps the most complete characters in literature were created by Dostoevsky long before the days of Freud, while Shakespeare and the Elizabethan and Restoration dramatists had insight into character which far exceeds those modern writers who derive their knowledge of human beings from psychoanalytical sources.

In this connection it is desirable, when dealing with modern characters in a situation of contemporary life, that at least some of the characters possess what is called "audience identification." This means that the members of the audience will be able to identify themselves with the characters, and vicariously suffer with or enjoy the experiences of one or more of them. This in turn produces the "involvement" of audiences in the play. The more the audience can participate in this way (even on a secondhand level) in the experiences of the characters, the more they will be absorbed in and enjoy the play.

In the case of costume or historical plays, the extent to which the audience can identify with the characters is of course more limited; but when, for example, the plays of Shakespeare are produced in modern clothes, it is much easier for the audience to "identify" with individual characters. Where there is no one in a play with whom the audience can identify, it generally fails. The peopling of a play with too many disagreeable or ignoble characters will definitely affect the impact of the play, unless these are portrayed so vividly and with sufficient theatrical excitement as to make them interesting. The portrayal of dull or mediocre people, while it can be tolerated in minor characters, may prove fatal if it extends to all the characters. "A common-

place play about commonplace people" is about the most
damning thing that can be said about a play. On the other
hand, villains, if their stature is great enough, such as
Richard III or Iago, can form the subject of important plays.

The playwright will often find it necessary either to evoke
dislike of a character on the part of the audience, or to
evoke sympathy or compassion. It was an old saying among
Hollywood writers that in order to make the audience
quickly dislike a character, it is merely necessary to have
him kick a dog or hurt a child. Dislike can be evoked subtly
by a hundred kinds of unsympathetic actions or attitudes.
Contrariwise, the opposite is true. Alfred Lunt once informed me that in working on a part, he searched for a
point where the audience could feel sympathy for him. He
found such a point in *Arms and the Man* at the moment he
is overcome with fatigue in Raina's bedroom in Act I, and
is left for a moment alone in the room and almost falls asleep.

A word which is constantly used in the theatre in connection with the writing of characters is "motivation." In theatrical parlance this means the reason why characters behave in
a certain manner. In creating his characters, it is important
for the author to reveal to his audience what makes his
characters "tick." The point of view of a character in a given
situation, the reason he possesses this point of view, and
why he takes certain actions as a result of it, are usually due
to some inner motivation which should not puzzle or be-
wilder the audience. In the narrower sense, we use the word
"motivation" to explain why a certain crime or behavior has
taken place. For instance, why did A murder his wife, or
why did B's wife run away from him? Specific motivation is
extremely important in the theatre, and if left out of a play,
usually produces the effect of incompleteness.

In considering the expression "motivation" we run into

another word now used somewhat haphazardly in the theatre, and this is "syndrome." This word is used in the sense of a series of episodes or events which create a change in the attitude or behavior of a character. The expression has been borrowed from medicine, in which the word is used to express a pattern of symptoms in a disease which added together assist in a diagnosis.

It is usual to assume that a series of events impinging on a character will cause this character to change, and that a play in which so-called character development does not take place, so far as the leading character is concerned, is regarded as faulty. However, in my opinion this is not necessarily true. I question whether in real life it is possible for a character to be changed by a series of events which can usually be depicted on the stage in the space of two to two and one-half hours. Indeed it is questionable whether the basic character of an individual is ever really deeply changed, except, possibly, by a long treatment of psychoanalysis. The effect of one or more dramatic events on an individual's character may be to modify it superficially, or even to create a different pattern of behavior—but really deep-seated change of character is not usually accomplished merely because of an experience or a group of experiences. The modern theatre, however, is full of examples of character development in which the character behaves according to one pattern at the beginning of a play and changes his pattern of behavior by the time the play is over.

Because it is fashionable at the present time to expect the author to produce a character change in almost every important role by the time the play is over, an actor is apt to state, "I don't care about playing this part because, even though I go through all the experiences of this play, I seem to be the same person at the end that I was at the beginning."

Many a thoroughly believable part has been turned down by important actors for this reason.

Excellent plays can be written which show character changes for the leading players, among which may be mentioned Othello, Kate in *The Taming of the Shrew,* Beatrice and Benedict in *Much Ado About Nothing,* Willy Loman in *Death of a Salesman,* Ephraim Cabot in *Desire Under the Elms,* and Nora in *A Doll's House.* On the other hand, equally good plays have been written about characters who do not change, and whose strength derives from the fact that no matter how greatly the character may be tempted to modify his behavior, he refuses to do so. Indeed, this kind of character often makes the best subject for tragedy. Examples are found in Job in *J. B.*, Tom Wingfield in *The Glass Menagerie,* Lear in *King Lear,* the Captain in Strindberg's *The Father,* and Bernardo Alba in *The House of Bernarda Alba* by Garcia Lorca. In another type of play, the character does not change but may actually waver and finally return to his or her original position of strength. An example of this is found in *Saint Joan,* in which Joan resolutely refuses to recant throughout her trial, but in a moment of weakness does so. However, this is momentary and within a few minutes she regains her original strength of character.

Some of the confusion which exists in regard to the words "character development" is due to the fact that in theatrical parlance these words are often given different meanings. For example, the English critic William Archer used the expression to indicate the clarification of a character as he perambulates through the play. He likened this character development to the development which took place in old-fashioned photography where the negative was placed in a developing bath, and the image on the negative—which was at first obscure or foggy—gradually took on definition until by the time the process of development was completed, the picture was clear in every detail. Applying this to the theatre, the character, when we are first introduced to him, is unclear, foggy or undefined, but as the play progresses, the character becomes clearer and clearer until he is fully developed.

An actor is perfectly correct in deciding it is an ungrateful task to play a part when it does not contain this or any other kind of development. Usually this is because the character is often a so-called "rubber stamp" and the actor continues to play this rubber stamp in each scene in which he appears throughout the play. The question of whether a character is fully conceived by an author, or is merely a cardboard figure, is quickly shown up by the test of whether this kind of development takes place in the play.

Of course where I have referred to character motivation and character development, I refer particularly to the main characters in the play. While it is possible in a novel to show the character development of dozens of individuals, the time and space limitations of a play usually do not permit this to apply to more than the most prominent characters.

Where we are dealing with a group of characters who are not generally known to the audiences and whose motivations are very special (as for example certain religious groups— such as the Mennonites in *Papa Is All* by Patterson Greene —with whose practices most audiences are not familiar), it becomes particularly important for the playwright to establish the character motivations in such a way that the audience can learn and understand them as the play progresses. Many plays fail for lack of a clear motivation which may be present in the author's mind, but which he has not made clear to the audience. This is particularly true of adaptations from European plays where certain concepts are not clearly understood in this country. It was a fact that, some years ago, when many European plays dealt with the subject of dueling, which involved questions of "honor" or "personal honor," it was very difficult for an American or English audience to appreciate why the settlement of such a difference of opinion should involve the forfeiting of life. Yet the same conditions existed many years ago both in the United States and England, so that when we are dealing with plays laid in earlier times, it is not usually necessary to clarify the motivation for such acts as dueling, which are difficult to understand in terms of today.

One of the striking differences between the modern theatre and the Victorian theatre which preceded it is the importance given in modern plays to plot and situation arising out of the development of the characters, in contrast to the plays of the earlier era, as exemplified by those of Sardou and Scribe in France (who set the fashion for other countries), in which the plot and situation came first and the characters were tailored to fit them. This same criticism may be made of Shakespeare, who purchased so many of his plots and then imagined his characters to fit them. However, he did this so superbly that the plots ultimately flowed from the characterizations. Shaw, in pointing out to me that, in contrast to Shakespeare, he always created his own characters and plots, remarked with a twinkle in his eyes, "After all, Shakespeare bought many of his plots, or had them ready made from history, so he was merely what they call in the world of motion pictures a 'dialogue writer.'"

In the theatre of today we have considerably less interest in plots and far more interest in character than was the case in the days of Sardou, who was a master of situation and suspense interest. He, of course, gave his people characterizations to a certain superficial extent, but that was not the prevailing artistic virtue of the theatre of his day. Ibsen

has been often described as the dramatist who first changed
the emphasis in the modern play from plot to character, but
this is not entirely correct. It was Turgenev, in his play
A Month in the Country, written about 110 years ago, who
first subordinated plot to character. This play may therefore
be regarded as the beginning of the modern theatre. When it
was produced by the Theatre Guild in New York in the
year 1930, with Alla Nazimova in the role of Natalia Pe-
trovna, it was apparent that here was the fountain from
which Chekhov had drunk deeply. However, the play was
not known outside Russia for many years after it was written
and produced there, so that the influence of Ibsen, Strindberg and others is correctly stated as the dominating influence in the change from the theatre of plot to the theatre of
character. (I have already pointed out that *The Pillars of
Society* by Ibsen is of interest to students as showing a
transition in Ibsen's style from the old kind of play of plot
to the new kind of play of character.)

It is a mistake to attempt to lay down any hard and fast
rule as to whether a play should be based on plot, situation
or character. The best plays use all elements. The question
as to which came first in the mind of the author in creating
the play is about as easy to answer as the familiar problem
of the chicken and the egg. One rule we can regard as important for the modern theatre; the author must make it appear that the plot arises out of the characters, and that the
author is not merely propelling a figure through a plot. But
this was also true of the older theatre. When Shakespeare
used the plot of an earlier story for *The Merchant of Venice*,
he attached plenty of good solid meat to the bones of Shylock, so that it is the character we tend to remember rather
than the plot. As to *Faust*, which was developed from the
earlier plot of *Ur-Faust*, it may be said that Faust himself

was more a repository for Goethe's philosophy than a figure of flesh and blood. In saying this, I am prepared to be torn to pieces as a heretic by all those for whom Goethe can do no wrong.

That plays stemming from character rather than plot are no modern innovation will be apparent from considering the plays of Molière, who selected characters motivated by one or another conspicuous vice, virtue or foible, and piloted them through plots arising from their own peculiar characteristics. Thus he provided a series of portraits including a miser, a would-be gentleman, an imaginary invalid, an overeducated female, a misanthrope, and a host of others whose comedic dilemmas stemmed almost entirely from their peculiarities as human beings.

Yet there is a distinction between these plays which spring from character, and those of the modern theatre which we label "realistic" or "naturalistic" as the case may be. This lies in the fact that in the earlier plays, behind the exaggerated qualities of the character is a sense of contrivance and artifice. In the modern theatre, the aim of the author is usually to use his characters in such a way as to make us, his audience, believe that what we see is actually happening. The moment we are aware of the artifice, we no longer believe the author. This is what we mean when we say that in the theatre of today, plot and situation are subordinated to truth in character. Yet tomorrow a genius may again appear upon the scene and write great plays based mainly on plot and situation. For we must remember that in the theatre we are not dealing with absolutes, but only with cycles and fashions.

On the stage the active characters or the "doers" are usually more interesting than the passive characters, to whom things are done. Consequently the active super-villain

Richard III is far more interesting theatrically than any whitewashed, kindly, mild-mannered man, no matter how true to life. Actors correctly evaluate characters according to whether they are active or passive, and usually shun the passive roles. This does not mean that passive characters may not be important to a play—merely that it is seldom possible to use them as leading characters, since they are more at home in novels than on the stage. The dramatic use of introspective characters is often made possible in the theatre by the convention of the soliloquy or, as it is called in the modern novel, "stream of consciousness." No one in real life speaks his thoughts aloud, yet we are usually ready to accept the soliloquy in the theatre without question. In the character of Hamlet, Shakespeare combines the active doer who overturns the Kingdom of Denmark, with the introspective thinker, whose thoughts and feelings spur him to move from playing a passive to an active role. His marvelous use of the soliloquy is largely responsible for this being made possible in the theatre.

On one occasion I had heard a rumor that Shaw was in the process of writing a play about Christ. The next time I called on him, I inquired as to the truth of the rumor. "Oh no," he replied. "You are referring to John Masefield. He is writing a play on the subject. I would never write a play about Christ." "Why not?" I asked. To which Shaw replied, "He is not a good theatrical figure. Throughout his life, other people were doing things to him. Now a good theatrical figure is somebody who does things to other people. Christ wasn't enough of a man of action for me to want to write a play about him." I did not think at the time to remind Shaw that many beautiful Passion Plays had been written about Christ, and that these would probably outlast many of Shaw's plays. On reflection, I felt that Shaw's appraisal of Christ as a dramatic character was superficial. A dramatist could actually make his very passivity an active ingredient of a drama. It would be necessary to find the best method of doing this, and this might well involve the dramatic use of the soliloquy.

The use of the "aside" in the theatre is an old device (which dates back to the Greek theatre) for the purpose of telling the audience something about the character or story that cannot be told in action. Modern writers avoid this, especially in realistic or naturalistic plays. In doing this they are losing a valuable extension of dramatic or comedic action, for when we witness only what a character does or says we may lose the more important facet of what he thinks. By the aside, so often used by the Elizabethans and the writers of the Restoration, we actually enlarge the field of the playwright and put a third dimension in his hands which, if skillfully used, can give us an insight to the inner man which we would not otherwise possess.

In a discussion with O'Neill on the subject of "asides," which he used with magnificent success in *Strange Interlude,* and with less success in *Dynamo* and *Days Without End,* he pointed out that a great actor was often able to read between the lines and indicate by his acting what the character was actually thinking, even when it was at variance with what he was actually saying. Putting it simply, one person greeting another might *say,* "How well you look today," while what he actually *thought* was, "You look half-dead."

O'Neill said he had relied too long on actors to indicate to an audience what the character was actually thinking under his lines, so he went back to the use of the aside, after finding that the use of masks, which he employed in *The Great God Brown,* was not entirely satisfactory. When I asked O'Neill how he reconciled the use of the aside with the reality of his plays, he pointed out that he disliked realism, and regarded much of his writing as a departure from the earlier Ibsen type of artificially created reality. Modern authors who have never seen *Strange Interlude* would be surprised to know how little the asides, some of them quite long, disturbed the sense of reality of the play. The audiences accepted them hook, line and sinker, and enjoyed particularly the times when the thoughts were completely at variance with what was spoken by the characters to others, a phenomenon they recognized as an everyday occurrence in their own lives. It is a pity that other modern playwrights have not followed O'Neill more often in the extensive use of the aside, for the third dimension which this added to his plays was a real contribution to the art of playwriting. Indeed, a brilliant use of added asides in Thornton Wilder's *The Matchmaker* made it a theatrical success in London and also in New York, where its earlier version, *The Merchant of Yonkers*, without these asides was a failure. In television the aside, or stream of consciousness, has far more often been successfully used than in the theatre.

The use of the "narrator" to describe characters, events, or the feelings of individuals in the play, while existing in some of Shakespeare's plays, has been reintroduced into the theatre from radio and television. Good examples of these are found in Williams' best play *The Glass Menagerie* and Thornton Wilder's *Our Town.*

There is room for any other innovation which the author's imagination can supply to delineate or clarify character. In the final analysis, skillful character drawing, along with suspense interest, is the *sine qua non* of every important play from the days of the ancients right down to the plays of today and tomorrow. And this condition is unlikely to change in the ages ahead of us.

CHAPTER IV

Writing and Rewriting Methods

W E are all familiar with the old saying that the best method of writing is to apply the seat of the pants to the seat of a chair. However, this old rule is one which is very hard to follow in writing plays. It seems almost inevitable that there is some reason why you should not, on any particular day, apply the seat of the pants to the seat of the chair. I myself have worked out all kinds of reasons why I cannot possibly write a play in a certain room. I cannot pace far enough back and forth in the room, or the ceiling is too low, or there is some other condition present which prevents me from writing. Indeed I have been looking for the ideal room to write in for the past thirty years. In my imagination it is the kind of room in which the moment you enter, the atmosphere is such that you immediately go to the table and begin writing. Any imaginative author can find any one of a dozen reasons why he cannot get to work. Molnar once told me that in order to live in his characters, it was necessary for him to stop living in his own life first— and dying was no fun. I believe that one reason why the rule of "the pants and the chair" does not usually apply to playwriting is because this form of writing differs from other forms in requiring a number of stages of creative thought before the actual writing can begin.

There are usually three periods or stages through which the author passes in writing a play. The first of these is the period of gestation, when the author is seized by the germ of an idea, thinks over what he intends to write, and decides how he is going to write it. In the case of a play, as compared with a novel, the entire question of structure or construction, or the way which is best to tell the story for the stage, is far more complicated than in the case of a novel. The second period through which the author passes is that in which he actually writes the play. Here he must settle down to back-breaking work, with the necessary continuity of time and place to write what he has spent so much time creating. The third is the period when, having read what he has written, the author has become a critic of his own work, and decides that some revision is necessary. This revision may also take a considerable period of time. Indeed, rewriting is often repeated a number of times, until the author is finally satisfied with his work.

Plays which seem to have been very easily written, are often actually quite deceptive. Ibsen often used to take at least a year to think over a play before he wrote it, and he often rewrote it or parts of it several times. The several re-written versions of A Doll's House have all been preserved and published, and it is interesting to note that each time Ibsen worked on the play, he intensified several of the dramatic situations. Many plays arrive in this country from Europe, especially those in printed form, which do not give the impression of having been rewritten. However, it may be said that very few of the finest masterpieces did not require some additional writing on the part of the author. Shakespeare, during some of his most prolific periods, was turning out two or even three plays in a year. Perhaps one reason he was able to do this was that he supposedly bought many of his plots from other authors and did not have to imagine them, thus cutting down on the amount of time spent in gestation. Much more creative effort would have had to be expended on his part had he started from the beginning and created the plots as well, as was the case with many authors who came after him. Yet the plots of Shakespeare bear the marks of creative rewriting right in the texts themselves. This is particularly shown in the magnificent techniques of entrances and exits and the sharp dramatic scenes which move with a dramatic speed and intensity seldom found in any other writer.

The craftsmanship shown by Shakespeare clearly indicates that he was an experienced man of the theatre, that he knew how to beat out the right rhythm for the mood of his scenes, and to use the best theatrical effects for his entrances and exists. Most people who work in the modern theatre regard as ridiculous the theory that these plays could have been written by Bacon or any other man who was not an ex-perienced theatre craftsman, for the techniques which are found in these plays could be learned only from actual ex-perience in seeing the plays come to life on the stage.

There is no record left of the writing methods of Shakes-peare, although it is commonly believed that he began to work by rewriting the faulty plays of others, and that some of his own early plays are indeed the rewriting of, or col-laboration in, the plays of other writers. This would account for the fact that he had no feelings of constraint regarding the use of their plots, whereas a playwright of today is far more concerned with the originality of his plot and will resent with great feeling the suggestion that he might have derived it from others. When I told Shaw that the exact modern plot of *Pygmalion* was to be found in *Peregrine*

Pickle by Tobias Smollett, he indignantly informed me that he learned this only after he had written his own play.

Every author has his favorite method of working and many of them differ. When St. John Ervine was a young man it was his habit to take very long walks which sometimes covered twenty miles a day. He told me that during the walk he experienced a warm glow of circulation in his body which helped him to imagine the deep emotional feelings of the characters in the play. He continued, "I was able to work myself up into an emotional state in which I could experience in my imagination the scenes and situations with the utmost freedom." In actual fact, the long walks released him from the constraints and inhibitions of everyday life and enabled him to create his characters with a flow of emotion which otherwise would not have been present. Thus it is that *John Ferguson* and *Jane Clegg* both represent plays in which characters pass through dramatic scenes of a high order; in *John Ferguson,* for example, each character plays a strong climactic emotional scene, and these added together made this one of the finest and most moving plays of its era. However, during World War I, Ervine lost one of his legs and he was no longer able to take these walks. He informed me that from that time on, he was no longer able to write plays which were based on deep emotion. He was, however, able to write comedies, and from then on his greatest successes were in the field of high comedy.

Eugene O'Neill derived something of the same physical exaltation from swimming. He could neither write nor live without the exercise of swimming, which kept him in superb physical trim during the most creative periods of his life. In Provincetown, he swam in the sea outside the Coast Guard Station where he lived, and in Bermuda, and Sea Island, Georgia, he also swam in the ocean. When he moved to California, he built a pool and continued his swimming there. It was only when he returned to New York, prior to his purchasing a house on the sea at Marblehead, that he interrupted this daily routine.

O'Neill made his writing an everyday job. He went to work in the morning at about 8:00 and he did not finish until around 12:00. He kept this up for long periods at a time—in other words, going to his writing was his daily life, just as a businessman might go to work in his office each day. It was because of this great devotion to the actual writing of his plays that he was able to turn out such a prodigious quantity of work. Furthermore, he made it a habit to stop writing on a play for a while after the completion of the first draft, and he would then return to it and fully rewrite it, often repeating the rewriting. I once asked him what he accomplished by this. He answered, "I am re-feeling the play. As I rewrite it, I do not just copy it from the earlier draft. I feel it over again. I re-create it." I supposed there was a certain amount of comparison between first and later drafts, and that some scenes which he felt to be in good condition did not have to be re-created. However, it would seem that this routine was an essential part of his writing method, and that he was not able to work any other way.

When he wrote me from California that he was having trouble with his writing because his hands were shaking so on account of illness, I sent him a Soundscriber dictating machine in the hope that he might learn to dictate his plays into the machine, afterwards to be transcribed by a typist. After trying it a few times, he gave up the idea as hopeless and continued to write the plays in longhand. As his hands trembled more and more, he would hold a pencil in his right hand and place his left hand on his wrist. This would prevent the hand from shaking, but the words grew smaller and smaller and harder and harder to read. His wife Carlotta, who typed most of his manuscripts from the time she was married to him, had the utmost difficulty in reading his handwriting, so small did it become. Thus O'Neill throughout his life illustrated the old adage that genius includes an infinite capacity for taking pains.

As a result of his method of writing and rewriting his plays, often several times in succession with a month or more in between, by the time O'Neill forwarded a play for us to read it was already in such excellent condition that there was very little to be done in the way of additional rewriting. However, like every fluent writer from Shakespeare to Shaw, O'Neill overwrote his plays, and knew that he was doing it. He therefore regarded the cutting of his plays as quite an important part of the procedure of writing them. He never hesitated to cut a play when, in the actual rehearsal, he found that the cutting was needed.

When I wrote O'Neill on the subject of cutting *Marco Millions* before we produced it, he replied as follows:

> You should have enough confidence in my ability to trim this play down to be able to predict for yourselves what the final product will be. After all, you are not dealing with any novice in the theatre, and anyone who has ever worked with me—Bobby [Robert Edmond Jones], Kenneth [Kenneth Magowan], Arthur [Hopkins], etc.—will testify that I don't have to be urged but am always on the lookout for helpful cuts right up to the last week of rehearsals. And the legend that I don't attend rehearsals is all rot. I didn't in the old Provincetown Players days because I was never in New York and when I was I was never "on the wagon." But of late years it has been different. Except in cases where I saw that my play was being given no chance and it didn't matter whether I was there or not, I have been very much on the

job. *Beyond the Horizon, Anna Christie, Hairy Ape, All God's Chillun, Glencairn* cycle, *Desire Under The Elms* and *G.G. Brown*, are examples of when I was. And I should most decidedly be there from the first day to last if I were doing stuff with you people because I would be genuinely interested.

O'Neill has a reputation, which was undeserved, of resisting the cutting of his plays. I did not find this to be the case until we placed *The Iceman Cometh* into rehearsal. By this time I felt an uncertainty in O'Neill's attitude at rehearsals. He had been ill and away from the theatre for nearly ten years, and did not seem to be quite as ruthless about cutting as he was with *Strange Interlude, Mourning Becomes Electra* and *Days Without End.* Of all the writers I have encountered, Shaw and O'Neill were both the most long-winded, and while their plays nearly always needed cutting, they seldom needed any rewriting after they were handed in for production. It is one of the tragedies of the later productions of O'Neill's plays that the necessary cutting which he would have performed, had he been alive at the time the plays were produced, was not done. As a result, he was blamed for repetition and dullness in many places where he would never have permitted it.

O'Neill did not wish his plays to be opened in out-of-town cities before coming to New York. Most of them opened in what is called "cold" condition in New York, and it was only with considerable persuasion that we were able to secure his consent to some of them first opening elsewhere. He did not like to see his own plays in the theatre with audiences, so most of his knowledge of what was going on was gained at rehearsals.

Shaw combined the enthusiasm for walking so characteristic of St. John Ervine, with a love of swimming which, in the latter part of his life, he enjoyed while spending summer vacations at Stresa. One of the most tragic moments in Shaw's life came at the time when he found it difficult to walk because this, in effect, made it difficult for him to think. Shaw seldom wrote in a regular fashion as was the case with O'Neill. He lived an extremely busy life, traveling a great part of the year, and engaging in public meetings and discussions, as well as a certain amount of social life with his friends. He was quite a gregarious man and, unlike O'Neill, he enjoyed company. Whenever he got ready to write a play, he seems to have shut himself up and worked extremely quickly on it. "Once he begins," Mrs. Shaw told me, "he works very rapidly indeed. He usually writes his plays in shorthand and gives them to his secretary Miss Patch to type. She knows how to read his shorthand and as a result, the plays are completed very speedily."

Despite Shaw's ill-natured remarks regarding Shakespeare's willingness to take his plots from where he could best secure them, Shaw himself was not averse to following the suggestions of Mrs. Shaw from time to time. It is well known that she suggested the plot of *The Doctor's Dilemma*, and he might never had written *Saint Joan* had she not constantly left books on the Saint around the house for him to read. As *Saint Joan* was one of Shaw's few non-iconoclastic plays, it is just too bad that Mrs. Shaw did not leave more volumes of history around to stimulate him.

I trust that my readers who wish to become playwrights will not fall into the mistaken belief that because Eugene O'Neill was fond of swimming and Bernard Shaw was an inveterate walker, they will have to become athletes in order to qualify as professional playwrights. I know some very excellent writers who will tell you that the reason they write well is because they do not take any exercise at all. They stay up late at night, and have no regular habits of any kind. (Dylan Thomas was the worst example of just such an author.) However, it may well be that the reason some writers fail in the theatre is because they lack the necessary discipline which is required for the strenuous job of writing a good play. A recent writer for the theatre, Brendan Behan, who seems to be leading a very spectacular life in England, appears to be writing plays such as *The Hostage* which are equally flamboyant, though contributing flashes of genius by his great knowledge of humanity in its less attractive manifestations.

Among the other prominent authors with whom I have worked, I will select Robert Sherwood, Maxwell Anderson and Sidney Howard to indicate their main differences in writing approach. In the following, I have had the assistance of their play representative, Harold Freedman, who has worked more intimately with them and other leading American playwrights than any other individual in this country.

Robert Sherwood, whose mother was a painter and from whom he derived a picture sense, created his plays from beginning to end in his mind, his main strength being his story, with the characters following suit. He did not attempt to write the play until it was completed in his thoughts in almost every detail. Then he wrote it in almost its final form and very little revision or rewriting was needed. Of the three plays on which I worked with him, *Idiot's Delight* needed the addition of only one speech and the necessary introduction to it, while *There Shall Be No Night* was substantially unaltered, as was *Reunion in Vienna,* despite a good deal of criticism from some Theatre Guild board members—to which he paid little attention. However, some verbal changes were made by one of the actors before the play came to

New York, to which Sherwood took strong exception, and his text was finally restored.

Maxwell Anderson was a writer first and a playwright second. Dialogue and scenes based on character and situation came easily with him. Structure and story were difficult, and came later. Hence his plays sometimes called for considerable rewriting because of faulty structure, but his scenes usually stayed intact. He was also very slow about rewriting.

When we opened Max's play *Elizabeth the Queen* with Alfred Lunt and Lynn Fontanne in Philadelphia, the script showed certain rather obvious deficiencies which we discussed with Max, who said he would rewrite some scenes and add some others. "How did you make out?" I would ask Max each morning before lunch. "Sorry, Lawrence," he would answer. "I had no luck. I just didn't feel like writing." The weather was fine in Philadelphia, and waiting for Max was an enjoyable interlude, but as the fateful day for our New York opening drew closer, and no rewriting was forthcoming, we began to grow more and more anxious. Finally we postponed the New York opening and moved to Baltimore. A torrential rainstorm which assaulted Baltimore and drenched us as we came to and from Ford's Theatre added to our depression.

On Tuesday morning after the Baltimore opening I met Max in the foyer of the Belvedere Hotel, and regarded him as an anxious farmer would a favorite cow that had gone dry. "How about today?" I asked, bitterly. "Here's what you wanted for Act One." He handed me some sheets, folded together. "Here's Alfred's new speech." Another sheet was handed to me; and so on until I was clutching in my hands the entire revision of the play. "When did all this happen?"

I asked in amazement. "Well, Lawrence," replied Max with an enigmatic smile, "I really only write well when it rains." No drought-ridden farmer was more grateful for rain than I was.

Sidney Howard wrote both from character and story. Plays such as *They Knew What They Wanted, The Silver Cord* (perhaps the most imitated play ever written by an American playwright), and *Ned McCobb's Daughter* all sprang from his creation of characters. However, Howard was a superb craftsman and with the expert training he received under Professor Baker at Harvard, he was able to mold his characters into stories that satisfied all the canons of technical playwriting at the outset. He knew, so to speak, all "the tricks of the trade," including the art of concealing them, and used them to the best advantage.

During the first ten years of the Theatre Guild's existence, our main task was to build up a standard of play producing which would encourage American authors to write plays which were equal to those being written by the best European authors of the time. During these years, most of the English and European plays which we produced came into our hands in very good condition; that is to say, they did not call for rewriting but could be produced in almost exactly the form in which we received them from their foreign authors. Of course what had actually happened had been that these plays had undergone a certain amount of rewriting in the theatres of Europe before they came into our possession.

As a result, it was our habit to produce our plays with four weeks' rehearsal in New York City, and we did not take the plays out on the road to "try them out," as the expression is used today. In other words, since little or no change was needed in the plays, it was possible to open them in New York City without difficulty after four weeks' rehearsal. We also used the same method with our American plays. Most of our greatest early plays were produced in this way. Among them I mention Molnar's *Liliom;* Shaw's *Heartbreak House* and *Saint Joan;* Howard's *The Silver Cord* and *Ned McCobb's Daughter;* S. N. Behrman's *The Second Man.* It was only toward the end of the twenties, when we began to receive more plays from American authors which were not in good condition, that we began to change our policy and open the plays in out-of-town cities. In order to open plays cold in New York, it was necessary to have a very different rehearsal schedule from that which prevails today. By the end of the second week we expected the play to be in such condition that we could see a "run-through" of it, and if any further changes were needed in connection with the writing, the acting or the direction, we had but two weeks within which to get it done. So while it seems surprising today that this could be accomplished without supreme difficulty, it was usually possible when the play was in good shape at the start of rehearsals.

Nowadays the tendency is to keep plays out of town longer and longer, and to prolong the time apportioned for rewriting unnecessarily. As an example, at the present time it is the habit to keep musical plays out of town for anywhere from four to six weeks. When we produced *Oklahoma!,* it played half a week in New Haven, and two weeks in Boston. The same was true of *Carousel.* It should be added that during this period we worked on the plays with the knowledge that they had to be ready within three weeks after they opened out of town. The work proceeded with far greater rapidity than is the case today.

The change-over of the Guild's method to opening plays out of town was partly a result of the flight of so many American playwrights to Hollywood with the advent of talking pictures. As a result, some playwrights no longer spent a long period of time in creating the plays, and an additional period in writing. Many of them tried to write their plays between Hollywood motion picture engagements, and as a consequence, the plays of even the top-flight dramatists often arrived in New York in semi-completed condition. This in turn made it extremely hazardous to try to open these plays cold in New York. The out-of-town opening took the place of that point in the creation of a play where the author looks critically at his own work. Consequently, many an author would await the presentation of his play on the stage at New Haven or some other tryout city before he would make any changes in the play. In other words, the authors used the reception which the play received in out-of-town tryouts to help them determine what rewriting was needed. Very often this was deceptive, for the reactions of out-of-town audiences could sometimes be misleading, and rewriting which was done to meet their criticism, either direct or implied, very often made the play less acceptable to the New York critics and audiences than the original play would have been.

Because of this, the so-called tryout can bristle with dangers for an author, especially if he is too prone to accept the acclamation of out-of-town audiences; which indeed may be due to an actress or actor whose popularity is arousing the enthusiasm of the audience, rather than to the play itself. This is one of the reasons why so many plays which have been successful in the out-of-town pre-Broadway engagements come into New York and are received with coldness and even hostility. Therefore, the out-of-town-audience reaction is sometimes a dangerous yardstick as to what re-writing is needed. The experienced author will usually seek the advice of associates in whom he has confidence and whose standards are satisfactory to him, and he will measure his own beliefs about the necessary rewriting against the point of view of others who have the same kind of standards that he has.

I pause here for a moment to state that, in my opinion, the putting of a play into rehearsal before it is completely written is unfair to everyone connected with the enterprise. Yet authors, managements, and agents often insist on this for one reason or another, such as the availability of an im-portant actor or a director. "Oh, we'll fix this in rehearsal" is the easy way they dismiss what may result in the ultimate destruction of the play. In dealing as extensively as I am doing here with rewriting in rehearsal, I do so only because it is one of the evils inherent in the present-day theatre, and it would be unrealistic to ignore it merely because as a con-dition, it should not exist at all. Since, as already touched upon, the final production of the play is the result of the collaboration of all the theatre artists—and the playwright is only one—the tryout and the rewriting which so often takes place as part of the collaboration seem to be almost essential under present-day conditions in the theatre.

One of the most bewildering experiences which an author can suffer is to listen to the so-called experts who inform him what his play needs, after it has opened in New Haven or Philadelphia, Manchester or Brighton. He can usually find just as many opinions as there are people with whom he consults. Notwithstanding the fact that many of these opin-ions are contradictory, the author who is sensitive to the re-action of those in whom he has some confidence may notice that a pattern of criticism emerges that helps him in making his decision as to what to do.

Fortunately, however, there are many experienced playwrights who do not need to measure the play against the opinions of their associates. Such playwrights are capable of making up their own minds, based on what they observe in rehearsal, and are often beginning to rewrite those portions which they feel need attention long before the play opens on its pre-Broadway engagement. However, it may be stated as a general rule that the more the play is readied for production prior to going into rehearsal, the less hectic rewriting in hotel bedrooms and sitting rooms will be required.

It often happens that an author who has written a play for a particular star or stars is guided to a considerable extent by their reactions to the play as they act it before audiences. It stands to reason that since the actors are required to make a deep study of the characters which they play, they become very familiar with these characters. I remember one occasion when S. N. Behrman was rewriting a scene from the play *I Know My Love,* which he adapted from the French play *Auprès de Ma Blonde.* It was felt that a certain scene needed rewriting, and Behrman complied with the request. Thereafter, Lynn Fontanne refused to play the rewritten scene, saying, "I have been acting in this play for several weeks, and I think I know as much if not more about this character than you do. She would never say the lines you have now written." She was correct. Under these conditions, little is left for the author to do, except to take the next train out of town, or hide somewhere!

Another example of Lynn Fontanne's valuable help was in connection with Robert Sherwood's *Idiot's Delight.* During one of the run-through rehearsals someone expressed the feeling that the play seemed to be too light for its signifi-

cant content. Lynn Fontanne, who appeared in the play with
Alfred Lunt, put her finger on the pulse of the situation and
suggested that Sherwood write an important scene for her
and the manufacturer of munitions, with the result that a
great deal of weight was added to the play. This is a further
illustration of the desirability of listening to the feelings of
actors and actresses, which are often valuable to a writer
when he is in the process of completing his work. Prior to
the insertion of this scene, the play had drifted perilously
between the delightful story of a group of chorus girls shep-
herded by Alfred Lunt, and lost in Italy, and the more serious implications of the oncoming war.

Another example of the value of the actor's point of view
arose in connection with our production of *Mary of Scotland*
by Maxwell Anderson, with Helen Hayes, Helen Menken
and Philip Merivale. As usual with Max Anderson's plays,
some slight rewriting was necessary. In Pittsburgh, where
we opened the play, we were in difficulties with the end of
the second act. Helen Hayes invited us all to supper in her
sitting room one night at the William Penn Hotel. "I have
an idea for that scene at the end of the second act," she said,
after we had eaten. "That's why I asked you up here. I
thought I'd feed you first in case you don't like my idea."
And then she explained that in the scene as written she had
too much to say and do as Mary, whereas Bothwell, played
by Philip Merivale, had too little. "By this time," explained
Helen, "they're all tired of me. I know I shouldn't say this
as an actress, but take most of the scene away from me and
give it to Philip." Helen's instinct was right, and Max accepted her suggestion, which, far from weakening her part,
made her big scene in the third act with Helen Menken
more powerful than before.

These examples show that you, as an author, must never

believe that if you are in trouble you cannot get a great deal of help from those who are connected with the production. Beginning with the director, you should pay considerable attention to his point of view, since the play is going to filter through to the audience through his eyes, or, in other words, as the director sees it. Then you will observe that your actors will ask you questions, and since most of these people are intelligent and experienced, the questions will usually be intelligent too. They may set you thinking about deficiencies in the writing of the characters which you have overlooked. It is fashionable for authors nowadays to feel they are above taking suggestions from actors. I could mention quite a few important authors who are deeply indebted to their actors, directors, and producers for extremely valuable suggestions. However, it is only human nature for the author to wish to create the impression that the play sprang out of his creative mind like Venus from the ocean, in perfect form.

As noted above, there are authors who actually turn over their script to a management or director in a semi-finished condition with the idea that the management will immediately cast it with some star actor or actors who are available, and arrange the booking of a theatre in the shortest possible time. This is because the pressure to obtain the services of such actors is so great that the important author will take the chance of submitting an incomplete manuscript, since he knows that the actors are fully aware that he can perfect the script later on.

One of the most interesting experiences we had in this connection was with the production of *The Philadelphia Story,* which was brought to us by Katharine Hepburn, who wished to play the leading role. Only one thing was wrong— the third act had not been fully written. The play was put into rehearsal without the third act, while Philip Barry betook himself to Florida to write it. Fortunately, it turned out eventually to be an excellent act, and *The Philadelphia Story* became one of the outstanding comedies of its time. Quite different was our experience with the play *Jane Eyre*, dramatized by Helen Jerome, which also engaged the interest of Katharine Hepburn but was so impossible to rewrite on the road that we did not bring it into New York.

One of the playwright's greatest enemies in writing his play is discouragement. This can take two forms: (a) discouragement because the play form is difficult to master; (b) discouragement because once mastered, plays are difficult to sell. When the author is having difficulty with a problem in his script, it is well to remember that his unconscious will often assist him if he will but give it a chance. Often a writer who is unable to overcome an obstacle in his writing will find that if he relaxes and "sleeps" on the problem, he will sometimes awake with the answer. The main lesson to learn is to keep trying. One is never defeated unless one gives up. There are almost as many remedies against discouragement as there are writers. Dorothea Brand wrote, "Act as if it were impossible to fail." Longfellow wrote, "The lowest ebb is the turn of the tide." Doubt is the reason for many failures. Shakespeare wrote, "Our doubts are traitors, and make us lose the good we oft might win, by fearing to attempt." Dr. Johnson is quoted as saying, "To strive with difficulties, and to conquer them, is the highest human felicity."

Playwrights in trouble can learn from the experience of Dr. A. J. Cronin, recounted by L. E. Watson in *Light From Many Lamps*. He was so discouraged while writing his first novel that he threw the manuscript into the ashcan. That same day he recounted the fact to a neighbor, a Scottish farmer, he met on a walk. The farmer pointed to a bog on his farm on which both he and his father before him had dug all their days but never made a pasture. "But pasture or no pasture, I canna help but dig. For my father knew, and I know, if you can dig enough, a pasture can be made here." Cronin rushed home and retrieved his manuscript from the ashcan. Working on it frantically, he completed it and sold it. The novel he had thrown away was selected by the Book Society, translated into nineteen languages, was bought by Hollywood and sold some three million copies. Cronin stated, "It altered my life radically, beyond my wildest dreams"—and all because of a timely lesson in perseverance.

Richard Rodgers, the world's best-loved composer of songs, had been trying to make up his mind whether to accept a position in the woman's underwear business—in which a brilliant future was said to await him, beginning at a secure salary of fifty dollars a week—or to take a chance on starving in an attic as a musical composer. Dick hesitated, then decided that if the *Garrick Gaieties* review was produced for a "run" in New York by the Theatre Guild, he would gamble on his music; this he did with the magnificent success that is now legendary.

Difficulties in selling a play to a producer are responsible for another kind of discouragement. Shaw once remarked to me that once a play was written, one should never wait to sell it before starting the next. "Remember that some plays are more salable than others; also that one-third of Shakespeare's plays were failures." Shaw waited for years to sell his first plays, as did S. N. Behrman and Moss Hart, as recounted in the latter's recent autobiography. My own remedy against discouragement is based on the saying of Jacobowsky in Behrman's play *Jacobowsky and the Colonel:*

"In every situation there are always two possibilities. One is labeled fear and doubt, and usually leads to ultimate failure; while the other is labeled courage and faith, and often leads to ultimate success."

Many authors are in the habit of preparing a synopsis of their work and committing it to paper before they actually embark on the labor of writing the play. One of the reasons for this synopsis is to enable the author to ascertain whether the play will possess a desired structure and, to use a colloquialism, whether it will "come out all right" or "finish" at the end.

Whether or not an author needs to write a synopsis depends very much upon his ability to organize his play without committing anything to paper. The novice will find that he will have to carry a long and complicated story in his mind if he wishes to proceed without a synopsis. Some of the most effective writers made the synopsis an important part of their work. Foremost among these was Eugene O'Neill, who almost invariably wrote a relatively detailed synopsis of his earlier plays. I remember on one occasion, he showed me a blank exercise book, of which he was extremely proud, and in which he had written the synopses of a large number of his plays. These were written meticulously in his small, well-formed handwriting. What struck me particularly at the time was the fact that each entrance of each character into a scene was marked with a symbol somewhat like an arrow, which indicated how carefully he had thought out the impact of each individual on each scene.

One of the disadvantages of making a synopsis is that it tends to freeze or constrict the author into his original pattern. Very often a character in a play will take hold of it and start to write the play itself, and with this kind of inspirational writing, the author will find himself writing the play in a direction which is quite different from that of the synopsis. If he tries to force the character into the rigidity of the synopsis, the results may be extremely bad, both for the character and for the play.

It is well known that plays by new writers often begin very well indeed. There is an excellent first act, with the characters and situations well delineated. However, the play begins to go downhill and eventually writes itself out. What has here happened is usually that the inexperienced author has been able to carry in his head in detail only the happenings of the first act. And he has not been able to carry on the concentration of thinking and creating necessary for writing the second and third acts in the same way. It is here that the synopsis becomes particularly valuable to the young writer, for having thought out his first act and written a synopsis of it, he can start to work on his second act in the same way and continue with the third act; that is to say, writing the synopsis will force him to concentrate his creative efforts on the details of his second and third acts, the same way he did with his first act.

It is unfortunate that the adage "Plays are not written, but rewritten" has become such a commonplace in the theatre. It encourages authors to be careless about their first drafts and look upon rewriting as a necessary concomitant to the play, whereas their plays would have a far better chance for survival if the same careful work was bestowed upon them before rehearsal as is bestowed by a first-rate novelist before publication. Indeed some playwrights have almost established a procedure of sending out a fair-to-middling first draft which their agent rushes over to the producer, with a statement that of course the draft is only partially ready but the author will do more work on it after the director has been chosen. Here the director is accorded some of the attributes of godhead, and the author tends to rewrite his incomplete play according to the kind of picture the director wishes to paint, or the leading actor or actress believes would help his or her characterization or personal popularity.

This practice in the modern theatre has resulted in two additional evils. One of these is that the director really steps into the position of a co-author, and takes over the control of the script just as though he were sitting perched in the brain of the author and directing the movements of his pen. As a result, a director with a penchant for violence in the early part of the play will have such a scene introduced into almost every play which he produces, the author being his willing slave in order to secure the services of so omniscient an individual. The second evil resulting from such a situation is that the director and the author come to loggerheads over the rewriting, and one or the other either walks out or they arrive at a stalemate. So great is the power of the director nowadays that the author often yields rather than lose his services, as a result of which the play is ultimately only a distorted picture of what he wishes to express.

On the other hand, let it also be said that many plays have been vastly improved as a result of the contribution made by the director. It is interesting to note that a conflict between the author and the director has recently resulted in some plays being provided with two endings. One of these was *Picnic*, which included William Inge's original ending, and the ending which was worked out with the director, Joshua Logan. Another play which indicated differences of opinion between the author and the director and was printed in both versions was *Cat on a Hot Tin Roof*, in which both Williams' original third act and the modified third act as a result of the direction of the play by Elia Kazan were included.

The printing of plays in this way represents a brilliant example of an author having his cake and eating it. Both plays were great financial successes as a result of the collaboration between the author and the director. Had the endings which the authors had originally written been used, it is highly questionable whether these plays would have been such outstanding popular and financial successes.

Another interesting example of the rewriting of a play as the result of a collaboration between director and author is found with the recent Pulitzer prize-winning play *J. B.*, by Archibald MacLeish. The play can be bought in two volumes, one of which is the original play written by Archibald MacLeish, while the other is the rewritten version of the play which may be regarded as a hybrid born of the union of director and author. Possibly, like most hybrids, this was an improvement on the original stock.

One of the strange results of the adage "Plays are not written but rewritten" is found in connection with certain plays which are based on an interesting idea but are not fully realized by the authors. These plays pass from producer to producer. Each makes a suggestion to the author, who thereupon rewrites it. Upon reading the rewritten version, the producer decides that it is not what he wishes, and the play is then sold by the energetic play agent to some other producer. As a result, a play may pass through several hands and by the time it gets into production, it may have taken on many new facets which so enrich the original play that it may actually achieve a box-office success. One play which participated in at least two productions, the second of which achieved a success which was not forthcoming with the first, was *The Innocents,* by William Archibald, based on "The Turn of the Screw" by Henry James.

A method of avoiding the bewilderment which too often

overtakes an author while his play is on the road and decisions are made as to rewriting, is to make out a rewriting
"timetable" which is gone over with the author and director.
I learned a good deal about the use for such a timetable in
connection with the rehearsals of *Meteor* by S. N. Behrman,
in which the need for an orderly treatment of the necessary
rewriting became paramount. As is usually the case where a
play requires additional work on the part of the author after
the initial performances, the author, producer, director and
others concerned with the production are in the habit of
meeting each evening after the performance to discuss what
should be done in order to improve the play. At such conferences a large number of ideas are usually bandied about,
some of them good, some bad, some indifferent, and some
positively harmful. An author, if he is at all sensitive, often
comes out of such a conference with his mind completely
confused. He is at a loss to know what should be done to
help the play, and, in fact, which person's point of view he
should adopt. This is especially true when the director is a
man of prominence and insists on having his point of view
prevail. The confusion arising from such a conference may
well be such that the author decides to do nothing at all,
since the conferees have divided into factions, one group
taking one point of view while another takes the opposite.

For this reason if the author cannot do so, it is desirable
for either the producer or director to sort out the results of
the conference and to prepare the writing program or timetable, or assist the author in preparing one. The various
scenes which require rewriting should first be given an order
of importance and a position on the timetable. For example,
if the first act requires the rewriting of a scene which should
go into the play as early as possible, because without it the
later part of the play is not being understood, then the

author realizes that this is his first job, and he works accordingly. In the case of *Meteor,* the day after our conference Sam and I sat down and wrote out a list of ten points which had to be tackled in order one after the other. This sorting out of the jobs to be done clarified the situation for Sam, who otherwise would have felt a great deal of confusion as to how much work he had still to do, and when he was to do it. That this method did not result in the success of *Meteor* did not mean that on other occasions it was not most valuable. Indeed, I have found this method of programing the rewriting with the author has proven extremely successful in all work of this character where it was called for.

I remember an incident regarding the rewriting of *Meteor* which illustrates some of the sufferings the author undergoes, along with his colleagues, in endeavoring to rewrite a play on the road. During one of the conferences which took place after midnight at Boston's Ritz-Carlton (the hotel where more plays have been rewritten than in any other place in the world), it was decided that Lynn Fontanne and Alfred Lunt needed stronger scenes of conflict and more moments of tenderness. Sam, who rose each morning at seven and produced a few pages of beautiful dialogue before breakfast, appeared at the theatre the next day with some sheets of paper. "Here, Lawrence," he said, "are six pages of conflict, and here are three pages of tenderness!"

Notwithstanding our efforts, the play refused to come together, and nerves became very tense as the days wore on and the dreaded New York opening drew closer and closer. One afternoon, at a rehearsal which had the ominous stillness of an oncoming storm, Philip Moeller, who was directing a scene which was obviously impossible to direct or act, suddenly began to sob and cried out, "I can't stand it any more! I can't stand it!" He then threw a fit of hysteria which had me running for water while others dragged him over to a couch. "Get him home as soon as possible," said Alfred Lunt, taking charge of the situation. "It's been too much for him, and I don't wonder at it." We helped the trembling Philip to his feet, and I started to walk back to the hotel with him. No sooner were we out on the street than Phil pulled himself together. "How do you feel now?" I asked. "Fine," he said, striding along and smiling happily. "If I hadn't thrown that fit of hysterics just when I did, one of our stars would have done it a minute later."

There are some authors with whom the preparation of a writing program will not work at all. Usually they are authors who are not strong on construction, but are nevertheless able to write individual scenes extremely well. In connection with at least two of the best known authors in this country who have had experience in the rewriting of plays, it was often possible to secure an excellent improvement in a play by saying, "In this place you now have a scene which lasts for only four lines—this scene should be at least three pages long." The author, faced with the necessity of writing a scene of this length, usually produces under his own steam something far better than anyone could suggest to him.

Indeed, this brings us to the crux of the rewriting situation. The only rewriting that an author should be asked to do is that which flows inevitably out of the script and characters. Those directors or producers who attempt to impose a different story or a different point of view on a play will usually create chaos. It take a good deal of experience on the part of the director or producer to realize that his main job is to stimulate the author to create the new writing which is necessary, and not to tell him what to do, or to dictate the writing which should be done. For this reason, when a play needs work, it is often a good idea merely to point out at first the defects of the script and ask the author himself to create scenes or situations to overcome them.

An author under the stress of rewriting must be careful to take his time on his rewriting and, on the one hand, not be so slow as to impede the production, but on the other hand, not be so fast that his rewriting is not carefully done and cannot be used in the play. I have had experiences with both of these kinds of authors, and, in general, would prefer to deal with an author who takes his time but delivers a carefully thought-out rewriting job, rather than one who quickly absorbs the ideas of his director or others, and turns in a badly conceived rewriting of what is needed to help the play. An inexperienced author who is attempting to make up his mind regarding what rewriting is necessary should be careful not to permit his vanity to prevent him from accepting the good suggestions of others, provided however that they are within the fabric of his conception of the play and will not cause distortion.

One aspect of the play which nowadays comes in for extensive discussion during the tryout is that of foul language. The young playwright, and the not-so-young playwright, of today often obtains a feeling of release by writing the speech of some of his characters with a plethora of four-letter words of the type usually found scrawled on the walls of men's toilets (and probably for the same reason). The shock value of such words was once considerable. Now many of them have grown tired, and provoke not so much irritation as discomfort on the part of audiences trained to regard the use of such language as either ill-bred or infantile. Shaw was the first to introduce the word "bloody" to the stage with shock effect in the exit of Liza Doolittle at the end of the tea party scene in *Pygmalion*. This word, which has a different impact on English ears as compared with American ears, is now about as shocking as the word "damn" in late Victorian days.

The Theatre Guild must plead guilty to co-operating with Sidney Howard in introducing the expression "son of a bitch" for the first time on the American stage. This was in *They Knew What They Wanted,* which was produced in the year 1924, and was used in proper context. However, the expression "son of a bitch" has nowadays lost its explosive quality by continuous use and abuse in the theatre. At the time this play opened, the effect on the audience was so shocking that it caused as much adverse comment as did Shaw's use of the words "not bloody likely" in *Pygmalion.* Unfortunately Richard Bennett, who played the Italian grape grower, was extremely nervous on the opening night on Broadway, and his nervousness took the form of repeating the expression every time he forgot his lines—and considerably more often than the script called for, thus making the play seem to be even more profane than the author intended!

The experienced producer never bothers the author too much about profanity—at first. He knows he is helping the author to feel that he has created rugged "he-man" and "he-woman" characters. By the time the play reaches Boston, the town authorities hand the management a list of words to be deleted, otherwise the play will be closed. No author wants his play shut down, so out they come, with the promise that they will be reinstated for New York. By the time the author has heard his play with two weeks of modified profanity in Boston, his ears have become accustomed to it and he usually does not want the words restored for New York. I call this "coming out in the wash," an expression which covers many incidents which happen when a play meets an audience, including overlong embraces, obscene gestures and bedroom postures which are usually out of place in a theatre which aims to be civilized. The author should remember that for every person who is amused by unnecessarily foul language, there are a dozen who are outraged.

One of the reasons for the pre-Broadway out-of-town tryout engagement today is because of the terror with which the opening night is invested in New York, due to the kind of commercial theatre which now exists and the fact that the play is generally made or broken by its opening night reception. This condition does not exist in any other country in the world (except to a lesser extent in London), and the wonder is that we have any theatre at all when we function under these abysmal conditions.

An important reason for the out-of-town engagement is to enable the actors to get some practice of what is called "opening night playing." The nervousness with which an opening night can affect an actor may result in his reacting in many different ways. For example, out of nervousness, he may gabble his lines. If he does this at the Philadelphia or Boston openings, the effect will not be too destructive, but if he does it in New York it may be fatal. It is possible, by giving the actors an opportunity to play the opening nights in different cities, for them to recognize the errors into which their nervousness leads them and to become conscious of and avoid these errors at the dreaded New York opening. When the careers of the actors and the author, as well as the recoupment of the large sums of money spent, depend upon the single opening night in New York without any respite or second verdict, their nervousness is inevitable and the need for the out-of-town engagement becomes apparent. Unfortunately the newspapers treat the opening of a play in the same way that they treat a street accident. It must be reported the day after it takes place irrespective of whether the critic has really had time inwardly to digest the play or to form a really trustworthy appraisal of what has taken place on the stage on the opening night.

In the English theatre, there are the so-called Sunday newspapers, which give certain of the critics some time to think over the play and even to attend it a second time and write a second notice based upon a reappraisal of the play. I venture to say that within the last thirty years, very few New York critics (other than those on *Variety*) go to see a play for the second time, or to witness it in the way in which it is played without the tensions and stresses of the opening night. This is notwithstanding the fact that certain critics write a reappraisal of the play a week or so later, and have ample opportunity to view it again. Thus it is that the critic who writes of the opening night with the greatest facility, with the greatest enthusiasm, or with the greatest erudition expressed in popular terms, influences the theatre to a far greater extent than those critics who have time to appraise a play carefully—not on the basis of the opening night, but on the basis of a later relaxed performance.

However, enough of this digression about the critical situation which the young author has to meet. Suffice it to say that the purpose of the pre-Broadway out-of-town engagement is to bring the play into the most approved form, and especially a form which will please the New York critics. This procedure will doubtless be continued long after I and my colleagues have passed out of the theatrical picture.

The author will wish to know the value of so-called "summer tryouts" in this country, for the purpose of providing additional opportunities for working on his play. My attention was called to the value of summer tryouts through the successful production of the early one-act plays of

Eugene O'Neill at the Wharf Theatre in Provincetown, Mass. After taking a trip through New England in the year 1930, I visited the summer theatre at Skowhegan, Maine, one of the oldest summer stock companies in the country, as well as the theatre at Dennis, Mass., which had just been built according to the designs of Cleon Throckmorton, who was the scenic artist of the Provincetown Playhouse. I decided that the summer theatre provided an excellent opportunity both for developing a repertory company, and for trying out new plays by new authors. As a result I built the summer theatre at Westport according to the plans of Cleon Throckmorton in the spring of 1931. During the first summer we also produced two new American plays; one of these was *The Comic Artist* by Susan Glaspell and Norman Matson, while the other was *The Bride the Sun Shines On* by Will Cotton. Both of these plays proved interesting and it was decided to transfer the latter play to New York. It opened in the fall of 1932 but received rather poor notices.

The next year we tried out several long plays, and one of these, *Chrysalis,* written by Rose Albert Porter and directed by Theresa Helburn, also found its way to the stage of the Martin Beck Theatre in New York. The same year *The School for Husbands,* an adaptation by Arthur Guiterman and myself of the Molière play, was performed in Westport and ultimately produced at the Empire Theatre in New York. Another Westport summer tryout, *Champagne Sec,* written by Robert Simon and me and based on the *Fledermaus,* was brought to New York and ran for a season, while the following year *The Pursuit of Happiness* written by Armina Marshall and me also ran for a season in New York, and has since played many stock engagements as well as a London engagement.

These results left no doubt in my mind that the summer

was an excellent time for trying out plays and perfecting them before they opened on Broadway. As a result of my experience in this field, over thirty plays have been brought into New York City after tryout performances at the Westport Country Playhouse. Furthermore, the Playhouse was responsible for the original production of William Inge's *Come Back Little Sheba,* which was the first of his long plays to be given a New York opening, thus introducing one of America's finest playwrights of today.

In view of the above, it may be stated categorically that a summer tryout may be immensely valuable to the new or untried author. However, this fact having been stated, it is also necessary to draw attention to many of the dangers to the unsupecting author which lurk behind the tempting façade of the summer tryout.

First of all, the management of the summer tryout must be carefully considered. If there is not connected with the enterprise someone who has his mind set on a major theatre production in addition to the summer theatre one, the results are liable to be negative, and may even be harmful. This means that the summer tryout production should be made mainly for the purpose of testing the values of the play and indicating where additional rewriting is needed. The first rule which I have learned in connection with the tryout of such plays is that it is essential for them to receive a minimum of two weeks and preferably three weeks of rehearsal. As this latter greatly increases the expense, it is sometimes possible to rehearse the two or three leading characters for an additional week before calling in the minor actors or actors who play the minor roles.

Another point to remember is that, if possible, a two- or three-week tour of the play being tried out in summer theatres is desirable, since it gives the author and the actors more time to consider the rewriting possibilities.

Another important point is to try to cast the play with the same actors one would like to use later on in New York. A striking example of this was the case of the very successful comedy *Life With Father*, which was first tried out in Skowhegan, Maine, and was brought into New York with the original actors, Howard Lindsay and Dorothy Stickney, and with very few changes in the cast. The same has been true of most of the successful Westport tryouts.

Another point to be borne in mind is that where a new and inexperienced author is concerned, it is desirable to provide him with an experienced director. This is not always necessarily true however, for very often the enthusiasm of a new director for a new script may produce better results than the work of the kind of director generally available for summer tryouts. For example, when we tried out *Come Back Little Sheba* at Westport, the director, Daniel Mann, had never directed a play before, but he made up in enthusiasm what he lacked in experience. What the author must particularly remember in connection with summer tryouts is that audiences and critics are always in a far less critical state of mind when visiting the summer theatres than is the case when the play arrives in New York. They must therefore be careful not to overestimate the audience response, since this can often be misleading.

Once the play has opened, the author can utilize his time for such changes as may be deemed necessary. The summer tryout should not be used to eliminate the out-of-town opening of the regular production which takes place later. It took nine weeks of playing on the road, after the summer tryout, to get Robert McEnroe's *The Silver Whistle* into the condition in which it ultimately became a Broadway success.

Playwriting is the most difficult of the writing arts, not only because of the actual writing of the play itself, but also because of what takes places after it is thrown to the lions of the theatre in the form of director, producer, actors and all the other collaborators whose creative artistry and egotism comes into play. These will be dealt with in a later chapter. The playwright may well envy the novelist, who encounters none of these participants in the accomplishment of his artistic work. And yet—!

CHAPTER V

Play Construction

(Part One)

ONE of the main differences between writing a novel and writing a play is embodied in the word *construction*. As used in the theatre today, this word means the arrangement of individual scenes, one after the other, so that the play builds in suspense until the story reaches its climax. The simile to a building is found in the fact that the play must have a strong foundation which must first be laid down at the beginning of the play, after which the structure is built scene by scene as one floor in a building is built above the next. There the simile ends, for when the building reaches its peak, it is finished, but when the play reaches its peak there is still usually more to be done by way of construction. However, as will appear hereafter, such form of construction may be modified according to the talents of the playwright, or even dispensed with altogether if he possesses the genius to get along without it.

Indeed, it is appropriate at this point to state that periodically attempts are made to write plays without reference to some or any of the so-called rules of construction. This is often a rebellion against the "well-made" play, as was the case with the expressionist plays in the early part of the century. Among the most successful of these may be mentioned Georg Kaiser's *From Morn Till Midnight*, Ernst Toller's *Man and the Masses*, John Lawson's *Processional* and

Elmer Rice's *The Adding Machine*—all produced by the Theatre Guild in the twenties. Chekhov, too, departed from the usual procedures and successfully invented his own particular type of structure by progressing his plays with contrasting moods, a method which has often been imitated but seldom with good results. (Shaw's *Heartbreak House* is an exception. Written on somewhat the same theme as *The Cherry Orchard*, the vitality of his ideas and language overcame the lack of structure.)

Today a new group of writers has come forward which again achieves a certain novelty by ignoring the age-old rules of construction. These plays have been fostered during the seasons of 1959 and 1960 in England, where a revolt against the standard drawing-room comedy has long been overdue. Among these so-called *avant-garde* plays are mentioned *A Taste of Honey*, by an eighteen-year-old factory worker, Shelag Delaney, and *The Hostage* by the somewhat spectacular Brendan Behan, who has transferred his flamboyancy to the stage with good results. Some audiences and critics (especially the London critics), bored with the current well-made play, have accepted these forms of playwriting which have released a new vitality in production, just as some audiences of the twenties accepted with enthusiasm the expressionist plays of that period. After the novelty wears off, however, writers and audiences in the past have almost inevitably returned to the older forms which are either rooted in the classics or represent the theatre at its highest point of effectiveness. Thus the theatre, like its rivals music and painting, seeks to free itself from the fetters of the past, often with good results.

Nevertheless, he who wishes to break with tradition in art will achieve the best results if he understands the tradition and breaks with it because he disagrees with it, rather than because he is not sufficiently skilled to achieve with it. Wagner's early opera *The Flying Dutchman* showed that he had mastered the technique of Italian opera before he supplanted it with his own. The young playwright of today who intends to introduce new forms in the theatre should be thoroughly familiar with the old forms; hence a knowledge of construction and its terminology is valuable both for those who intend to use it and those who intend to discard it.

The word *scene* has three meanings in the theatre. The first is geographical, and means the locale where the action takes place. The second refers to a part of an act, or division of the play, as indicated by the expression "Act One, Scene One." The third use of the word is in connection with a confrontation or meeting of two or more characters in a play in which some conflict or event usually takes place. The Act or Scene may consist of several small individual scenes; indeed, in the French theatre, the playwright usually writes or prints his plays with a new scene heading whenever a new character meets other characters on stage.

Every scene in the second and third sense of this word should partake of the same characteristic as the play itself. It should have a beginning, a middle and an end. The scene must preferably advance the story. The main characters at the end of the scene should, if possible, have reached a different position in relation to each other than that which existed at the beginning of the scene. Preferably the scene will build to a climax, either dramatic or comedic. A scene which does not advance the story usually seems static, even if the characters physically run all over the stage while they play it. When a series of scenes each progresses the story, the play is said to move or build. The latter is especially true if each succeeding scene progresses out of the scene or scenes which preceded it. This structural form is like the house that Jack built, since each scene logically flows from a scene or scenes which came before it. Many good plays have been written, however, which do not slavishly follow this pattern. Now and again a scene may also be included which does not advance the story, but may provide necessary atmosphere, or time to change costumes, or provide comic relief. In general, however, the rule holds true. Build the scenes successively on the preceding scenes in order to progress the story.

I have found in my experience that, given characters which live on the stage, *suspense interest* is the one essential of the play which cannot be dispensed with. A play with suspense interest grips your attention and holds you spellbound to the edge of your seat. A play without it will cause you to be restless, inattentive, and uninterested in the outcome. A novel usually has suspense interest, though it is not as important as in the theatre. When you get tired of reading the novel, you can close the book and pick it up again later. Not so in the theatre. There you must sit in a seat, usually not the most comfortable, for periods often extending over forty minutes for each act, and sometimes longer. Your back grows tired, your limbs feel numb. The play must run in competition with your progressively increasing tiredness. This it can do only by becoming progressively more interesting and exciting.

This is the miracle that suspense interest performs. It keeps you in your seat, eagerly awaiting the development of the play. A writer may do away with acts, scenes, or any of the stereotypes of the theatre, but he cannot eliminate suspense interest.

There are a few simple rules about suspense in a play.

Suspense is best obtained by placing a person or a situation in jeopardy, or by a threatening disaster or menace which hangs over a character or characters. Teachers of playwriting have well named the means by which this is accomplished, the hanging of a sword of Damocles or threat over the character or situation. Suspense is additionally obtained by adding additional threats or swords of Damocles over the character, until the audience is hard put to it to guess any way for the character to escape his fate.

Suspense is continued in a play by hanging additional threats or swords of Damocles over the character whenever one of these threats or jeopardies is removed. In other words, the character is not permitted to escape from a dilemma which threatens to engulf him, without plunging him into another and preferably greater dilemma. The author should keep these threats and jeopardies up as long as possible, and as close as possible to the end of the play. He should intensify them if he can before he relieves them.

Suspense interest does not necessarily depend on the so-called "sword-of-Damocles" technique. There is a built-in suspense interest in every character who is liked by the audience which desires to know the outcome of the story and its effect on the character. This is especially true of comedies, when the suspense interest can often be expressed by the question, "What is going to happen next?"

In rewriting a play, insufficient suspense interest can usually readily be built up by increasing the threat or jeopardy in which a character is placed. In creating suspense interest, the writer should be sure that he hides the mechanisms by which he obtains it. If it is too obvious, the audience will not be affected by it.

Suspense interest is sometimes obtained by bewildering the audience, feeding it small portions of information, one piece at a time, so that the audience will be held by a desire to know more about the characters and situations. Many plays, seemingly incoherent or difficult to follow, are acceptable because of the natural curiosity of the audience to penetrate the well-written fog.

In speaking of suspense interest we must also consider the duration of the threat. If it lasts throughout the play, or most of the play, we call it a "long-range" suspense interest; if of short duration, it is called "short-range" suspense. The latter is of far less importance than the former. A play in which the main character is repeatedly threatened, and released from threat almost immediately thereafter, will lack the build of the long-range threat which is intensified by additional threats, some of which may be short-range. As an example of the former, in William Inge's play *Picnic* the character of the wandering ex-football player Hal is a long-range threat to the contemplated marriage of the daughter Madge and the banker's son Alan; a threat lasting throughout the play and intensified by scenes in which the mother and the fiancé attempt to get rid of Hal without success. In O'Neill's *Mourning Becomes Electra* the daughter Lavinia is determined to avenge the murder of her father through her mother, and the suspense lasts throughout the play as the tragic consequences of her revenge envelop all the principal characters, ending with her self-immolation at the final curtain.

Another method of developing suspense is based upon requiring a character to make a decision affecting either his life or the lives of others. This is the basic suspense interest of all courtroom dramas, where the decision is made by a judge or jury based on evidence, or plays where a character makes a choice based on events which affect his judgment. The most obvious form of this on a short-range basis is found

in the casket scene in *The Merchant of Venice,* where the
suitors' choice of the gold, silver or lead caskets is based on
their evaluation of the quality of the metal. The riddle scene
in Gozzi's *Turandot* is another example. In the modern
theatre, examples of this form of suspense interest on a long-
range basis are found in the long-discussed intention of
Harry Hope, the saloon keeper of O'Neill's *The Iceman
Cometh,* to walk through the neighborhood; in Professor
Higgins' decision to attempt to make a lady of Eliza Doolittle in Shaw's *Pygmalion;* and in Tracy's decision as to which
man she will marry in Philip Barry's *The Philadelphia Story.*

The material and the story actually determine the *shape*
or *form* of the play. If it is a story that can be told only in
four acts, this simply means that it will call for a certain
number of scenes and intermissions. If it is a story with a
dramatic or comedic climax at or toward the end of the
middle of the play, it may take the form of a three-act play.
In any event, the stage is adaptable enough to take care of
all forms or shapes of plays, or even no form at all, so long
as there is suspense interest.

In the last sixty years, the three-act play has become the
most popular form for dramas or comedies. In Shakespeare's
day there were often as many as thirty changes of locale,
because little or no scenery as such was used. In modern
musical plays, the two-act form with many scenes and a
single intermission is generally used, while in the so-called
four-act play, it is usual to perform the first two acts in
succession with a single middle intermission.

In the Greek theatre, it was thought highly desirable to
have *unity of time and place* and to use a single set. This is
because by locating the action of the play in a single place,

the author could keep on building the suspense continuously without changing the locale, thus avoiding interruption to the flow of feeling, and assisting the dramatic build of the play to its climactic conclusion. Euripides' *The Trojan Women* is written in this way, and so are such plays of Ibsen as *A Doll's House* and *Hedda Gabler*. Unity of time, or continuous action, is also valuable for somewhat similar reasons. However, the use of unity in time and space is a difficult technique, and often creates a playwriting problem by forcing the story artificially into a single locale.

The modern unity of place in what is called the "one-set" play is often imposed upon us by the stagehands' union. We know that every set is going to cost so much to build, and with more than one set, a crew of sixteen stagehands or more must be employed in the United States. Up go the running expenses, so that the play must enjoy much more popularity at the box office in order to live for a "run." Thus we have the curious fact that in the United States the economics of labor reach right into the theatre and tell the playwrights what they have to do in order to earn a living. One way to overcome this difficulty is to write plays which do not require too many sets and heavy realistic scenery. The same number of stagehands needed to move two large sets can also move ten or more small set pieces. Since we are in trouble whenever we have a play with more than one set, we might just as well have several sets, as far as the stagehands' expenses are concerned.

Actually, the playwright can make his own rules about the number of sets needed, but should remember that if he has written a play which calls for absolute realism, it takes time and costs a good deal of money in building and in supplying stagehands to move rapidly from one set to another. This imposes a limitation of about four box sets as a maximum. It is correct to say that so long as the play is in three acts, calling for three box sets, it might as well have ten smaller sets, for the production costs will be about the same. This is because if the author calls for more than four sets, we are forced to suggest the scenery by using only small parts of the locale, and to rely on the audience to supply the details, which they are usually more than capable of doing. Indeed in the Chinese and other Eastern theatres, the scenery is left entirely to the imagination of the audience.

As already stated, the author, before deciding on the form of the play, may make a *synopsis* of the story itself, and then figure out, after he has written it, just where he wants to place the different scenes and curtains. This will help to tell him what type of act formation his story calls for.

The foundation of the play structure is laid down at the opening of the play. The remarks which follow regarding exposition and the other events which take place at the beginning of the first act, and constitute the foundation, are equally applicable to all forms of plays and musical plays without limitation as to the number of scenes or acts in the play. (I exclude, however, the one-act play, which usually covers an episode and in which a far greater condensation is needed.)

In the earlier days of the theatre, a great deal of importance was given to the subject of the *opening exposition.* When the curtain rose on Act One, you listened to the old-fashioned exposition, which generally supplied background information on the time, place and characters of the play. In the days of Sardou, this was often done by a maid and butler who conversed while they dusted the room, or arranged the flowers. When this type of exposition became too hackneyed, another type took its place. According to Professor George P. Baker, "the dramatist is writing supposedly for people, who except for plays on a few historical subjects, know nothing of his material. If so, then as soon as possible the playwright must make them understand who his people are, where his people are, the time of the play, and what present and past relations of his characters cause the story." This type of exposition was popular in the theatre of twenty to thirty years ago. Eugene O'Neill and other playwrights trained by Professor Baker gave a considerable amount of time and effort to such exposition. *Anna Christie* is an example, which began with a scene in a saloon in which everything was laid out in detail for the audience as to who the characters were, and the situation they were in.

Today this kind of exposition is usually unnecessary. This is largely due to the impact of television. The audiences of today have seen so many plays and stories on television and in motion pictures that they are far more aware and play-conscious than the audiences of twenty to thirty years ago. It is, therefore, no longer necessary to lay out an elaborate pattern of exposition. The audience picks up the requisite information very rapidly, and becomes impatient with the old type of exposition. Through television we have learned to begin our play immediately with something dramatic which will hold the interest of the audience, and we either let the exposition come along later, or make it part of a dramatic opening scene. The audience will be held by something happening between people which is exciting in itself, and will be even more curious afterwards to find out or learn about these people. An example of this kind happened with Guy Bolton's adaptation of *Anastasia*. Bolton, who is a splendid craftsman, was worried by a long scene of boring exposition with which the play started. It was only at the middle of the first act that the audience became interested in the characters, when a very strong dramatic scene took place. After the New Haven opening, Bolton resorted to the technique of television and removed this dramatic scene to the beginning of the play, and placed his scene of exposition, explaining who the people were, later on in the act. This is the preferable way, under modern conditions, to start any play, whether it be a comedy or a drama. Begin, if possible, with some kind of action, some kind of excitement.

Additional exposition may be fed into the play throughout the first and second acts. It is usually difficult to provide a scene of exposition in the third act unless this is in the form of dramatic conflict. In writing exposition, the author should beware of two characters telling each other something which both of them know, in order that the audience may be made aware of a past situation. If such exposition is needed, it should be revealed in the form of an argument or conflict about the past, instead of in statements of fact.

Some writers prefer to begin a play with an unimportant *opening scene* because of the latecomers who disturb the rest of the audience. In my opinion, this is wrong. Many managements nowadays do not seat latecomers at the beginning of the play, but try to find a place later on in the first act where the disturbance does not matter so much, and seat them at this time. Opening scenes should not be written for the benefit of latecomers. I suggest that writers might always include a stage direction in their first act: *At this point latecomers may be seated.*

Another good rule for the opening of the play is to avoid having the characters on stage discussing people we do not know, and about whom we do not care. This, in my opinion, is also an obsolete form of exposition, but one which sometimes cannot be avoided. It is a safe rule that if the author wants to discuss somebody at length, he should find some reason to bring him on the stage first. Then he can talk about him afterwards as much as he pleases. This rule may also be due in part to the advent of television, which forces the author to take short cuts, as he does not have time to describe his characters in detail before they appear, without creating a static effect.

In the first fifteen minutes of every play, an important experience happens to the audience. Its members sit in the theatre somewhat grimly, wondering what kind of play they are going to witness—even if some of them have heard about it favorably from the newspapers or from friends. They have paid a considerable sum of money for their tickets and they are trying to make up their minds as to what kind of play this is, and how they are expected to react. This is why what the author does in the first fifteen minutes is very important, as it gives the audience the clue to the kind of play they are seeing. If the play is a comedy, it is best, in the first few minutes, if the author possibly can do so, to provide a comedic incident or situation, to set the audience at ease, and to let them know that they are going to enjoy something amusing. It is by no means an easy matter to provide an amusing situation at the beginning of a play, but if the author can do this, it will put the audience in a laughing mood from the very beginning, and the laughter will come more easily for the rest of the play.

In attempting to start a play off on the right foot, we must be careful not to go too far in one direction, and lead the audience into the wrong mood. For example, if the play is a comedy with serious overtones, it is desirable to indicate this at the beginning of the play by a scene which will include not only the comedic aspects but also some of its serious implications. In other words, the opening should reflect the fabric of the play which is to come later, and should not be misleading. I may add in passing that it is extremely upsetting to an audience if the mood changes entirely during the progress of the play, as from comedy to drama, or even from comedy to farce, although a change of this latter kind is more acceptable than the former. In the English theatre the audiences are more accustomed to a change from comedy to farce than is the case in the United States, where for some mysterious reason our critics are prone to complain of this.

A recent musical play, *Bells Are Ringing*, the book of which was written by Betty Comden and Adolph Green, may be cited as an example of the need to set the correct mood at the beginning of the play, and the use of a *Prologue* to accomplish this. On the pre-Broadway engagement, the opening took place in a little sub-cellar which was shabby and run-down, and it was from this place that an answering service was operated by Sue. The cellar looked like the setting for a serious play of the genre favored by the Group Theatre, and it took a long time to coax the audience into a receptive mood for a musical play. The difficulty was overcome just before the play was brought to Broadway (where it ran for over two years) by adding a musical Prologue with a group of colorfully dressed girls, all seated at telephones and receiving messages, while singing the title song, "Bells Are Ringing." As a result, there was telegraphed a foretaste of what was to come, and when the curtain rose on the sub-cellar, the audience was in a receptive mood and no longer in the state of apprehension which had formerly interfered with the enjoyment of the play.

While it is a general rule that when the play is a comedy it should begin in a comedic mood, and when it is a drama it should begin in a dramatic mood, this is not always the case. Only recently a comedy written by Joseph Fields and Peter De Vries from the novel *Tunnel of Love* was singularly successful by breaking this rule. The play, which is a comedy of manners, begins with a strong dramatic scene lifted bodily out of the third act, and serving as a prologue. It shows the main characters in serious conflict, with the wife leaving the husband. The rest of the play is devoted to showing how the husband and wife reached this climactic situation, and there was no difficulty in shifting the mood of the play from this dramatic scene to the ensuing scenes of comedy. During the pre-Broadway tour of the play, the author was tempted to try what would happen if this dramatic scene was omitted, and for one evening he yielded to this temptation. He restored the scene very quickly when he found that without it there was no tension between the two characters, and no indication to the audience of the direction in which the play was going. The same results might, of course, have been accomplished by different means, but I cite this to show that when it serves a useful purpose, all rules in the theatre may be broken by those who can do so successfully.

In the Restoration comedies, it was often the custom to provide an amusing Prologue to beguile the audience into the correct mood for enjoying the play. A modern example of such a Prologue is found in the rhymed verse adaptation fashioned by Arthur Guiterman and me, of Molière's *The School for Husbands*. When the play was tried out at Westport originally, it had no Prologue. The actors, dressed in their period costumes, started the play with a serious scene, and the members of the audience would listen grimly and think, We are not going to be amused by this. And even when the play began to amuse them, we could not coax them into laughing for the first twenty-five minutes, no matter how funny the play became. The moment the audiences saw the costumes, they felt they were in the presence of a classic, like a play by Shakespeare, or an imitation of Shakespeare, and they made up their minds to take it seriously. After a few days we decided to write a Prologue for Sganarelle, the leading character of the play, which was played by Osgood Perkins, one of the finest comedians of the day. This Prologue said, in effect, "Ladies and Gentlemen, don't be frightened, we are here to entertain you. Don't be afraid to laugh at this play, it was written to amuse you, it has amused people before, and it will again." The effect was magical, and the Prologue was retained. The same technique was used with good effect in a recent musical play, *Candide*, by Lillian Hellman, where the same problem existed and was solved in the same way by means of a Prologue in the style of Restoration comedy.

The use of a Prologue is especially valuable to introduce a point of view about a play or to explain an event which took place either before or after the play, and which will color the understanding of the play itself. Very often a play is set in the past and there seems to be no modern application of its theme or contents. By means of a Prologue dealing with an event of today, the play which follows can be laid in the past and yet take on modern significance by having its present application pointed up by the Prologue.

An amusing use of the Prologue will be found in Bernard Shaw's *Fanny's First Play,* where a group of dramatic critics discuss the play, which device enabled Shaw to lampoon the foibles of the various drama critics of his day as well as to introduce one of the leading characters.

In *introducing the characters*, it was once fashionable to provide what was known as a "build-up" for the entrance of the leading characters. In an exaggerated form this was done by references to the character who was about to enter, and in the case of historical plays, a herald would often appear and announce the character; and the leading actor would enter on stage with a flourish of trumpets. In the modern theatre, where such antics do not usually take place, there is a more subtle way of introducing the leading characters with some kind of importance. One of these is by awaiting expectantly the arrival of a character, as is the case with Hickey at the end of the long first act of O'Neill's *The Iceman Cometh.*

By the time the writer has reached the middle or end of Act One he should preferably, though not necessarily, have introduced his leading characters and started the main situation of the play moving toward the end of the first act. If the play has a theme, or something to say which the writer feels is important for the understanding of the play, it is desirable to introduce this before or during the middle of the first act. As a result, the audience realizes that it should be on the watch for those parts of the play which pertain to the theme.

By the end of the first act, we should have a pretty clear idea of the direction the story is taking. If it has a theme, this may also be emphasized in the last scene or curtain of the first act. The action should move toward the curtain situation, which should highlight, if possible, the direction in which the play is going.

As already stated, young or inexperienced writers can usually write a good first act. The second act is often not as good, and the third act often falls away to vacuity. This kind of play is the hardest to correct, because it starts off with so much promise that audiences expect it to get better in the second act, and best in the third act, or at least as good as it was in the second act. How is the author to correct his play under these conditions? One way is to demolish the first act, take the best material out of it and place it into the second act, or even into the third act. Another way, but much the harder way, is to improve the second and third acts, leaving the first act alone, or modifying it slightly so that the expectations it has raised with the audience will not be so great.

What has been stated above as to the opening of the play applies equally to the two-act, three-act and four-act play. However, the balance of the first act usually calls for the consideration of a number of facts, and these will be discussed later on with reference to the three-act play, which is the most usual form in the theatre of today. We shall now deal briefly in more detail with the *two- or four-act play.*

The two-act play, which may also be a four-act play, with a single intermission located about the middle of the play, represents a form which is used only occasionally in the theatre of today. In both cases, it is better to refer to the play in terms of halves, rather than scenes or acts, because in effect the first half of the play may contain a number of scenes and the same may be true of the second half. Indeed, the use of the word "half" is in itself a misnomer because, in general, in this type of play the first part should generally be at least a third as long again as the second part. In other words, from the point of view of timing, the play should be more than half over by the time we arrive at the single long intermission. Experience has shown, especially with musical plays, that a long first part, followed by a short second part, is usually the more satisfactory division of the play; it is certainly more satisfactory than the reverse.

By the time we reach the intermission in a two-act play

we should know all the main characters, and we should be so deeply into the main situation that at the curtain of the first part of the play we are in a state of strong suspense as to how the story will continue.

This is well illustrated by the famous musical play *Oklahoma!*, in which, before the curtain falls at the end of the first part, Laurie has a dream which is in the form of a ballet, in which Curley is killed by Jud, who carries her off. At the very end of the act, after the dream is over, the two contestants for her love have a moment of defiance, and the curtain falls on the question of whether or not Laurie's forebodings will come true at the Box Social party to which they are all departing.

The musical play *Carousel* was also divided into two parts, and even stronger suspense interest was provided by the fact that, as the procession of young men and girls streams across the stage to go to the picnic at the end of the first part, the sailor Jigger shows the carving knife which he has stolen to Billy Bigelow as they walk off just before the curtain falls. The presence of this fearsome weapon forebodes the killing of someone in the next act.

Much of what has been written above is applicable no matter into how many scenes or acts the play is divided. Thus a play might be written in eight or nine scenes without the author indicating any act divisions. It will be up to him or the director to decide, in the playing of the play, where the intermissions shall come, and these will tend to be selected in accordance with the same rules which apply either to three-act plays on the one hand or two-act plays on the other.

We shall discuss the three-act play in the next chapter.

CHAPTER VI

Play Construction

(Part Two)

ARISTOTLE'S time-worn dictum that a play should have
a beginning, a middle, and an end lends itself quite naturally
to the *three-act play*, which is the most popular form in the
theatre of today. Such a play may be constituted by any
number of scenes. However, it presents the characteristic
of being divided into three divisions, with intermissions between the first and second division. It is also desirable in this
form of play to provide a strong suspense interest at the end
of the first act, and to provide a climactic scene or crisis
at the end of the second act.

There is an old formula for the structure of the three-act
play or comedy, said to have originated in France, which
runs, "In Act 1, get your characters up a tree; in Act 2, throw
stones at them; and in Act 3, get them down again." I shall
dwell on this formula, as I have found that it works well for
certain kinds of plays, and especially for comedies. In my
opinion, however, it needs elucidation. I would rewrite the
formula to read, "In Act 1 begin as soon as possible to get
your characters up a tree, at the same time letting your audience know what kind of characters you are dealing with,
and what kind of a tree (problem) it is. In Act 2, throw
stones at them, but begin with the smaller stones and then
throw stones which are larger and larger, until by the end of

the second act you almost knock them out of the tree. Then at the beginning of the third act, either continue to keep them there or start to bring them gradually down, but do not let them get safely down until the end of the play."

What is meant by "throwing stones at the characters"? This actually means getting the characters into trouble or placing them in a dilemma. The "stones" usually represent incidents which create suspense interest, and the "tree" represents the main problem or dilemma of the play. The formula represents a simplification of the form of many comedies and is not always applicable, especially in connection with dramas or tragedies, where the stones are apt to be thrown at the character throughout the entire play until the very end. Another formula for the three-act comedy is "boy meets girl, boy loses girl, boy gets girl again." This formula suffers from the defect that when used, the experienced theatregoers, and especially the dramatic critics, know just what to expect, and unless considerable invention is shown in the story itself or in its telling, it is too easy to guess what is coming.

Experience has shown that in the three-act play we should be introduced fully into the beginning of the main problem of the play by the time the curtain comes down at the end of the first act. The author should not, in this form, merely introduce a group of people in Act One and then start to show their main problem in the second act. The problem may only be indicated, but the first-act curtain should preferably come down on a situation which is the main situation of the second and third acts. If the author does not do this, he may have an incomplete or lightweight first act with insufficient suspense interest to carry over successfully into the second act. (Successful examples are shown in the endings of the first acts of Shaw's *Candida* and *Man and Superman.*)

Having already established the problem of the play by the end of Act One, we have considerable time available without relieving suspense interest at the opening scenes of Act Two. This is a place in the play where the playwright is free to use less important material for his purposes, if he wishes to do so. Generally speaking, however, the main or central situation of the play should start again at the beginning of the *second act* and should grow in excitement and intensity until it reaches its climax at the end of the second act.

Care should be taken *not* to begin the second act with the most important or dramatic scene of the act, because this will usually result in the second act running down or diminishing in interest, unless it is possible to build in importance and impact later on. When we speak of the second act running down, we usually mean that the climax of the main situation is reached before the end of the second act. In such a case, the later part of the second act will be anticlimactic.

In following the rule which was mentioned earlier, viz. by the end of Act I, get your characters up a tree and in Act II you can throw stones at them, do not make the mistake of throwing your big stones at the beginning of the second act, or you will have a falling off of interest at the end of the second act. I remember in the case of S. N. Behrman's *The Pirate,* based on an original play by Ludwig Fulda, there was great trouble with the second act, and indeed, I received a telephone call from our co-producers, who were in charge of the production, telling us that they thought the play should be abandoned on the road. I visited it in Washington, D. C., and found that a very strong comedic quarrel between the leading characters, played by Alfred

Lunt and Lynn Fontanne, took place at the beginning of the second act, after which there was no place to go and the rest of the act dribbled off into vacuity. It was suggested to Behrman that the situation could readily be remedied by postponing the strong quarrel from the beginning of the second act until its end. Sam agreed, and after rewriting it brilliantly, the play came into New York and ran the rest of the season. What had happened to change the picture was simply this. The biggest stones were thrown at the characters at the end of Act Two, instead of at the beginning.

Where the author finds that his second act drops in interest from the middle to the end of the act, he is faced with an extremely difficult situation, as the play will be in grave danger. Experience has shown that where the climax of a second act is reached about the middle of the second act, the story begins to lose interest during the last part of the act. This is because nothing is quite so disappointing as an anticlimax at this point. The audience underlines this disappointment during the intermission, and will not listen to the third act with the zest which would otherwise be present. Indeed most plays fail under these conditions. It was for this reason that the late Arthur Hopkins, one of our most experienced directors and producers, wrote a book entitled *How's Your Second Act?* which emphasized the fact that a play without a good second act seldom succeeds in the theatre. This has sometimes been misunderstood as meaning that the second act should be better than the third act. This is not the case. A good second act followed by a better third act is perhaps one of the most desirable forms to attain.

When the author is faced with the fact that the climax of the second act comes in the middle of the act, he can solve his problem in three ways: he can, if possible, move it to the end of the second act; he can possibly create an even greater climax to follow it; or finally, if there are no other factors which prevent it, he can turn the play from a three-act play into a two-act play with an intermission after the climax in the center of the play. In other words, he may solve the problem by doing away with his original second act altogether. In this case the first half of the play consists of the original first act followed by the first half of the old second act, ending on its climax. The anticlimactic scene or weak scene which ended the old second act now becomes the first scene of the second half of the play. This scene, although it may be weak in itself, will hold the interest of the audience far better if it comes after the intermission instead of before it.

It will be helpful at this point, in indicating to authors what not to do, to consider what happened to *Love's Old Sweet Song*, which was jointly directed by Saroyan and Eddie Dowling. This play, one of Saroyan's most charming efforts, was written in loose form in three acts. Any eccentric actor who appeared at our office might stimulate Saroyan to write in scenes for that actor, very much as one might build a vaudeville show by putting in a "number" for any comedian who applied for a job. The danger into which we were drifting because of Saroyan's position as director became very apparent when, one fine day, a lady parachute jumper appeared at the Theatre Guild office and was shown in to Saroyan. "Could you jump from the roof of the stage with your parachute and land on the stage at the end of the second act?" asked Saroyan. "Because if you can, I will make you one of the characters in the play." Since the lady couldn't without breaking her neck, we were mercifully spared this addition to the play. However, Saroyan discovered an old friend on the street, a Greek comedian who had appeared as a comic in some films, and by providing him with a lawn mower and an American flag, Saroyan introduced him into the play with extremely happy results!

We opened in Philadelphia with disaster, for while the first half of the play was excellent, it reached a climax in the middle of the second act after a long speech by Walter Huston as a medicine vendor, and from there on this act ran steadily downhill. The feeling of the audience at the end of the second act was one of extreme disappointment, for they had just seen the weakest part of the play where they should have seen the strongest. After Saroyan made a number of attempts to remedy the situation, it finally occurred to me that if the play, which was in three-act form, could be played as a two-act play, our intermission could take place in the middle of the play, and at the point about halfway through where the second act reached its climax. It is never possible to tell whether an operation of this kind will turn out successfully, and the only way to ascertain is by trying. Saroyan therefore agreed to slice the play in half, and it became a two-act play instead of a three-act play. Since it was extremely loose in form, this operation, instead of hurting it, turned the trick and converted what had been a failure into a success. That part of the play which was weakest, instead of being at the end of the second act, now became the beginning of the second half of the play, and from this point on the play steadily improved until the final curtain.

When we opened in Baltimore with this new arrangement, we received excellent notices, not an easy matter, for Baltimore was a town where the critics were not noted for their indulgence. I felt happy as we brought the play to New York, feeling that the out-of-town tryout, with its consequent financial losses, had nevertheless justified itself since we had apparently solved all our problems. Alas, however, I had reckoned without our Saroyan. Two days before the play was due to open in New York he arrived at the theatre with his play agent, Pat Duggan, and the two of them sat in the smoking room of the Booth Theatre and expounded their point of view to the rest of us. Saroyan, it appeared, had demonstrated his ability to write a two-act play with *The Time of Your Life.* It was now considered desirable that he should demonstrate his ability to write a play in three acts— yet here we were putting it into two acts! Terry Helburn and I pointed out that we had already demonstrated that the play was extremely weak in three-act form but was excellent in two-act form. We were met on all these scores with stubborn obstinacy by Saroyan.

As we teetered in the face of uncertainty, Saroyan made an impassioned speech: after all, it was his play and if it was a failure, he would have to take the responsibility for it. His reputation was at stake, and he felt that he must insist on his right as an author that the play should be presented in three-act form. Finally, to make his point very clear, he added, "And I'll be very glad to buy out everyone here who has money invested in the play, so that I will own the entire play myself." Pat Duggan, who, thank the Lord, preserved his Irish sense of humor, winked at me and suggested that we have a chat in the hallway. "I just want to explain one thing to you," said Pat. "Please don't take up his offer. He hasn't the money to buy you out, and even if he had, I wouldn't let him."

The matter was discussed back and forth, with Saroyan's friend the late George Jean Nathan, the dramatic critic, joining in, and it was agreed that since Saroyan's reputation was more important than anything else, we should accede to his request rather than "destroy a great work of art." The result was that *Love's Old Sweet Song* opened the following night with a weak second act, and the critics, except for two, lashed it severely. The next day Saroyan called me on the telephone and remarked, "You had better put the curtain back the way it was in Baltimore!" Alas, we had missed the boat. Thus was "lost" one of the most delightful plays Saroyan has ever written, and if anyone wishes to revive it, I strongly recommend that he present it in the two-act form with which we should have opened the play in New York.

(It is one of my regrets that Saroyan has spoiled so much of his own work by attempting to be both author, director and producer of his plays. He was always an exciting and colorful personality, right in many big ways and wrong in many small ones. He has never been mediocre, dull or conventional, and I would gladly put up with his temperamental antics for the sake of another good play. It is still not too late for him, jolted as a producer and director, to add a series of fine plays to those he has already written. That he may do so, and turn them over to producers and directors who know their business, is the fervent hope of all who admire his talents, among whom I beg to be included.)

The second act in a three-act play should usually end on the climax or high point of the dilemma, or the situation which has yet to be resolved by the characters in the *third act*, which latter act usually contains the resolution of the problem before its end. However, there is another type of three-act play where the author keeps building the intensity continuously, so that the denouement comes at the very end of the play. We observe it mostly in tragedies (as in *Hamlet* or O'Neill's *Desire Under the Elms*) or in mystery melodramas where usually the tension is not released until the very end of the play.

In order to persuade the audience back into the spirit of the play after the second intermission, it is desirable to open the third act with a scene of strong conflict in the case of a drama, or a scene of strong comedy in the case of a comedy. In some cases, scenes can have the quality of both of these. For example, in O'Neill's *Desire Under the Elms,* the party scene in which Ephraim Cabot participates in a wild dance brings the audience quickly back into the spirit of the play. A similar effect is created with the beginning of Act Three of *Ah, Wilderness!* in which the youth Richard meets the young prostitute Belle.

There is one rule regarding the latter part of the play which seems to be true for every form of play, and also for vaudeville and any other kind of entertainment which runs for the entire evening. Somewhere before or about the middle of the third act, or the latter part of the second act in the case of a two-act play, a rousing or exciting scene should take place on the stage. It is my own theory that such a scene is needed to shock the audience out of the lethargy into which it tends to drift after being seated in the theatre for over two hours. A perfect example of this was the rousing song "Oklahoma!" in the musical of that name. Without this song, which was introduced into the play during rehearsals, the latter part of the second half of the play tended to become lethargic. A similar note of high excitement was introduced into *Carousel* by the famous ballet which took place at the precise moment when the audience needed "waking up." Of course in musical plays, which can be constructed on more or less artificial lines, it is relatively easy to provide a climax of this kind at the point desired. In a dramatic play or a comedy it is not so easy, since this must be done without distorting the play.

As a substitute for, or in addition to, the above, a similar effect can be obtained in the third act by introducing a new and highly entertaining character who, by the originality of his attitude and dialogue, will provide a lift to the third act and so-to-speak "wake it up." Perhaps the best example of this is the introduction of "Gentleman Johnny" Burgoyne in the latter part of Shaw's *The Devil's Disciple,* a character who usually runs away with the play.

The last part of the third act, in general, constitutes a resolution of the play, either in the form of a happy ending in the case of a comedy, or a tragic ending with a spiritual lift in the case of a tragedy. It is also fashionable at the present time to provide an ending to a play which is neither all black nor all white, but leaves something to be decided by the audience. Such a resolution is found in Leonard Spigelgass' recent comedy *A Majority of One,* where Mr. Asano and Mrs. Jacoby are brought together in a comedic scene which, while it suggests that they will probably continue and may possibly even develop their relationship after the play is over, leaves the actual ending to the imagination of the audience. A somewhat similar ending exists in *Sunrise at Campobello* where the audience is brought, in the last third of the play, to the scene where Roosevelt prepares to make his nomination speech, and the play reaches the conclusion of the third act by FDR walking confidently down the platform to the rostrum and greeting the audience. That Roosevelt does not make the speech itself, in order to reach the climax of the play, is a triumph of playwriting on the part of the author, Dore Schary, who felt from the outset that the victory of FDR over his illness and despair at the beginning of the play would constitute a high climax to the play itself.

In most plays, the resolution of the problem to which the play is addressed usually takes place in the last part of the third act. If it takes places at an earlier point, the end of the third act is liable to be anticlimactic, and the audience becomes restless and does not desire to await the end. This is particularly true in the case of comedies, or in the case of plays where the end can be too readily foretold in advance. This can sometimes be remedied by adding suspensive lines or incidents which stimulate the further curiosity of the audience, so that they will remain seated until the end.

We shall now consider the other kind of three-act play, already mentioned, in which the characters do not come down from the tree after the end of the second act, but have stones thrown at them throughout the third act, and until the very last part of the act where the final resolution takes place. In such plays, the general rule is preferably that each succeeding part of the play shall exceed in tension that part which has gone before it. The opening of the third act should, if possible, start with even greater tension than that which ends the second act, while the final climax or denouement can take place in the last five or ten minutes of the play, as with the classical examples of *Hamlet* and *Othello*.

I also emphasize that the *curtain situations* or so-called *curtains* of plays, whether they consist of two, three or four acts, are of extreme importance to the success of the play. If weak, they tend to leave the impression that the entire act is weak. If strong, they help to make the audience forget any weakness in the play which preceded them. In the best form, the playwright makes an effort to write a curtain situation which will have a direct dramatic reference to the theme of the play and will point up at the end of each act what is coming in the next act. Such curtains are often extremely effective, but may sometimes tend to be artificial and to have the effect of being contrived. This effect of contrivance is also emphasized by the fact that many plays are written with a so-called "punch line" at the end of the act. A similar attempt is made in comedies to end each act with a hilarious comedy situation or line of dialogue producing laughter on the part of the audience. Here again the effect is often felt to be contrived, which is not surprising, since this is actually the case. How often have I heard a director say to a writer, "What we need for this curtain is a big laugh." One is reminded of the retort of Owen Davis to a director who made this remark to him. He is said to have replied, "For instance?" Shaw was one of the best exponents of the telling curtain line and situation. Examples of these are found in nearly all of his earlier plays.

The second type of curtain is one which is deliberately untheatrical. The technique here is to place the carry-over scene just before the curtain (this is the scene which will give suspense) and then deliberately go out of the way to bring the curtain down on a remark such as "It's a fine night tonight." The best examples of this kind of curtain are found in *John Ferguson* by St. John Ervine, a play full of strong climactic situations. However, at the end of each act he brought the curtain down on a line which had nothing to do with the story of the play, but might be the kind of line a character would say in the situation, but talking against it. Here are some examples of the curtain lines in *John Ferguson.*

Act I curtain: "Put a shawl over your head, daughter, and wrap yourself well from the night air."

Act II curtain: "It's all right, Hannah, dear! Andrew's away to fetch your da!"

Act III curtain: "It's colder the day nor it was yesterday! Ay, Son."

The third kind of curtain is one which I do not recommend. It is to bring the curtain down on a scenic "effect" or an effect created by properties or by artificial means. The trouble with such curtains is that they are usually dependent upon the ability and carefulness of the stagehands. One of the curtains of Elmer Rice's *Adding Machine* depended upon such a scenic effect. No matter how hard we tried to make this effect work properly, it usually proved disappointing.

Indeed, it may be stated as a general rule that "effects" which are produced on the stage by mechanical or electrical mechanisms nearly always defeat their purposes, and cannot be relied upon nearly as much as the interaction or conflicts of human beings. This is because the better the effect, or the more surprising, the more the audience wonders how it was produced and is usually not carried away by it. This of course is not always true, but like most of the rules here, there is sufficient truth in it to warn the playwright against ending an act on an "effect" which may or may not come off.

The *intermissions* between the acts of the play are extremely important and are not usually given the attention they deserve. An intermission in a play has two values. First, it gives audiences a chance to move out of their seats and roam around, so as to provide a muscular release on their part, if they so desire, and it enables them to take care of their physical needs. So when a playwright thinks of writing a play which requires the audience to stay in the theatre for hours without an intermission, he should know that this is not a good idea from many practical considerations. Secondly, an intermission is a punctuation. It emphasizes a point in the story when the members of the audience are no longer at the receiving end, but are given an opportunity to think over what has happened up to this point, and to evaluate it. Whenever I read a new play, I always put it down after I have read the first act and again after the second act, and I consider my feelings about the play after each act. This is what the audience does. If you leave your seat at the intermission in the wrong mood, in a half-sour mood, in a bewildered mood, or in a depressed mood which is not overcome by the excitement of wanting to know what is coming next, then you might well feel you would rather go home than stay to see the rest of the play. So the playwright has to remember that the situation and suspense at the curtain of each act should create high excitement in the audience, and make it possible for members of the audience to talk about other matters, or to drink, or even to eat in the intermission, and yet want to return eagerly to their seats again. Intermissions in the wrong place or under the wrong conditions (such as mood) can sometimes wreck a play.

While the intermission is an interruption, and too many of them are not desirable, the emphasis they give to the curtain situation is extremely important. The wrong emphasis can mislead the audience. The right emphasis can excite the audience and carry it more deeply into the play. If there is a weak spot in the play, the author should not stop for the intermission at this point but keep his story moving along until he arrives at a strong point in the story, which an intermission will underline.

A device often used in the theatre is the *Epilogue,* a scene or monologue at the end or completion of a play, the purpose of which is usually to make an author's farewell greeting to the audience, as in Shakespeare's *As You Like It,* in which Rosalind addresses the audience in her wedding gown; or to explain something which happened after the events of the play had taken place, as in the case of Bernard Shaw's *Saint Joan.* In this instance, when the play seemed so long as obviously to need cutting, I asked Shaw why it would not be logical to remove the Epilogue. "Not at all," he replied, "I was writing about *Saint* Joan, not Joan. Her story was not ended with her burning, but with her having achieved sainthood some hundreds of years later." And it enabled Shaw to add the great postscript to his greatest play, "Oh God, that madest this beautiful earth, when will it be ready to receive thy saints? How long, O Lord, how long?"

In Elizabethan and Restoration plays it was often the fashion to end the play in a dance of the characters; the "jig" was especially favored in Restoration comedies, in which Nell Gwyn made her popular reputation. (Perhaps some writer of gloomy dramas of today will reintroduce this convention to send the audience home in a happy mood!)

Before completing these remarks on play construction, I should like to refer to some other considerations which properly form part of this subject. These include the *dialogue, invention,* and *surprise.*

There is a bite, a condensation, to good dramatic dialogue which contrasts with the leisurely dialogue generally used in novels. When the spoken sentence meanders, it loses its force. When a character is angry, the words can spit out like bullets from a machine gun. When the character is in a reminiscent or philosophical mood, the words can be uttered with a rhythmic flow. Long speeches are often an advantage. They sustain an actor, hold him up in the same way that a good song sustains the singer. Never be afraid of lengthy speeches as long as they are in the correct mood and rhythm. The playwright has only to fear that the actor will be afraid of them, and by rushing through them or "gabbling" them, prevent the audience from properly hearing them or understanding them.

If the playwright has a good ear, he will write sentences with the correct timing for comedy. One or two additional words in a sentence will "kill the laugh." I have noticed that authors who are in the habit of telling amusing stories in their social life usually understand the art of "timing," for they practice it with the telling of each humorous anecdote, which usually ends in a "laugh." No one can teach comedy writing or a sense of humor. We either have it or do not.

Invention is a quality in telling a story or writing a play which consists in deviating from the expected development of a situation which can usually be foretold by the audience and, taking them by surprise as it were, plunge them into the unexpected. In terms of playwriting this is often called a "twist" or "turn," which may or may not increase the suspense interest. An example of the use of invention is found in the capture of the two villains by Dogberry in *Much Ado About Nothing*, who confesses the trick played on Claudio, and as a result of which the denouement of the play follows.

Another aspect of invention lies in the so-called *surprise*—the introduction of a character who was unexpected or unheralded, or even had no possibility of being present, yet whose introduction into the play is fraught with consequences for the main characters. We have already mentioned the introduction of Burgoyne in *The Devil's Disciple*. Shaw was given to the use of surprise in many of his plays; for instance, in *Captain Brassbound's Conversion* by the unexpected advent of the Sidi at the end of Act Two which changes the entire course of the play; the return of Doolittle in Act Three of *Pygmalion* with a fortune at his disposal; and the arrival of the burglar in *Heartbreak House*, who turns out to have been a former sailor under Captain Shotover who was married to the Captain's housekeeper.

There is a tendency to believe that surprise will always be attained by the introduction of a new, unexpected scene or situation. When audiences have begun to believe in a certain set of facts, as evidenced by the play, it is difficult to cause them to change their minds much because of the introduction of a new character or situation. This calls for what is termed *preparation,* and most surprise situations require this preparation for their believability. Reduced to the simplest terms, this means that somewhere earlier in the play (without giving the surprise away) information is given to the audience which, when the surprise takes place, makes it conform with the earlier information, so that the facts fall into place and are believable. An example of this is found in Shaw's *Captain Brassbound's Conversion,* in which the surprise of Brassbound's relationship to the Judge, Sir Howard, is carefully prepared for early in the play.

Surprise based upon the deception of the audience up to the point of the surprise is always dangerous. This leads us to a general discussion of *deceiving the audience* and under what conditions this is feasible or desirable. The formula for most detective stories and plays is for suspicion to rest on one or more characters who appear to be guilty, but in the denouement of the plot they turn out to be innocent whereas the party on whom there is no suspicion turns out to be guilty. This "trick" has become so commonplace that it is now seldom effective.

It is permissible to deceive the audience under conditions where the characters in the play are also deceived in the same way, so that the situation is unraveled for all of us together. However, it usually spells disaster if the characters on stage know the real situation or truth, but the author deliberately sets out to deceive us. It is also true that when we know the truth, but the characters on stage do not, the deception of these characters is interesting to us, as in Frederick Knott's play *Dial "M" for Murder.* In the case where the audience and the detectives are searching for the guilty party, we have a "whodunit" beloved by television. In the case where we know the guilty party but the characters on stage do not, we have a "Will-they-catch-him?" type of suspense interest, in which we watch the deception of the characters on stage with interest.

By using *formulae,* it is readily possible to contrive or construct a play following rules which have been used a thousand times before. However, when a formula is the basis for the writing, the play will tend to be peopled with cardboard individuals whose purpose it is to carry out the formula. This in turn will usually result in a play which never comes to life, and the resulting work, while it may be technically perfect, will not live and breathe on the stage. A perfect example of this occurred with Eugene O'Neill's play *The First Man,* written after he had taken Professor Baker's playwriting course at Harvard. The play obeys all the rules of standard playwriting, but none of the characters comes alive and the play was one of O'Neill's greatest failures. The formula play also suffers from the defect that it is usually readily predictable, since formulas become tired in the hands of tired writers, and are all too familiar to our critics and trained audiences of today.

Too much stress cannot be made of the fact that what has been written here must not be regarded as playwriting formulae, but as examples of structures which have been successful in a great number of important plays. The above rules of construction are particularly useful when the writer finds that he is in trouble, and that his play needs some rewriting. They will help him to decide where his scenes of greatest tension should preferably take place, and such other information which he needs and which he can gauge or measure from the past experiences of other writers. I remember talking with Sidney Howard about the difficulty many writers have in starting to write a play which then begins to write itself, so that the third act seems to have little or nothing to do with the first act. "That often happens with me," said Sidney. "All you have to do is go back and rewrite the first act so as to make it fit the third!" How simple and practical, yet how often playwrights are bewildered by this situation!

Finally, each and every playwright can make his own rules. G. B. Shaw once stated to me, "I believe I can write a play in which two people sit down to talk with one another and the conversation will keep going on for two and a half hours, with possibly two or three other people joining in the conversation, and this would make a perfectly good play." The answer is that this might be true, depending upon who writes the dialogue. Shaw's dialogue was often, at the time when he wrote it, so interesting to audiences that he could create and hold a suspense interest by sheer talk. In actual fact, his play *In Good King Charles' Golden Days* is not very much more than an animated conversation between successive groups of characters, yet it was strong enough to run nearly a year in a small theatre in New York. However, very few people can write dialogue as suspenseful and brilliant as Shaw's, and this idea is certainly not recommended to the budding playwright who, by using it, may throw away most of the advantages provided in the theatre by plot, dramatic build and suspense interest. For in the last analysis it is these which give the play the high excitement which is not to be found in any other form of literature.

CHAPTER VII

The Playwright's Role in Production

IT has already been explained that a playwright's work does not end with writing the play. Thereafter he should continue to stand behind and work on his play during its production, and especially during rehearsals. This period constitutes an acid test for the writer, for if he fails or is unwilling to collaborate with the other artists who are involved, his play may never reach the boards in anything approximating the form in which he conceived it. As already stated, four of the world's most important playwrights—Shakespeare, Molière, Shaw and O'Neill—usually made it their business to stay with the play until the curtain rose on it at the opening night, and the same applies to most other successful if less-known playwrights. Consequently, no book on playwriting is complete unless it deals with the incubation of the play from the manuscript to the stage.

The playwright who has found a producer capable of doing a first-rate job of collaboration is lucky. Due to the high costs of present-day theatrical production, many so-called producers (managers in England) are really unworthy of the name, since their main ability is to raise the capital needed for the production, which is then turned over to others to produce. If the producer knows his business, he will serve, so to speak, as the captain of the producing team and be a pillar of strength for the author to lean on. He will also decide disputes between the other members of the team, and this with authority, since he is the "owner" of the play by contract when it is considered as property, and once purchased, the author cannot make changes in the play without the producer's consent (and vice versa). If the author is inexperienced but has an experienced play agent, the agent can also be of valuable assistance. Under the American Dramatists Guild contract, the author has the right to veto the employment of the *stage director* (called the producer in England), the *actors,* the *scenic artists,* and the *costume designer.*

While the producer and author may flatter themselves that they are selecting the stage director, it is usually the stage director who actually does the selecting. This is because there are only a handful of expert stage directors, and their services are greatly in demand. Assuming that a competent director has been found who is enthusiastic about the play, the author can afford to rely heavily on him for advice regarding the selection of the other artists. The ideal director is one who tries to serve the play, and uses his efforts to bring out the meaning and intentions of the author. He is, in other words, the servant of the play. Unfortunately, some stage directors today simply take the play and use it to serve their own directorial purposes, bending it to their own conception rather than that of the author. For this reason, the author should be assured that the director visualizes the play in the same way that he does before the director is actually engaged.

It is desirable to select the actors after the director has been secured, otherwise he may not agree with the casting, and confusion can result. On the other hand, where extremely good actors wish to appear in the play, it is sometimes better to let them have a voice in the selection of a director, since it often happens that certain actors will not work with certain directors. In connection with the casting, the following generalities may be offered in the way of advice.

Try to obtain actors who have creative imaginations, and will add something to the roles. An excellent imaginative actor is always better than a man or woman who looks the part, but gives nothing more than an adequate representation of the character. This latter is called "type" casting.

Where the character is written in a one-dimensional plane, it is best to use actors who will round out by their own personality the characteristics which are missing in the writing.

In the case where a character is so extreme as to be almost unbelievable, be sure to avoid selecting an actor who is of the same "type" as the character, since by adding the living personality to the written personality, we are apt to arrive at a completely unbelievable character. The expression "casting against type" is used to indicate the kind of casting which should be done in such cases.

The playwright should not expect to find in the actors exactly what he wants, and become irritable with the actors because of this fact. Eugene O'Neill was seldom satisfied with the actors in his plays. In writing them, he had imagined ideal actors playing the characters, and no actors ever quite filled the bill. The author should beware of expecting the impossible from an actor.

The author should be careful to work through the stage director and not deal with the actors personally. If he attempts to discuss the play with the actor without the approval of the director, the actor may become confused and the director will be impeded in his work.

The playwright must not only concern himself with the *scenery,* but also with the *lighting* which will be employed to establish the various moods of the play and the time of day.

In writing a description of the scenery, the playwright should remember that the more he states, the more he is apt to confuse. He is not a set designer, and should not attempt the designer's work. He should describe clearly the kind of place and atmosphere he wishes the scenic designer to create on the stage, and pay special attention to the playing spaces and where he wants the entrances and exits. Shakespeare used less stage direction than almost any other playwright, and his plays have not suffered noticeably as a result. In Victorian days he was cluttered with cumbersome scenery which almost destroyed the swift movement of his action. Today the tendency is to use as little scenery for Shakespeare as possible, as in Elizabethan days.

Remembering that the purpose of the theatre is to enhance life and not to limit it, the author should not demand of the scenic artist that he be too literal or realistic in his scenery, unless the play especially calls for it. Of course if he is writing for what I call the "kitchen sink" school of drama, then he should by all means include every detail including the sink, and every domestic utensil that belongs in a kitchen. But even in this school of writing, the play will improve if the scenic artist will produce the *effect* of a kitchen without actually putting the kitchen itself on the stage.

Good scenery for a play should never fail to whisper to the audience unconsciously that it is looking at theatre scenery—but the scenery should whisper and not shout. This applies to almost every kind of play, but especially to comedies and poetic plays.

The playwright will have completed his work if he sets up his most desirable arrangement of chairs, sofas, benches, windows, fireplaces and so forth, but he should not be obstinate about their position if the director wishes to change them. In general, the most important scenes in the play should be played closest to the audience. A distance of ten feet inside the set may easily reduce by one-third the dramatic intensity of a scene played at this point. In the days of Restoration Comedy, the scenes were played by the actors standing literally over the footlights, but we must remember that these footlights were candles. The rule holds true, however, that high-comedy scenes are more effective when played close to the audience. Low-comedy scenes can be played all over the stage.

Bernard Shaw had a habit of refusing to recognize the existence of a stage at all, and described his scenery from the viewpoint of a person in the room or place where the play is set. Before his innovation, it was the custom for playwrights to clutter up their manuscript with stage directions such as "Enter L. C." for "Enter Left Center," and "X R. R." for "Cross Right Rear." The less we have of this to contend with in reading the play, the more we will be able to enjoy it. Shaw also had a habit of setting up his characters by means of chess pieces on a chessboard and moving them from one place to another, thus directing the play himself. I know of no director who ever improved on Shaw's directions in this respect.

Elaborate stage directions are confusing both to the reader and actor. "What are you doing?" a stage director once asked an actor who was making an extraordinarily painful grimace. "I'm following the author's directions," was the reply. "I'm smiling *callously."* Some directors make it a rule to cross out all such directions before going into rehearsal, on the grounds that they merely confuse the actor. I do not agree with this. In certain instances, when the lines taken alone are capable of misinterpretation unless the stage directions are also given, I believe these serve a useful purpose.

The author should take great care in selecting the scenic artist. The American dramatist has a veto on his selection. Scenic artists are chosen for a variety of reasons: they may be the best for the play; they have contributed scenery to a large number of "hit" plays; they will sweeten the play, they will toughen it; they are inexpensive; they are engineers and will make swift changes possible; and finally, they are friends of the producer or director who likes working with them. These are all good reasons, and should be respected by the author.

There are a number of scenic artists whose work has enhanced almost every play on which they have worked. Perhaps the greatest of these was the late Robert Edmond Jones who, more than any other American scenic designer, provided an atmosphere which surrounded a play and lifted it from its mundane dimensions to the heights of pictorial beauty. One of the most notable of his sets was for Eugene O'Neill's *The Iceman Cometh,* the interior of a sordid saloon which, by the magic of his artistry, was transported into a scene of shimmering beauty without ever causing the audience to lose sight of the ugly reality of the barroom. Less talented scenic artists are sometimes the enemy of the author. But more of this anon.

The following are some facts of which a playwright should be aware in setting his scenes for a play, or in looking over scenic sketches or attending scenic or dress rehearsals.

Do not place a large window or opening in the back wall

of the set, except where the set is in use for only a short time, or the window can be masked with curtains. It bothers an audience to look directly into light for a long period, and it also tends to silhouette the actors.

Do not use black drops or black sets unless there are large areas of contrasting coloring in the balance of the scenery, costumes, or properties. The "color" black not only strains the eyes to look into it, but it also creates a mood of depression. I once witnessed a production of *Macbeth* at Stratford-on-Avon. It was directed by John Gielgud, who should have known better. The walls of the scenery were painted a funereal black, and the effect on the audience was to create a feeling of unadulterated gloom. Instead of Shakespeare's strong drama coming over to the audience in terms of dramatic excitement, the mood set by the scenery and lighting put the onlookers into a condition of morbid depression. I stumbled out of the theatre wondering what had happened to one of Shakespeare's best plays. It had collided with the black scenery, and came off second best.

Remember the old theatre rule, actors cannot play comedy in the dark. If necessary, the scenic artist can set a mood of darkness at the beginning of a comedy scene, then gradually bring up the lights. In general, brightness lifts the spirits of an audience, darkness depresses it.

While discussing the need for brightness for the playing of comedy, I may mention that in the original production of *Oklahoma!* Jerome Whyte, the musical production stage manager for Richard Rodgers, provided the musical comedy lighting of that period, while John Haggott, the Theatre Guild production stage manager, provided the usual dramatic lighting. The combination of this double lighting under Rouben Mamoulian's direction produced a burst of light on the stage at the opening which never failed to lift the play and its audience. On the other hand, an underlit production of *Porgy* in London made it impossible for the critics to see the faces of the Negro actors and to understand their dialect. The play was a complete failure, largely on this account.

Allow the scenic artist thirty seconds at the beginning of an act to light the scenery, after which insist that he light the actors and the play. Even then, watch him, or he may start the play or the act in the wrong mood.

The use of three or more "box" sets, as in many of Shaw's plays, is to be avoided under modern theatre conditions, especially where quick changes are needed. Where there are a number of sets, the scenic artist is forced to use his imagination to produce his effects with small units. This also applies to musical or spectacular plays, where combinations of painted drops, set pieces or platforms are used to obtain rapid scenery changes.

The high cost of scenery and stagehands has increasingly forced the dramatist to write his play for one set. This sometimes increases the potency of the play by providing unity of place, as in the ancient Greek theatre. In many instances, however, the reverse is true, and the audiences become tired of looking at the same set. In such instances, variations of lighting become important to provide a variety of mood.

Do not rely on scenic effects for an emotional climax. Sometimes they come off, more often they don't. Human emotion to express a climax is more certain of achievement and more moving to an audience. In general, the more excellent a mechanical or electrical effect, the more the audience will pass out of the mood of the play to wonder how it was done. But a bad effect is even worse.

Do not expect the scenic artist to be an interior decorator, even if the set calls for interior decoration. A good scenic artist is an artist of the theatre, not a room decorator. He should create a room of the kind the play calls for in terms of the theatre. This involves simplification, but more essentially it involves the creation of scenery which will point up the play by providing the proper mood, playing spaces for the important scenes, and so forth. In the days of Belasco realism, every effort was made to produce the effect of reality on the stage. For this the late David Belasco should be praised rather than condemned, for he came into the theatre as an innovator at the turn of this century, and at a time when lighting and scenery were in the age of innocence. However, he ultimately made realism an end in itself, which defeated his original purpose. He once conducted me over the set of a French restaurant which was appropriate to the play he was producing. "Every piece of furniture on this stage," he remarked, "was brought over from Paris. Even the table linen, wine glasses and the knives and forks came from a Paris restaurant. All this at a cost of some twenty thousand dollars!" I remarked that the young Theatre Guild was putting on plays with nonrealistic scenery at a cost of less than a thousand dollars a set. "Ah, my boy," he sighed, "you can get away with it, I can't. They expect this of me."

Belasco built realism to a point where it finally engulfed him. We may note other trends today which will similarly engulf the theatre of our time if we do not call a halt. I refer particularly to our overcomplicated scenery and stage lighting and overpaid and overmanned stagehands.

Do not try to crowd too much scenery on a theatre stage. Many young playwrights, especially those coming from television, will describe a set consisting of a four-room apartment, a bathroom, a street, a back door, a front door, and the house next door. If the author *must* have such a set, for heaven's sake do not attempt to change it during the play, or there will be a major catastrophe.

Do not let the scenic artist provide sets which will dwarf the actors. Many scenic artists like their sets to be as high as possible—sixteen feet is beloved by the fraternity, despite the fact that most rooms are seldom over fourteen feet high, while modern rooms usually run about nine to twelve. The lighting of the top of the scenery, instead of the actors, is also something to be avoided.

The scenic artist is either the author's friend or his enemy according to the extent to which he uses his art to enhance the play. If he is becoming overwhelming, he may be reminded that no play has ever succeeded because of its scenery.

The scenic artist can be the play's worst enemy by designing scenery which is too heavy, or too complicated, or too expensive. And he can positively cause the play to close weeks before necessary by calling for too many stagehands. He can also deprive the author of his royalties on tour by making the scenery so heavy or difficult that the play cannot travel because of the expense, or the time taken in setting it up, or because the bulk costs so much in railroading and trucking that only a lunatic would want to send the play on tour.

Robert Edmond Jones, the greatest of all American scenic artists, was also the most economical. The simplicity of his single set for *Othello,* which toured for two years, should be an inspiration for the young scenic designers of today who are not spoiled by the Broadway appetite for extravagance and vulgar display. (As I write these lines in the year 1958 a musical monstrosity has just closed in New York with a loss of nearly five hundred thousand dollars, largely spent in scenery, costumes, and stagehand-rehearsal expenses. Do not tell me tearfully that the producers wanted it. Someone connected with this dizzy disaster must have felt the scenery could overcome the deficiencies of the book.

Lighting experts are now being used increasingly in the American theatre. In my opinion they tend to complicate the production, and increase the expense of operation. Most of the world's great plays were produced without their help. It is the scenic artist's job to light his shows, and if he fails to do so, it is usually because he is too busy, too lazy or too inexperienced. In the interests of truth, it should be added that in plays where little scenery is used, lighting becomes increasingly important; and that a few rare souls exist in this field who can simplify lighting and reduce expenses rather than increase them. In general, however, the darker the play, the more electrical equipment is called for by the so-called experts!

The development of the off-Broadway theatres, if they can survive economically, may be of service to the young playwright (and even the older playwright) as far as scenery is concerned. Such theatres, being small, and their owners operating without much capital, are forced to resort to the exercise of imagination in the scenery of the plays they produce, being unable to compete with Broadway where scenery is "the real thing"—scenery in which too often extravagance takes the place of suggestion, reality takes the place of atmosphere, and money takes the place of art. Imagination is the rarest quality in the theatre, and the least expensive. It is rarely found in the scenic artist with an unlimited budget.

In the early days of the Theatre Guild we had an opportunity of contrasting two methods in two plays, each calling for a scene in a cathedral with large pillars, and each designed by the brilliant scenic artist Lee Simonson. In the first instance he built a complete cathedral section on stage.

The three columns weighed several tons, and indeed were so heavy that one of them broke the chains by which it hung and nearly killed some stagehands. The other cathedral was for the original production of *Saint Joan*. The set consisted of the huge base of a column which one could imagine as projecting upwards for a hundred feet. It stood against the gray background of a stone wall painted on a canvas drop. Some colored lights projected the effect of light coming through a stained-glass window high up in the cathedral. The audiences imagined a cathedral so large that only a small portion could be seen on the stage. The cost was infinitesimal, and the effect far more successful.

Elaborate scenery and ever rising costs of production and operation are making it difficult for the experimental theatre to survive. The theatre of youth and innovation is forced to live off-Broadway—and starve even there. The blame is on everyone's head, and not the least on the unionization of the theatre's business managers—the very men whose duty it is to keep the costs of the other unions within bounds, but who cannot now do so without getting into trouble themselves, and being stigmatized as "anti-union" by the other unions. So long as this condition exists we need not be surprised that theatre costs have risen five times, whereas the cost of living has not more than doubled. But this is as nothing compared to what will happen in the future, when the great foundations, such as Rockefeller and Ford, enter the picture! The scenery unions are waiting for them with open arms—and embraces. (I exclude from the above generalization those excellent general and company managers who work devotedly for the best interests of the theatre and the enterprises which employ them. Thank heavens, there are many such!)

When it comes to the selection of the costume designer, except in unusual circumstances, the author had better leave this to the producer and stage director. So many factors are involved, of a business as well as an artistic nature, that the author finds his greatest asset is to be able to play the role of "critic," after having explained to the costume designer the general and specific costuming he looks for. It is also better for him, if possible, not to become involved in those controversies between the actor and the costume designer which so often arise in the theatre.

So much for the scenery and costumes—now for *rehearsals!*

It is the duty of the playwright to attend all rehearsals, to which it may be added that a writer would be a fool to stay away, especially since he can demand his living expense away from home or on tour for participating in the production under his Dramatists Guild contract. (Some authors in the past have brought their entire families along with them, including children and nurses, and run up enormous hotel bills, a practice I do not recommend.) The author will preferably watch the rehearsals in the theatre and make his notes, which he will talk over with the director at the end of each rehearsal. He should not discuss the roles or the play with the actors, except with the express authority of the director, who should preferably be present. The author is warned that the actor may not understand him unless he is versed in theatre language. Despairing at one time of ever being able to communicate with the actors, a certain director used to confine his remarks to single words such as "louder," "quieter," "lift it," "drop it," "angrier," "happier," and so forth—words almost impossible to misunderstand. Remember that the less said, soonest *minded.*

Once the play goes into rehearsal there are certain stages in the production when the presence and decision of the author are especially needed. These are the initial reading of the play, the first "run-through" rehearsal, and the out-of-town opening or openings.

The purpose of the *initial reading* of the play is to enable all concerned to become acquainted with one another and with the words of the play in the mouths of the actors. During the reading and thereafter, the management can decide whether actors are miscast and should be changed. It is also sometimes possible to note what rewriting or cutting may be needed, even if decision is deferred as to this.

The purpose of the *initial run-through,* which if possible should take place in about fourteen to eighteen days after the first rehearsal, is to enable decisions to be made which will affect the final days of rehearsal. These may include correcting wrong interpretation, or wrong casting which may still be changed (usually at considerable expense), and the question of script changes. Care should be taken not to make drastic decisions as to such script changes unless these are obvious and can easily be done before the opening. A well-known stage director once remarked that it was impossible to tell the taste of the dinner when the meal was only half-cooked. However, an audience of chefs might hazard a good guess.

Some directors like to have a run-through before an audience before the play opens; others object. In my opinion this can often be helpful if the audience is well selected and includes some skilled individuals whose reactions will be respected. Such audiences usually raise the morale of the actors and help them in their final rehearsals. The opposite result can also take place if the audience reaction to the run-through is not favorable. The work done by the actors, which can either be energetic or lackadaisical, is usually accelerated as the result of the run-through. In the opening of plays "cold" in New York, and especially in off-Broadway plays, several run-throughs are almost essential for a smooth opening.

The *out-of-town opening*, if there is one, is most important for the author. After it an appraisal of the performance and the play takes place at which decisions are made in almost every branch of production. These decisions will necessarily include judgment of the writing itself. Care should be taken that such decisions are made with the consent of the producer as well as the director; for, as already stated, under his contract the author cannot make changes in the play to which the producer does not agree. As a practical matter it is usual after the initial opening of the play, and each evening after the performance is over, to hold meetings at which the producer, author and director are present. The author has the right to attend such meetings, and if the director or producer or both have a tendency to make decisions without him, he should insist on meetings which he can attend. The following of these simple rules will avoid each individual going off in different directions and performing work which has not been approved and which has to be undone later.

A play seldom is produced in this country today in which a certain amount of rewriting is not necessary. The reader is referred to my remarks on this subject in connection with rewriting methods in pre-New York and summer theatre try-outs in Chapter Six. A final word of advice in regard to such rewriting. The playwright should not permit the pressures under which he works on tour to result in making wrong decisions which have to be rectified later on. "Look before you leap into your rewriting" is a good adage for all concerned in play production, but especially for the author to whom these remarks are particularly addressed.

CHAPTER VIII

Adaptations and Collaborations

(*Dramatic and Musical*)

THE adaptation of plays is an art which is almost as old as the seven Roman hills. There is the best of evidence, which is found in the plays themselves, that much of so-called Roman drama and comedy was adapted from earlier Greek plays which were undoubtedly what we would call today the "smash hits" of Athens.

Adaptations usually take two forms. One of these is the selection of a play which is written in the language of a given country and then translating and adapting it to the language and stage of another country. Another form of adaptation is to select a well-known novel (or, Lord help us, even a motion picture!) and then adapt it for the stage. In many periods of the Victorian theatre, adaptations from novels were extremely popular, as evidenced by the success of *Rip Van Winkle, Uncle Tom's Cabin,* and *The Count of Monte Cristo.*

In dealing with the transfer of a play from the theatre of one country to the theatre of another country, it is to be noted that the adapter has not only the task of translating the play from one language to another, but also of making the play understandable to audiences in the second country. Therefore, in some cases, the adaptation may be almost a collaboration for all practical purposes, especially in the case where the adapter takes the characters of the country for which the play was originally written and transforms them into characters of his own nationality. It was the custom for many years, when plays were adapted for the American theatre from England or the Continent, to make all the characters Americans and set the play in the United States. This was often disastrous.

The Theatre Guild was one of the pioneers in insisting that foreign plays be laid in their own countries, thereby adding an additional dimension due to the novel and colorful characters of other nationals. This was done in the case of Molnar's *Liliom,* which had failed in London when it was peopled by English characters. The New York production was set by the Theatre Guild in the Budapest of the original play, and was a great success. The reverse took place in *Carousel,* the musical version of *Liliom,* in which substantially similar characters were transferred to the United States. In making this adaptation, Rodgers and Hammerstein had the blessings of the author, Molnar, who realized that by setting the play in an earlier time period, with the use of picturesque costumes, an equally colorful effect could be obtained in the American musical theatre. Indeed, the adaptation amounted to substantially a new play with new dialogue and a better ending supplied by both the authors which completely converted the Hungarian Liliom and Julie of Budapest into the American Billy Bigelow and Julie of the State of Maine.

The extent to which a writer should adapt a play freely depends upon the nature of the play, the adapter's own creative abilities, and such arrangements as he can make with the foreign author. Many disputes arise in connection with such adaptations, and the American author who wishes to adapt freely should make quite sure that his contract with the foreign author permits him to do so. The adapter of a foreign play has a great advantage over the adapter of a novel, in that the play structure has already been worked out in the country of origin, and those scenes which are especially valuable because they play well are usually pointed out to the adapter.

The extent to which the adapter may require a free hand is rather amusingly illustrated by the story of how Bernard Shaw adapted the play *Jitta's Atonement*, written by his friend Trebitsch. Shaw made a complete departure from the original play, which was tragic, and turned it into a comedy. In explaining to me why he did this, he stated that the German and Austrian audiences for whom the play was originally written liked a subject of this kind dealt with in the form of tragedy. He stated, however, that the audiences of England and the United States would never accept the material in this form; therefore he turned it into a comedy. But it did not succeed either in England or the United States, despite the talents of its adapter.

The writer who is faced with the problem of adapting a play from a foreign language, must look very carefully into the question of whether it would be better to permit the characters to remain in the country of origin, or to change their nationality to that of this country. Here we must balance various factors one against another. For example, if he is adapting the play from the French or German and setting it in France or Germany, he must consider the question of whether actors are available to play these French and German characters in this country. Nothing is so distressing to my ears as a company of actors all pretending to speak with foreign accents in order to create the impression that an American adaptation of a French play, for example, is laid in the city of Marseilles. On the other hand, if such a play is transformed to a United States locale, it may lose its colorful foreign quality and gain little as a result. One of Sidney Howard's most successful adaptations was a play called *The Late Christopher Bean,* in which he very successfully transferred the original French setting of the play to an American milieu. Some foreign subjects are unsuited to a successful transfer to our stage, as witness the recent rapid demise of *Chéri,* based on stories by Colette.

The adaptation of novels is a form which is always prevalent in the English and American theatres. It is interesting to note in this connection that the ability of a writer as a novelist is by no means a criterion as to his ability as a dramatist. Perhaps the best example of this is Henry James, who as stated earlier made several abortive attempts to write plays, but whose novels have turned into extremely successful plays, such as *The Innocents, The Heiress,* and *The Aspern Papers.* When he is dealing with the adaptation of a novel to theatrical form, the writer must call into play all his knowledge of technical playwriting in order that the novel may be presented in the best theatrical manner. As a rule, novels contain a far larger number of characters than plays. The adapter must therefore pick from the novel his main characters and situations and concentrate on these, with the consequent diminution of minor characters and incidents. He must remember also that many thousands of people will have read the novel and will be disappointed if he has omitted from his play those elements from which the reading public derived its greatest enjoyment.

Perhaps the best rule to follow, in view of the practical exigencies of the theatre, is to select one, two, or three characters from the novel whose story will provide the best acting parts, so that when the adaptation is completed, it will not be difficult to find the best actors or stars to play these parts. Indeed, reverting to the older plays mentioned earlier as adaptations of novels, these were successful in the theatre not because the adaptations were particularly good plays, but because they provided the best actors of the day with the best parts of the day, such as Joe Jefferson in *Rip Van Winkle* and James O'Neill in *The Count of Monte Cristo.*

One of the best examples of an adaptation made from material supplied by another person is that of *The Diary of Anne Frank,* by Frances and Albert Hackett. Indeed, this splendid play was much more than an adaptation—it was a dramatic creation for the theatre inspired by the diary of a little girl who probably could never have put her story into dramatic form had she lived to be a hundred.

One of the reasons that motion pictures do not usually serve as a good source for dramatic adaptation is because most of these pictures, before they reach the screen, are so tortured by the directors, actors, front office men and others who are involved in the production of a motion picture that what usually appears on the screen has become sterilized and stereotyped so that it is quite unexciting for the theatre. On the other hand, where such material is successful, it is often due to the excellent work of the director, and not the writer. I shall therefore not waste much time on the subject of adapting motion pictures into stage plays. Except under the most unusual conditions, such adaptations are stale and unprofitable. Quite recently a Japanese movie, *Rashomon,* was transformed from a successful motion picture into an entirely unsuccessful play. Anyone familiar with the elementary principles of playwriting would know in advance that such a play was bound to fail with its audiences, for lack of any kind of sustained suspense interest.

Stories are generally made into motion pictures because the medium is best adapted for that purpose, and while it is not outside the bounds of possibility that a magnificent play may be made from a motion picture, it is in my opinion somewhat unlikely. On the other hand, where a fine motion picture has been made from a novel, an equally good play has been made from the same novel. An excellent example of this is *The King and I,* based on the biographical novel *Anna and the King of Siam.*

The collaboration of two writers does not seem to have existed in the Greek or Roman theatres, and perhaps the first pair of collaborators to come to our attention are Beaumont and Fletcher, who flourished in Elizabethan days and whose plays are still given. The story of the collaboration in the musical theatre of Gilbert and Sullivan is well known, as well as the reasons which caused them to part company. These generally include the fact that Sullivan felt the intellectual and satiric character of Gilbert's writing got in the way of his fullest expression of emotions as a musician. Regrettably no important play, either musical or otherwise, resulted from their break-up. If anything, experience suggests that if collaboration produces good results, the writers should continue to collaborate.

The Diary of Anne Frank will serve as a good focal point to discuss the question of collaboration between husband and wife. There seem to be two schools of thought on the subject, one being that the closer you are to your collaborator, the better the results, while the other school believes that the reverse is true. Having worked with a certain modicum of success and failure in both ways, if I am not an authority on the subject, at least I speak from experience. Frances and Albert Hackett have been married for a number of years and their marriage has resulted in some fine collaborative efforts which include, in addition to *The Diary of Anne Frank, Up Pops the Devil,* and *The Great Big Door-*

step. Bella and Samuel Spewack are another couple also given to collaboration and have written some excellent plays, including *Kiss Me Kate, My Three Angels* and *Boy Meets Girl.* In my own experiences, my collaboration with my wife Armina Marshall included the successful *The Pursuit of Happiness* and several less successful efforts. In my opinion, collaboration between husband and wife is only feasible when there is a very great mutuality, and a clear understanding as to which aspect each of the collaborators will especially devote himself and herself. The greatest difficulty arises when there is a difference of opinion and neither wants to give in. On the other hand, my collaboration with two authors, Philip Bartholomae and Guy Bolton (whom I did not know at all at the time) resulted in the musical play *Tangerine* which ran two seasons in New York and one on tour!

In the case of the successful musical play *Tangerine,* the three authors collaborated in the following peculiar manner. After meeting together and deciding on the various scenes, I would make the first draft of the dialogue and mail it to my collaborators. They would then rewrite it and send it to me, after which I would rewrite it again. We would then have a meeting and come to a final decision. This method sounds complicated, but it avoids a great many disputes.

Both musical plays and "musicals" are properly classified under collaborations since it is only once in a lifetime that a single writer composes the book, music and lyrics. (This was true of Noel Coward in his musicals *Bittersweet* et cetera.) Generally speaking, the writing divides itself into the book or libretto, the lyrics and the music. Some authors, such as Oscar Hammerstein II, contribute the book and lyrics, or the lyrics alone; others such as Cole Porter and Irving Berlin, the music and lyrics. Others such as Comden and Green contribute either book or lyrics or both. The choreographer is often added to these collaborators, as in the case of Jerome Robbins or Robert Fosse, both of whom also function as directors.

With such complicated arrangements, it is not hard to understand why so few good musicals are written and produced. Success almost invariably depends upon a good book, which is even rarer to find than a good score. It may be said that a good score seldom survives a poor book, while the opposite is often true. (The notable exception to the above is *Fledermaus,* the score of which certainly outshines the libretto.)

Because of the difficulty of creating original librettos, as well as the growing increase in the costs of producing musical plays, it is usual to base the musical "book" on an existing play, as was the case with the Theatre Guild's *Porgy and Bess,* based on *Porgy; Oklahoma!,* based on *Green Grow the Lilacs;* and *Carousel,* based on *Liliom. My Fair Lady,* based on *Pygmalion,* is another outstanding example. In such cases there is, so to speak, an additional collaborator—the original author on whose play the musical is based.

Prior to the advent of *Porgy and Bess* the American musical theatre was lacking in so-called "book shows." Often what started out as a logical story was so pulled apart in production that it ended as a mixture which was neither logical nor story. This was because the book, usually with no stature of its own, became a battleground between contending stars and their agents for the best positions and songs. Actors and actresses were engaged with promises that they would be provided with so many songs in the best positions (scene curtains and act curtains). Once the musical was set for rehearsal, the fight for position began, and it is small wonder that the book and the book writer were relegated to minor roles. This was of course not true of all musicals.

Reverting to an earlier "story" form, *Oklahoma!* started a revolution in this field by introducing ballet as an inherent part of the production technique, including the staging of the songs as well as special ballets, and also by abolishing the so-called "spots" for singers and dancers, the latter up to this time being usually interpolated into the musical play to provide specialty numbers which often had no relation to the story at all. The songs and ballets progressed the story, which provided a logical suspenseful continuity.

When the collaborators take an old play and adapt it for a musical, it is usual for the composer to indicate first the places where he imagines musical treatment is desirable. On the other hand, it is often the lyric writer who notes where the best songs can be written and placed. In the adaptation of *Oklahoma!* it was Oscar Hammerstein who first conceived the song "Oh What a Beautiful Morning" as a poetic lyric. Rodgers wrote one of his most beautiful melodies for the song. "How could I help it with such a beautiful lyric?" he is reported to have said. On the other hand, many composers have melodies in their portfolios and will provide them when needed. Thus in this respect there is no rule. It is, however, usually desirable for the composer, in looking over the original play, to select those parts which he would prefer to set to music, song or dance, rather than to stick in his music like currants in a cake. (In my one experience in collaborating as a writer on a musical, the hit song "Sweet Lady" was interpolated into the score of *Tangerine,* being obligingly written by Frank Crummit, who played the male lead.) In general, it is the experienced book writer who usually controls the position of the songs, choreography and dances, but a strong lyric writer or composer can also be expected to dominate the situation according to his relative ability.

Addressing myself to the book writer, whether he be the author of an original book or the adapter of an old play: the proper placement of the songs or dances is usually at the top of situations, when a point is reached which is strong enough to be prolonged in a song. Preferably, though not necessarily, one or more of the singers leaves the stage at the end of the song, and a new scene begins. If possible, the song should progress the play, though this too is not necessary. It should, however, arise out of the character and situation, and not constitute a drastic interruption merely for a song. The same applies equally to the introduction of ballet. Hammerstein used the dream ballet in *Oklahoma!* to show what Laurie was thinking. He is quoted as saying, "With a song or ballet, you can convey a character's thoughts. Actually a dream ballet can contribute a great deal to a play in a manner similar to the soliloquy as used by Shakespeare." The famous song "My Boy Bill" from *Carousel* was written and staged in substantially the same manner as a Shakespearean soliloquy. Agnes de Mille on the same subject stated, "I introduced terror and fear in the musical comedy *Oklahoma!* through dance. The dream ballet provided the necessary suspense for the second act, and added conflict." Thus these integrated songs and ballets progress the play, and distinguish the modern musical from its predecessors, such as *The Geisha* or *The Merry Widow.*

In general, the writer of a musical selects an "escape" period which will provide an opportunity for colorful costumes and scenery. However, the opposite can be equally true, as witness the success of *West Side Story* with its gang warfare and drab costuming and scenery. Indeed, we tend to rebel against insipid or sentimental musicals which, since

Porgy and Bess and *Oklahoma!,* have departed from the saccharine tradition of *The Student Prince* period by introducing one or more killings.

The dialogue of the musical play requires a condensation far beyond that of the ordinary play. However, the playwright usually leaves to the lyric writer and composer the development of emotional feelings between the characters, such as the love ballads, which need not be repeated in dialogue.

The position of the director is increasingly important in the staging of a musical, since it is he who will usually umpire the disputes which may arise between the various collaborators, with the producer acting as a court of appeal. If he is a man who has the confidence of the writers, he can use them for his over-all visualization of the musical. When he and the producer are not strong enough, the song writer or some other important individual will attempt to take over, often producing an overweighted effect in one department or another.

Probably the reason why we have not had more collaboration in the theatre is because the very act of collaborating imposes a special difficulty—the difficulty of getting along with another human being in the enormously complicated area of creative writing. If one member of the collaborative team has a special talent for one part of the job, such as a talent for structure, while another member of the team has a special talent for another part, such as characterization, then there can be a division of labor which makes for ease of collaboration. However, if each collaborator fancies himself to be an expert in every department, and differences of opinion arise, the difficulties of collaboration are multiplied as compared with those of the single author who has only himself to argue with. To the young author who is attempting to collaborate with another, I would add the advice to do so only if he feels that he will gain from the collaboration knowledge and strength which will enable him to write better by himself later on.

As a final remark on the subject of adaptation, it should be remembered that while a writer's personal ego may require him to be the author of every word, line, situation and even the story itself, yet some of our greatest writers for the theatre have not hesitated to seize on material wherever they could find it. I reiterate to the point of boredom that Shakespeare bought many of his plots, and may be said to have adapted them for the stage. His creative genius in transforming them into the greatest comedies and tragedies of all time should reassure all adapters that their artistic horizons are unlimited.

CHAPTER IX

Types of Plays

So far as I know, no one has made any serious attempt to classify the various kinds of plays which exist, and which have appeared on the stage during the past thirty years. By means of such a classification it is possible to explain the relative importance of the various kinds of plays, and the points to which an author should pay particular attention in case he undertakes to write a play falling into one or other of these categories. Here again the playwright is warned that there is nothing to prevent him from starting a new category if he has the creative originality to do so. Indeed, since the theatre is hospitable to anything new, he may stand a better chance for success if he finds some new way of telling his story. He should be warned, however, that he will be working in a field in which many have experimented. For example, he might think it entertaining to write his play backwards. This has been done successfully already by George S. Kaufman and Moss Hart in *Merrily We Roll Along*, and by George O'Neil in *American Dream*. Or he may wish to start his play in the middle and then go back and write the beginning. This too has been done before—for instance, in Joseph Fields' adaptation of 'Peter De Vries' novel *The Tunnel of Love*. This need not deter him from using either form again, if he feels it will be helpful.

I will now refer to each category of play by a short title, and list a number of the plays, with their authors, which fall under these classifications. Many more plays could, of course, be added to these lists.

1. THE DRAWING-ROOM COMEDY

The Philadelphia Story	Philip Barry
The Last of Mrs. Cheyney	Frederick Lonsdale
The First Mrs. Fraser	St. John Ervine
The Circle	Somerset Maugham
Biography	S. N. Behrman

The drawing-room comedy is rapidly disappearing from both the American and British theatre, largely because people are rapidly disappearing from drawing rooms. Or perhaps it would be more correct to say that the drawing rooms themselves are disappearing as life becomes more proletarian. And since drawing rooms are disappearing, authors seldom write about them. In the twenties, however, the denizens of the drawing rooms were a very gay set indeed, especially the English ones. They drank tea with fervor and exchanged epigrams with the curate and the country folk, and the small talk was rapid and delightful.

One of the best writers of drawing-room comedies was Frederick Lonsdale, whose series of plays kept two generations of English actors balancing teacups. Another and more serious one was Somerset Maugham. Indeed his play *The Circle* is perhaps the highest example of this kind of comedy. On this side of the Atlantic, Philip Barry was also a talented worker in this field, and his comedy *The Philadelphia Story* will stand the test of time as one of the best examples of the contemporary drawing-room life which existed and still exists in the Main Line suburbs of Philadelphia.

It is my opinion that this type of play may return to the

modern theatre sooner or later, when our audiences begin to tire of plays about southern psychopaths and northern neurotics. As long as there are intelligent people in the world, whether they live with or without the benefit of servants, their conversations and actions will always appeal to some literate authors and audiences. Plays of this type usually have little or no importance, although one American author, S. N. Behrman, has used this form to provide trenchant criticisms of American life. One of his best plays, *Biography,* while laid in a studio instead of a drawing room, contained most of the ingredients of this kind of play, but it also contained much social criticism. The same cannot be said of the plays of Noel Coward, which fluctuated between drawing rooms, balconies and bedrooms, and furnished a certain amount of heat but very little light on the thought of the day. Unfortunately, due to the lack of opportunities to appear in such plays, the theatre's stock of comedy performers capable of playing "high comedy" is rapidly dying out, being replaced by the uncharming realistic actors who now portray angry young men and neurotic young women.

In writing these plays today, the author will do well to avoid making his play too light in content. On the other hand, the entertainment value of such plays is such as to continue to make them a fashionable medium for social criticism, provided that the author possesses the necessary wit and the director and actors the necessary comedic skill.

2. ARTIFICIAL COMEDY

As You Like It	William Shakespeare
Much Ado About Nothing	William Shakespeare
The Country Wife	William Wycherly
The Way of the World	William Congreve
Love for Love	William Congreve
The School for Scandal	Richard Brinsley Sheridan

She Stoops to Conquer	Oliver Goldsmith
Lady Windermere's Fan	Oscar Wilde
The Importance of Being Earnest	Oscar Wilde
You Never Can Tell	Bernard Shaw
The Philanderer	Bernard Shaw
Blithe Spirit	Noel Coward

These plays, which follow an English tradition beginning with the rapid-fire witty exchanges between Beatrice and Benedict in *Much Ado About Nothing*, represent the highest standards of comedy in the English theatre. In America we have never come close to achieving success in this field, our wittiest exponent of the art of repartee, S. N. Behrman, usually going beyond the artifice to deeper implications. The modern drawing-room comedy of the English and American theatre may be regarded as a lineal descendent of the English artificial comedy, and has often been written by young Irishmen laughing their way into English society.

3. *THE CHARACTER SITUATION COMEDY*

My Sister Eileen	Joseph Fields and Jerome Chodorov
Happy Birthday	Anita Loos
The Man Who Came to Dinner	George S. Kaufman and Moss Hart
Twentieth Century	Ben Hecht and Charles MacArthur

In these plays, which are based on entertaining situations and amusing characters, there is no attempt to provide any theme of importance. While comedies of this kind come along once or twice a year, and are usually extremely successful financially, their happy fate is to end up as successful motion pictures and to live over and over again in television.

4. THE COMEDIES AND DRAMAS OF FAMILY LIFE

I Remember Mama	John van Druten
Life with Father	Howard Lindsay and Russel Crouse
Ah, Wilderness	Eugene O'Neill
Call It a Day	Dodie Smith
Long Day's Journey Into Night	Eugene O'Neill
Five Finger Exercise	Peter Shaffer

This kind of play usually calls for a leisurely approach and the key word for the playwright is "nostalgia." In most of these plays, the author usually sees his childhood through rose-colored glasses, and the audience is persuaded to enjoy the recollection of an irate but lovable father, or a lovable and managing mother. The appeal of childhood and parental love is of universal interest, and the wonder is that more plays are not written on this subject. That many do not find their way onto the boards is generally due to the fact that the family which is represented often enjoys a degree of mediocrity which is boring to the extreme. Eugene O'Neill's *Ah, Wilderness,* which was written as a result of a dream about his childhood, is a perfect example of this rosy view of adolescence.

5. THE HORROR SUSPENSE SITUATION PLAY

The Desperate Hours	Joseph Hayes
Night Must Fall	Emlyn Williams
Kind Lady	Edward Chodorov

The formula for writing this type of play is to portray a lovable character for whom the audience has sympathy, and then place this person, who is helpless and defenseless, into a situation where a terrible gangster or fiend is either going to kill or torture her. (It is usually a "her.") One of

the best examples of this type of play is *Kind Lady,* in which
an old lady was mentally tortured into relinquishing rights
to all her money. It is seldom that these plays achieve any
importance beyond their considerable entertainment value.

6. THE RELIGIOUS PLAY

The Miracle of Saint Anthony	Maurice Maeterlinck
The Miracle	Karl Volmoller
The Passion Plays	Anonymous
Abraham and Isaac	Anonymous
The Eternal Road	Franz Werfel
Murder in the Cathedral	T. S. Eliot
J.B.	Archibald MacLeish

This category, which includes passion plays, miracle plays
and the medieval plays of the church, usually has for its
purpose the promotion of religious doctrines, and has always
intermittently existed in the theatre. The famous passion
play of Oberammergau has drawn audiences for hundreds
of years, and a similar passion play is an annual event in
California at the present time. Archibald MacLeish's play
J.B., which has recently been acclaimed in New York City
and won the Pulitzer Prize, is an example of this kind of
play, and its acceptance by audiences shows that there is
still plenty of room in the theatre for the expression of religious thought. In passing, we should not forget that the
religious plays performed by aborigines for animal food cer-
emonies go back in time to our remote prehistoric ancestors.

7. MORALITY PLAYS

Everyman	Anonymous
Back to Methuselah	Bernard Shaw
Liberty Jones	Philip Barry

The morality play is akin to the religious play, and usually
takes the form of an allegory. *Everyman* is of course the

most noted play of this kind. It is a form which was once quite popular. I remember seeing a morality play in New York, the title of which I have forgotten, in which Vice appeared on the stage dressed as a woman with a snake around her neck, followed by Virtue dressed in a snowy-white gown. Vice and Virtue engaged in a long argument which was settled by a man dressed as Greed appearing on the side of Vice, while a child dressed as Innocence appeared on the side of Virtue. Then of course Lust would enter the scene, usually a young man attired in a leopard skin, and Vice and Virtue would engage in a tug-of-war to capture his interest. Childish as this seems, this type of play is recurrently popular and may be with us again at any time. Indeed, the opening play of Bernard Shaw's *Back to Methuselah,* with its scenes of Adam and Eve and the serpent, followed by discussions with Cain, is reminiscent of the early morality plays, and Shaw used this form to project his idea that Mankind must somehow succeed in living for hundreds of years in order to achieve some kind of fruitful existence. This example shows that the morality play can readily be employed to carry a preachment which need not be limited to the simple form first described above. *Liberty Jones* by Philip Barry, with its naïve use of Black Shirts, Brown Shirts, and Blue Shirts, is mentioned as a type of modern morality play to be avoided.

8. THE MURDER MYSTERY OR MELODRAMA

Dial "M" For Murder	Frederick Knott
The Bat	Mary Roberts Rinehart and Avery Hopwood
air	Bayard Veiller
	Patrick Hamilton

'ch are often very successful commer-
ive very little interest except as a way

of passing the time. They rate in the theatre on about the same level as detective stories in literature, and very often a detective story is an important ingredient of this kind of play. In the usual formula for these, a crime is committed, and we ascertain which of several people has done it. While such plays are popular and often financially lucrative, they have seldom been written by important playwrights.

9. THE COURTROOM DRAMA

On Trial	Elmer Rice
The Trial of Mary Dugan	Bayard Veiller
Witness for the Prosecution	Agatha Christie
The Caine Mutiny Court Martial	Herman Wouk
Inherit the Wind	Jerome Lawrence and Robert E. Lee
The Andersonville Trial	Saul Levitt

This type of play depends for its interest on a trial which takes place on stage, with a character whose punishment, whether it be the death sentence or a term of imprisonment, depends upon the outcome of the trial. This play is in somewhat the same category as the murder mystery melodrama, and usually serves the purpose of entertainment in a similar fashion. However, this form of play can be used to carry a much more important type of theme, such as *The Andersonville Trial,* in which not only is the alleged criminal on trial for his life, but a type of crime is exposed to the audience to make us aware of some form of social wrongdoing which has been accepted historically for one reason or another. Thus, the courtroom drama can produce important plays, whereas the murder mystery play seldom does.

10. THE SATIRE ON MARRIAGE

Getting Married	Bernard Shaw
Why Marry?	Jessie Lynch Williams
Private Lives	Noel Coward
The Marriage-Go-Round	Leslie Stevens
The Seven Year Itch	George Axelrod

These plays have sometimes influenced public opinion in changing the popular attitude toward divorce, and also in improving the status of women in marriage. Where they have been directed against the institution of marriage as a whole, however, they have usually failed. Marriage, while still a controversial subject in the United States, is usually taken seriously on the stage. It is viewed entirely differently in France, where the approach to the subject is based more on the humors of adultery, representing a sophisticated attitude toward marriage prevailing in Roman Catholic countries where divorce is difficult or impossible to obtain. (But see my later remarks on The Comedies of Marriage and Adultery, No. 25.)

11. THE WESTERN

The Girl of the Golden West	David Belasco
Green Grow the Lilacs	Lynn Riggs

The first Western I remember was *The Girl of the Golden West,* an attractive melodrama written by David Belasco at the turn of the century, and made into the opera by Puccini. This play contains almost all the traditional accompaniment to all Westerns—the miners, the cowboys, the saloon, the good girl, the bad girl, and a sufficient infusion of sheriffs and shooting to provide the ideal suspense interest in stories of our picturesque western frontiers.

Westerns have developed from their early beginnings into

a formula, and by repeated repetitions of the same story in motion pictures and television, they have become the most stereotyped stories of the American scene. Before the days of motion pictures and television, the Wild West was represented by paperback thrillers which sold for a few cents and were the delight of the small boys in the neighborhood. Elevated to a form of literature by James Fenimore Cooper, they have since been down-graded by the western movies and the Westerns on television. Yet it must be admitted that our western frontier, which has so captured the imagination of the people of the world, should be cherished by playwrights rather than reduced to its lowest common denominator.

A few years ago, the Theatre Guild produced a television play called *The Last Notch* by Frank Gilroy, which possessed both poetry and a powerful theme. A motion picture was also produced with an equally fine theme—the famous *High Noon*, which has served as a model for other motion pictures of similar caliber. Westerns naturally lend themselves more to motion pictures and television than to the theatre. However, there is no reason why, if a writer could produce tomorrow a Western with psychological characters instead of cardboard figures, it would not be welcomed in the theatre. Indeed Lynn Riggs' *Green Grow the Lilacs*, with its cowboy setting which gave birth to *Oklahoma!*, is a case in point. Unfortunately, the subject of western life is nearly always treated in such infantile fashion that the material has now become more suited for children than for grownups. A few years ago someone formulated the idea of producing a program of what were called "adult Westerns" for television. Starting off with promise, this program rapidly lowered the age of the adult, which ultimately dropped to the age group of fourteen, and now the movies and television programs in the field are generally catering to the taste of fourteen-year-old adults. I believe that the very deluge we are now encountering in television will ultimately wear out this type of play, after which we may hope for a revival in a really adult form.

12. *THE REPORTORIAL PLAY*

Dead End	Sidney Kingsley
Men in White	Sidney Kingsley
Detective Story	Sidney Kingsley
Counsellor-at-Law	Elmer Rice
Five-Star Final	Louis Weitzenkorn
Yellow Jack	Sidney Howard
The Last Mile	John Wexley
Street Scene	Elmer Rice
The Miracle Worker	William Gibson

Reportorial plays are the kind which show on the stage what a camera might do were it taken into a given milieu and photographed what was going on. Many of these plays differ from other plays in the group by having more quality, because the writer had a point of view to express in connection with them. The reportorial talent, if combined with a point of view which illuminates life, can make plays of this kind an extremely valuable contribution to the theatre. Its best exponents, such as Sidney Kingsley, have not usually been satisfied merely to purvey the excitement which takes place in a hospital, in a police station, or in an alley by the river, but have often added an important point of view. Sidney Howard's striking play *Yellow Jack* illustrates my meaning when I say that such plays are capable of providing a theme which goes far beyond their documentary quality. Thus while *Yellow Jack* painted a picture of the men who worked to overcome the scourge of yellow fever, it also illustrated his basic theme of the teamwork and self-sacrifice of dedicated men and women in the army medical corps and in the hospitals. *The Miracle Worker* is a successful latecomer in this group, and illuminates the greatness of the human soul by dramatizing in vivid terms the early life of Helen Keller.

13. THE POLITICAL AND SOCIAL SATIRE

Born Yesterday	Garson Kanin
Of Thee I Sing	George S. Kaufman, Morrie Ryskind, George and Ira Gershwin
I'd Rather Be Right	George S. Kaufman, Moss Hart, Lorenz Hart, Richard Rodgers
Processional	John Howard Lawson
Both Your Houses	Maxwell Anderson
The Apple Cart	Bernard Shaw
State of the Union	Howard Lindsay and Russel Crouse

Political satire is a strong and potent weapon for the improvement of society, provided that it is pointed at defects in our social system and attacks them with sufficiently savage laughter and ridicule. The trouble with most American political satires which have been written to date is that they are not savage enough. Satire goes beyond merely making fun of or laughing at the thing which is satirized. Aristophanes was a brilliant satirist, as was Jonathan Swift, and they did not stop merely at laughing gently at the social abnormalities which they decried. They hit them hard and riddled them with ridicule.

Our American satires are generally based on the acceptance of a situation, and then making gentle fun of it. Thus there is not a line written in the gentle satire *The Solid Gold Cadillac* which might tempt Wall Street to change its practices. Nor did *Born Yesterday* or *State of the Union* do anything to clean up politics. In *Of Thee I Sing*, Kaufman and Hart had a good laugh at the expense of the Supreme Court. It is possible that this may have led the way to the ultimate packing of the Supreme Court by Franklin D. Roosevelt, but the mere ridiculing of the Justices and the Vice-President does not represent the kind of savage attack which makes satire effective.

Perhaps one of the most popular political satires which has ever been written is Gogol's classic, *The Inspector General*, which ridiculed the dishonest bureaucracy of Czarist Russia by introducing into a small village which reeked of corruption a pair of adventurers, one of whom pretends to be the Inspector General dispatched from Moscow to look into what is happening. The bogus Inspector General collects money from everybody in order that they may be permitted to continue with their rascality. The end of the play finds the real Inspector General arriving just after the counterfeit Inspector General has departed. However, it must be admitted that this play did not put a stop to corruption in Russia or anywhere else!

There was never a time in the history of the world when we needed savage satire in the theatre as much as we do right now. There is so much going on in the world which is criminally ridiculous, that one misses greatly the existence of good satirical writers who will attack these problems as Aristophanes did with laughter and ridicule instead of with melodrama or drama. While we have not yet developed the enjoyment of satire on the part of the audience in the way the French and the English have done, yet I believe this moment to be right for the beginning of American satire on a grand scale—satire of the kind that will point out the idiocy of the world in high places in a way that may bring about some desirable changes.

A few years ago the Theatre Guild produced a play, *The Love of Four Colonels* by Peter Ustinov, which was a very good example of the art of satirizing governments. Later on, Ustinov wrote another political satire called *Romanoff and Juliet* which also won praise in the American theatre. Ustinov is an Englishman, and it remains for other Englishmen to follow in his footsteps. In the United States we seem to be without any writers with the mental perspicacity to begin at the point where Ustinov has left off. The field is wide open!

14. THE ROMANTIC COMEDY

Kismet	Edward Knoblock
Romance	Edward Sheldon
The Swan	Ferenc Molnar
Reunion in Vienna	Robert Sherwood
Arms and the Man	Bernard Shaw
The Devil's Disciple	Bernard Shaw
Anastasia	Guy Bolton

This is a type of play which was once extremely popular, but of latter years has lost its appeal. However, the success of Guy Bolton's *Anastasia* and others indicates that romance *per se* is not dead in the theatre. This is a field which could well be exploited by authors who are trying to write on an important subject; for instance, as Shaw did in *Arms and the Man* and *The Devil's Disciple*. Taking *Arms and the Man*, Shaw used what was a romantic situation and made it frankly anti-romantic. He made fun of the hero worshiping which was part and parcel of the admiration of the military man Sergius, and contrasted him with the character of Bluntschli, the little Swiss in charge of the food and supplies, whom he turned into an anti-hero. Thus, while utilizing all the beauty of scenery and charm of costume of the romantic comedy, Shaw bent it to his own end, as indeed many other authors have since attempted to do.

Robert Sherwood, in *Reunion in Vienna,* also used a romantic story to score an unromantic point, as he did in
Idiot's Delight. The attraction of this kind of play, quite
apart from the love story, is the fact that it brings to the
stage the beauty of costume and settings which form a
pleasant counteracting influence to the drab realism which
occupies so much of the theatre today.

The authors of the musical play *My Fair Lady* informed
me that one of the reasons they believe that huge audiences
enjoyed the play was because the Ascot number and other
portions of the play gave the public an opportunity to observe people wearing pretty dresses again in the theatre.
That is an interesting observation, but why should it sound
so revolutionary? The fact is that we have tended to banish
well-dressed people from the stage. We have left the theatre
a far more dull and drab place than we found it. This is
not necessary, for the costume play or the romantic play
lends itself to the portrayal of almost every subject in a
form which attracts the public to the theatre.

15. THE HISTORICAL SATIRE

Caesar and Cleopatra	George Bernard Shaw
The Great Catherine	George Bernard Shaw
The Man of Destiny	George Bernard Shaw
Amphitryon 38	Jean Giraudoux, S. N. Behrman
Tiger at the Gates	Jean Giraudoux
The Road to Rome	Robert Sherwood

This type of play owes much of its success to Bernard
Shaw. It was his custom to take a historical subject for the
expression of his sociological and other sentiments. The
writer who enters this field may aim high with little fear of
competition at the present time.

16. THE HISTORICAL PLAY OR DRAMA

Saint Joan	George Bernard Shaw
The Lark	Jean Anouilh
Abe Lincoln in Illinois	Robert Sherwood
Sunrise at Campobello	Dore Schary
Valley Forge	Maxwell Anderson
Mary of Scotland	Maxwell Anderson
Elizabeth the Queen	Maxwell Anderson
Disraeli	Louis N. Parker

Shakespeare's historical plays

Richard of Bordeaux	Gordon Daviot
Maria Stuart	Friedrich Schiller

The field of the historical play is also well worthy of exploitation by the playwrights of today. History is a subject which is perennially interesting, because it is perennially changing. This is because we, too, are always changing. With our greater knowledge of psychology, and our deeper understanding of what makes people behave, our authors can take a historical subject and write of it in the light of the knowledge we possess today. *Saint Joan, The Lark, Abe Lincoln in Illinois,* and *Valley Forge* are all examples of the rewriting of history in terms of today's knowledge. Max Anderson's plays, *Mary of Scotland* and *Elizabeth the Queen,* also gave the author an opportunity for writing in verse. One factor which makes for the popularity of such plays is that the ordinary theatregoer is able to spend an evening in the company of kings, queens and other historical personages. He is made familiar with far greater events than those which take place in the lives of ordinary people, and so these kings and statesmen, when they appear on the stage, seem to have greater stature than we have. Furthermore, the more positive they are, the more important they seem. The doer in the

theatre, the man of action, is the most interesting man, and
that is the reason why historical plays are usually interesting,
re-creating, as they generally do, the great deeds done by the
great personages of the world.

17. THE PLAYS ABOUT THE ENTERTAINMENT FIELD

The Royal Family	George S. Kaufman and Edna Ferber
Stage Door	George S. Kaufman and Edna Ferber
Merton of the Movies	George S. Kaufman and Marc Connelly
Boy Meets Girl	Bella and Samuel Spewack

Plays about the world of entertainment have furnished
high comedies with delightful acting roles for generations.
George S. Kaufman and Edna Ferber have been particularly
happy collaborators in *The Royal Family* and *Stage Door*
and have avoided the usual pitfalls in this kind of play, of
which there are many.

Practically every playwright who has had his plays produced feels called upon to write a play which will show the
public the ridiculous nature of the theatrical world and the
absurdities to which he has been exposed. The same is even
truer of the Hollywood writer, almost every one of whom
has a play in his portfolio which exposes the rascality of the
motion picture industry. The reason why the general public
is usually uninterested in such plays is because they are on
the outside looking in, and cannot identify themselves with
the subhuman species that usually people them.

In my opinion, the more we can maintain a feeling of dignity about the theatre, the more we behave with reticence,
the more the imaginations of our audience can play on the

kind of people we are, and on our good qualities as well as our bad. There are many remarkable attributes in the characters of the people who work in the theatre—a sort of minor heroism which happens all the time among members of the theatrical profession. Actors and actresses will drag themselves to a performance under conditions of illness where the ordinary businessman would long before have deserted his post—and this without regarding themselves as heroes or heroines. It is highly undesirable to cheapen the profession by which we live, and to make our lifework seem unimportant or contemptible.

The publicity of the Hollywood picture companies has greatly cheapened the characters of their actors and actresses, and indeed the entire aura of the motion pictures. The old folk saying "Familiarity breeds contempt" is an accurate statement. Authors who care about the theatre should avoid writing the kind of play which fouls their own nest—although I maintain their full freedom to do so if they so desire.

18. THE PLAY OF UNIQUE AND OFFBEAT CHARACTERS

The Show-Off	George Kelly
Craig's Wife	George Kelly
The Miser (*L'Avare*)	Molière
	(Jean-Baptiste Poquelin)
The Would-Be Gentleman (*Le Bourgeois Gentilhomme*)	Molière
	(Jean-Baptiste Poquelin)
The Imaginary Invalid (*Le Malade Imaginaire*)	Molière
	(Jean-Baptiste Poquelin)
Guest in the House	Hagar Wilde and Dale Eunson
The Merry Wives of Windsor	William Shakespeare
Harvey	Mary Coyle Chase

You Can't Take It With You	George S. Kaufman and Moss Hart
The Remarkable Mr. Pennypacker	Liam O'Brien
Arsenic and Old Lace	Joseph Kesselring
Old English	John Galsworthy

This kind of play is usually based on the use of an unusual and theatrically effective character, such as Falstaff or Rip Van Winkle. Plays like *Craig's Wife* and *The Show-Off* are based on characters who may be said to be universal in terms of the highly special. We have probably never met anyone who was quite as big a show-off as the character in George Kelly's play of that name. He is a monstrous show-off, yet we recognize him because we have met him on a lesser scale. However, we must beware of picking out over-sized people, for there comes a point when such characters will be unbelievable, unrecognizable and unidentifiable to the audience.

These plays of unique characters also include comedies of eccentrics or offbeat people, which have lately become quite popular in our theatre. These plays are most appealing when the characters are recognizable, even if their eccentricities are carried to an extreme. Thus, the comedic bigamy of *Mr. Pennypacker* and the charming lunacy of *Harvey* are both enjoyable and ultimately believable.

19. *THE POLITICAL AND SOCIAL DRAMA*

The Diary of Anne Frank	Frances Goodrich and Albert Hackett
Watch on the Rhine	Lillian Hellman
The Little Foxes	Lillian Hellman
Another Part of the Forest	Lillian Hellman
Idiot's Delight	Robert Sherwood
There Shall Be No Night	Robert Sherwood
No Time for Comedy	S. N. Behrman

| *Time Limit* | Henry Denker and Ralph Berkey |
| *Justice* | John Galsworthy |

The importance of this kind of drama speaks for itself. We must be careful, however, to distinguish the kind of social drama which is referred to above, and that which was very prevalent throughout the thirties, and was referred to as "socially conscious drama." The plays listed above represent the finest writing which has been done for the modern theatre. The main danger in writing them is that they tend toward propaganda. The good ones do not lecture or propagandize. *The Diary of Anne Frank,* one of the finest plays to be written in our times, does not contain a word of propaganda. When this play was first given in Germany, the audience, after it was over, was silent for several minutes, and then walked quietly out of the theatre because they were so moved by, and ashamed of what they saw on the stage.

20. *THE PHILOSOPHICAL OR METAPHYSICAL FANTASY*

Six Characters in Search of an Author	Luigi Pirandello
Right You Are If You Think You Are	Luigi Pirandello
Pigeons and People	George M. Cohan
Outward Bound	Sutton Vane
Death Takes a Holiday	Walter Ferris
The Passing of the Third Floor Back	Jerome K. Jerome
Wings Over Europe	Robert Nichols and Maurice Browne
The Skin of Our Teeth	Thornton Wilder
Time Is a Dream	Henri-René Lenormand
Hotel Universe	Philip Barry
The Tenth Man	Paddy Chayefsky

This kind of play opens up the walls of the theatre and carries the audience into a world which is as wide as the imagination of the playwright. In actual fact, the author becomes a magician. Nothing is beyond his powers. He can carry you up to the heavens and show you what is going on in a star, or he can show you what is happening in the underworld or in a place that hasn't yet been discovered. Taking *Six Characters in Search of an Author* as an example, the characters the author is creating come out on the stage and discuss with him the way they want him to write about them. The use of the legend of the Dybbuk gave importance to Chayefsky's *The Tenth Man*. This metaphysical type of writing, of which the Europeans are particularly fond, enable us to say truly of the theatre that it is much larger than life, because it is also the home of the human imagination, and of the mysteries of existence. Authors who set their sights high should realize the importance of writing this kind of play, far too few of which are being written in America.

21. *THE FAIRY TALE*

Princess Turandot	Carlo Gozzi
Peter Pan	James M. Barrie
Mary Rose	James M. Barrie
The Blue Bird	Maurice Maeterlinck
Mrs. McThing	Mary Coyle Chase

This kind of play, popular at the beginning of the century when James M. Barrie's *Peter Pan* and Maeterlinck's *The Blue Bird* were written, represents another dimension in the theatre which is somewhat similar to that described above. It is given only to few authors to possess the poetic imagination which makes possible such a complete work of art as Barrie's *Peter Pan*. It is therefore idle to suggest that this kind of writing is one which suits every talent. If this is the kind of play you are capable of writing, you will want to write it. Mary Chase, whose brilliant comedies *Harvey* and *Mrs. McThing* showed that she was capable of combining reality and fantasy, is one of the few writers in this country who possess this rare gift. More power to her pen.

22. *THE FOLK COMEDY, FOLK DRAMA, OR FOLK LEGEND*

The Playboy of the Western World	John Millington Synge
Riders to the Sea	John Millington Synge
Deirdre of the Sorrows	John Millington Synge
Spreading the News	Lady Gregory
Cathleen ni Houlihan	William Butler Yeats
Juno and the Paycock	Sean O'Casey
Green Pastures	Marc Connelly
Rip Van Winkle	Dion Boucicault
The Lost Colony	Paul Green
The Scarecrow	Percy MacKaye
Orpheus Descending	Tennessee Williams
The Rose Tattoo	Tennessee Williams
The Dybbuk	S. Ansky

This is a field in which American writers have not played any conspicuous part, although the late Percy MacKaye wrote many plays about the Kentucky mountaineers. *Green Pastures* may be classified as a folk legend and is an outstanding example of the possibilities of success of such plays in our theatre. One reason why folk plays have not found much encouragement is because they are not usually appreciated in the large cities or theatre centers, where the climate is more suited to sophisticated fare. Thus such plays as *Johnny Appleseed* and *Dark of the Moon* have never been given the welcome they deserve. On the other hand, our provincialism leads us to swoon over the folk plays of other countries, such as the Scotch play *Bunty Pulls the Strings* by Graham Moffat, or the Irish *Playboy of the Western World* by Synge.

A group of Russian-Jewish folk comedies, mostly laid in Poland, flowed from the pen of Pinski. Before the first World War, a group of actors known as the Sicilian Players toured through Europe in a program of Sicilian folk plays which excited the attention of the theatregoers of other countries, mainly because of the passionate nature of the acting of their leading actress, Mimi Aguglia. In one of their plays, I witnessed a performance in which she attempted to strangle her lover by springing at his throat and biting him. This type of play, however, is not recommended to the young American writer, who may witness something of the same sort in Tennessee Williams' *The Rose Tattoo*. It is curious in this connection that some of the best folk plays in the United States have been written in the last few years by our most advanced authors, such as Tennessee Williams and Truman Capote. Unlike the usual folk play, which shows the simple passions of peasant folk, these plays bristle with amorous complexities. While they are not written about sophisticated people, the points of view of the authors in writing them are extremely sophisticated.

23. PLAYS OF THE REGIONAL THEATRE

Bus Stop *Picnic* } (Kansas)		William Inge
A Trip to Bountiful (Texas)		Horton Foote
The Rainmaker (Midwest)		N. Richard Nash
Green Grow the Lilacs (Oklahoma)		Lynn Riggs

They Knew What They Wanted (Napa Valley, California)	Sidney Howard
Papa Is All (Pennsylvania Dutch)	Patterson Greene
Porgy (Charleston, South Carolina)	Dorothy and DuBose Heyward
Our Town (New England)	Thornton Wilder
The Time of Your Life (San Francisco)	William Saroyan
Tobacco Road (The South)	Jack Kirkland and Erskine Caldwell

Plays of this group are always endearing if they are well done. America is a varied and wonderful country and its people are equally varied. There is, in actual fact, no such thing as an "American." We have New Englanders, Southerners, Midwesterners, Westerners, and a host of minor classifications, such as Hoosiers and Crackers. Plays which represent our national life, and also sections of our country, include some of our best modern writing. We must also include among these plays comedies and tragedies based on the emigrants who have peopled our country, such as the Italian-Americans, the Greek-Americans, and the Irish-Americans.

It seemed at one time as though the authors of such plays would make the greatest contribution to the American theatre, but I rather suspect that the failure of the Broadway sophisticates to pay too much attention to their efforts has resulted in a diminishing interest in them. However, more recently, William Inge, who hails from Kansas, has shown us in his plays *Picnic, The Dark at the Top of the Stairs,* and

Bus Stop that plays about the ordinary people of the Middle West can attract the attention of the entire country, when the characters are portrayed with artistry and compassion. Some of our best native writing is found under this category, which lends itself both to poetic and philosophic treatment. It is a field which cries for more attention from our playwrights.

24. THE SOLDIER AND SAILOR COMEDY

No Time for Sergeants	Ira Levin
Mister Roberts	Thomas Heggen and Joshua Logan
The Teahouse of the August Moon	John Patrick and Vern Sneider
What Price Glory?	Maxwell Anderson and Laurence Stallings
Sailor, Beware!	Kenyon Nicholson and Charles Robinson
South Pacific	James Michener, Joshua Logan, Richard Rodgers, and Oscar Hammerstein II
Stalag 17	Donald Bevan and Edmund Trzcinski
Command Decision	William Wister Haines
On The Town	Betty Comden and Adolph Green

The fashion for this kind of play began with the writing by Maxwell Anderson and Laurence Stallings of the comedy *What Price Glory?* after World War I. Since that time the American theatre has witnessed a succession of soldiers and sailors who have appeared on the stage, strutted for their bawdy hour or so, and retired into oblivion. Nevertheless, some of these plays have achieved a stature far beyond the horseplay which is characteristic of this type of entertainment. Among these may be mentioned *The Teahouse of the August Moon,* with its brilliant satire of the American mind

at work in the East, and *Mister Roberts* with its explora-
tion of the ennui which forms part of the horrors of war.
Such plays usually constitute very good entertainment, but
they never go very far beyond amusing and reportorial
writing. Some of them have failed badly in England, which
refuses to enter into the spirit of this form of comedy, as in
the case of *Mister Roberts*. But *The Teahouse of the
August Moon*, with its gentle satirizing of Americans, was
an outstanding London success.

25. THE COMEDIES OF MARRIAGE AND ADULTERY

Janus	Carolyn Green
The Seven Year Itch	George Axelrod
The Tunnel of Love	Joseph Fields
Private Lives	Noel Coward
The Voice of the Turtle	John van Druten

These plays are differentiated from such plays as *Why
Marry?* by Jesse Lynch Williams or *Getting Married* by
George Bernard Shaw, since they make no attempt to pon-
tificate on the subject of marriage but deal entertainingly
with the many problems which arise when two people, a
man and a woman, agree to live together for better or for
worse. Most of such comedies deal with the "for worse"
aspect of the situation. This kind of play has usually been
a somewhat rare bird in the garden of Broadway. This is
often because the reception committee of New York drama
critics has been somewhat lukewarm in welcoming them.

Plays about marriage and adultery are far more commonplace in Roman Catholic countries than in the United
States and England. The reason for this is because marriage,
generally speaking, is indissoluble in these countries, so that
in order that the relationship can be made possible, more
liberty is permitted by way of infidelity. In the United States

and England, however, where it is relatively easy to secure a divorce, unfaithfulness is not regarded as a joke but is taken seriously, and the Gallic treatment of the subject is generally frowned upon. I was once asked why it was that so few French boulevard plays succeeded in America, and I was forced to give the explanation that those who write critically about the theatre in New York take their family life seriously, or are unmarried, or have no children. They are, therefore, sticklers for the sanctity of marriage, especially the bachelors who know nothing about the subject, and show by their bachelorhood how frightened they are of an institution which, in their opinion, requires them to be faithful to one and the same woman for the span of their mortal lives. Thus it is that the success of *The Seven Year Itch* in New York startled the theatrical world and has since been followed by a handful of other plays in which the bonds of fidelity were made sport of by tongue-in-cheek authors.

Partly due to this attitude toward marriage, which begins at the top and works its way downward in the mass-amusement industries, young people go into marriage in this country with the idea that if there is ever the slightest suggestion of adultery, they must rush to the divorce courts, break up their homes, turn their children into waifs and then start again with another husband or wife with whom the same thing too often repeats itself. Thus one of the reasons for our abnormally high divorce rate is because our entire theatre, motion pictures, and television are geared to create this sugar-coated idea of the subject, instead of permitting our authors to show marriage as it really is.

For this reason, there are few plays produced in the American theatre in which the subject of marriage is treated in the way intelligent people would like to see it treated. On the contrary, it is one of the sacred cows of the theatre, and woe betide the producer who runs contrary to our critical tradition in this respect. However, there is some hope that our reviewers, many of whom do not object to plays portraying abnormalities, may become equally tolerant on the subject of marital vows. Notwithstanding this present condition, which I do not conceive will last forever, I strongly urge authors whose bent lies in this direction to write on the subject if they wish to do so. Not much good has ever come of accepting a tradition in the theatre, but good has often come from breaking it, as witness the career of Bernard Shaw.

At one time I wrote Shaw about the difficulties I was having with my own plays, many of which were satires on marriage and represented an unorthodox or "free thinking" point of view. The following, which was written by him thirty years ago, is equally true today.

> The plays are very good: I read them all through with undiminished appetite; and so did my wife. But you will find the same difficulty with them as I did with my Philanderer. The circle of freethinkers to whom your outlook on family life is commonplace is astonishingly small. It is hard to imagine that men with the morals of tom-cats and the conversation of camp followers are so convinced of the sacredness of indissoluble monogamy that they are unable to understand a play in which legalities do not settle everything; but they are mostly like that; and even critics who have picked up what I may call problem play jargon are as scandalized as Victorian governesses when their own cackle is brought home to them on the stage.

26. THE SOCIOLOGICAL PLAY

Inherit the Wind (The Scopes trial)	Jerome Lawrence and Robert E. Lee
They Shall Not Die (The Scottsboro trial)	John Wexley

Winterset (The Sacco-Vanzetti trial)	Maxwell Anderson
Mrs. Warren's Profession (Prostitution)	Bernard Shaw
Damaged Goods (Syphilis)	Eugene Brieux
Pillars of Society (Business greed)	Hendrik Ibsen
An Enemy of the People (Political corruption)	Hendrik Ibsen

All of these plays represent a criticism of society, and of specific evils to which the playwright was drawing attention, partly inspired with the hope of correcting them.

The American public is more apt to accept this kind of play as a reason for making changes in our social system than it will accept the more entertaining plays of satire, which it generally refuses to take seriously.

My nickname for the first three plays is "civil liberties plays" because the desire to protest infringement of our civil liberties is mainly the reason for writing them. In the best sense, they are not propaganda plays, because they use character and artistry to demonstrate the points they are trying to make.

27. PLAYS OF LABOR CONDITIONS

Strife	John Galsworthy
Waiting for Lefty	Clifford Odets
The Adding Machine	Elmer Rice
The Weavers	Gerhart Hauptmann
Pins and Needles (revue)	Arthur Arent, Marc Blitzstein, Emmanuel Eisenberg, Charles Friedman, David Gregory, and Harold J. Rome

Plays under this category are recurrently interesting to the socially minded theatregoer. Such plays are usually successful according to economic conditions at the time they are presented, and generally succeed when written in terms of the theatre and not in terms of propaganda. However, during the depression of the thirties, successful plays were written in terms of vivid realism and the Group Theatre particularly distinguished itself in producing such plays, of which Clifford Odets was a leading proponent. These plays were valuable in drawing the attention of the public to the problems of the day. One of them, a form of entertainment known as the living newspaper and entitled *one-third of a nation,* made a vivid impression.

28. *THE FARCE AND FARCE COMEDY*

Charley's Aunt	Brandon Thomas
Springtime For Henry	Benn W. Levy
Three Men on a Horse	John Cecil Holm and George Abbott
Room Service	John Murray and Allen Boretz

The farce or farce comedy has almost disappeared from the American stage, but exists in England in various forms, being still the backbone of the Christmas pantomime. It is also kept alive in revue sketches and television. While often highly amusing, this form does not lend itself to the treatment of important subjects.

29. *THE EXPRESSIONIST AND AVANT-GARDE PLAY*

Man in the Masses	Ernst Toller
From Morn Till Midnight	Georg Kaiser
The Dream Play	August Strindberg
Waiting for Godot	Samuel Beckett
The Chairs	Eugene Ionesco

The Killer	Eugene Ionesco
The Hostage	Brendan Behan
The Connection	Jack Gelber
Make Me an Offer (musical)	Mankowitz, Norman and Heneker
The Balcony	Jean Genêt
One-Way Pendulum	N. F. Simpson

These plays, the grouping together of which may well be questioned, have in common mainly a lack of conventional structure. They deal in important and unimportant subjects, in more or less coherent form. The latter groups of plays, the so-called *avant-garde,* are almost anti-theatre in their contempt for forms which have characterized the best plays of the past. In my opinion some of them are born of a despair of attempting to achieve anything of importance for humanity in a world which they expect will shortly be blown to smithereens. (How they will have wasted their time if their prognostications prove incorrect!) A survey of a few of these latter plays in England and the United States in the season of 1959–60 leaves one with the belief that the writers have achieved a substantial feeling of superiority by thumbing their noses at respectable social institutions, law and order, good manners, and nicety of language. It is possible that from this iconoclasm some new thinkers will arise, and I sincerely hope so.

30. THE POETIC PLAY

Romeo and Juliet	William Shakespeare
Macbeth	William Shakespeare
King Lear	William Shakespeare
Dr. Faustus	Christopher Marlowe
Liliom	Ferenc Molnar
Cyrano de Bergerac	Edmond Rostand
He Who Gets Slapped	Leon Andreyev

The Cherry Orchard	Anton Chekhov
The Sea Gull	Anton Chekhov
Strange Interlude	Eugene O'Neill
Lazarus Laughed	Eugene O'Neill
Marco Millions	Eugene O'Neill
The Moon of the Caribbees	Eugene O'Neill
Green Grow the Lilacs	Lynn Riggs
The Glass Menagerie	Tennessee Williams
Street Car Named Desire	Tennessee Williams
The Lady's Not For Burning	Christopher Fry
Come of Age	Clemence Dane
Paolo and Francesca	Stephen Phillips

In Chapter I, I have already given the reasons why I regard the poetic play as the highest form of theatre experience. At the risk of being repetitious, I affirm my belief that the unconscious effect of poetic expression on audiences in the theatre affords them the greatest of all satisfactions, and that this is irrespective of whether the dialogue of the play is couched in poetic language or verse, as in *Macbeth* or *King Lear,* or is poetic in its conception although written in prose. I hesitate to attempt to define what I mean by "poetic in its conception" but I believe it would include the beauty of the world, the nobility of which the human soul is capable, and the finest expression of love in its aspects of fulfillment on the one hand, and self-sacrifice on the other.

Plays which are distinguished for their beauty of language, are becoming increasingly rare on the stages of America and England. We may hope for a return to this kind of writing when authors and audiences tire of mediocre language spoken by mediocre people.

31. THE PLAY OF SEXUAL PERVERSION
OR SENSATIONAL VICE

The Green Bay Tree	Mordaunt Shairp
Prisoners of War	J. R. Ackerly
The Captive	Edouard Bourdet
Cat on a Hot Tin Roof	Tennessee Williams
Suddenly Last Summer	Tennessee Williams
Earth Spirit (Erdgeist)	Frank Wedekind
Pandora's Box	Frank Wedekind

One of the easiest methods of achieving novelty in the theatre is by exposing defects in human nature about which society in the past has imposed reticences in the hope that such reticences will prevent the spread of practices which are felt to be harmful. Where this involves shutting our eyes to evils, the shattering of taboos is highly desirable, as was the case with the subject of venereal diseases, which was considered unmentionable until the advent of Ibsen's *Ghosts* and Brieux's *Damaged Goods;* and prostitution prior to Shaw's *Mrs. Warren's Profession.* The letting in of light on subjects which should be aired is highly desirable when this produces either a remedy or an enlightened social attitude. I have already indicated my feelings that this can be carried too far in the theatre, and that writers should avoid a tendency to mistake sensationalism for importance of subject matter. Thus, cannibalism by children is so rare an event that I doubt that the production of plays on the subject will put a stop to a practice that is almost nonexistent.

The writing and presentation of plays on sexual perversion is no new experience in the European theatre. Wedekind depicted almost every form of perversion in his two sensational dramas *Earth Spirit* and *Pandora's Box.* These plays, the latter of which is a sequel to the former, exploit the sexual life of Lulu, a frigid woman who ultimately becomes a prostitute, and they contain scenes which include the exponents of a variety of sexual perversions. Indeed, in *Pandora's Box* almost every character on stage is one of a different type of sexual pervert. When I witnessed this play in Berlin, I paid special attention to the audience. It was hard to tell who were the most perverted, the people who made up the audience or the characters in the play, since this was the kind of audience the play attracted. This experience has undoubtedly prejudiced me against plays on this subject, which I have since come to regard as unhealthy for the theatre.

In concluding this chapter, I would like to point out that my dicta in regard to these various categories of plays represent personal opinions expressed by one who has labored long in the vineyard. I venture to say that if a budding author will consult with a dozen individuals engaged in the theatre, he will receive a dozen sets of opinions which differ from my own. However, the writer must learn to make up his own mind, not by remaining ignorant of the views of others but by taking them into his own consciousness, digesting them, and independently arriving at his own conclusions.

CHAPTER X

Writers and Television

T ELEVISION, which extends our sight, hearing and speech over countries and continents, is a modern miracle which was dreamed of by Western scientists only in the last fifty years, and as yet its potentialities for the service of mankind have been barely scratched. It has already achieved wonders in the fields of education, entertainment and public service, despite the fact that it has been in actual large-scale use for less than fifteen years in the United States, and for considerably shorter periods in other countries. That the medium has already reached some modicum of maturity in the few years it has been with us, is overlooked by its critics, who fail to remember how long it took the silent pictures, talking pictures, and radio to grow out of their swaddling clothes.

Television is an exciting revolutionary new medium for the playwright which is already contributing to the enlargement of theatrical entertainment, and will undoubtedly progress along lines similar to the theatre itself as it grows in maturity. The playwright should therefore consider the medium seriously, not only for its present, but also for the future which undoubtedly awaits it.

In the United States at this particular moment of writing (1960), the medium has fallen into some areas of disrepute. This should not blind us to the fact that follies are a normal accompaniment to youth. In the short time the medium has been with us it has already achieved some notable accomplishments. Among these may be mentioned the lectures and panel discussions which are providing opportunities for millions of our citizens to enhance their educations in their own homes. It has also provided many important play programs which have stimulated both the production of existing theatre plays and the writing of new plays which are especially written for this medium, and are increasingly improving in quality. Some of our leading industrialists who are sponsoring the writing and production of new American plays which provide entertainment of quality and good taste may be likened to the earlier patrons of the arts in Elizabethan days who subsidized their own superior acting companies, such as the Earl of Derby and the Lord Chamberlain's men, who were the backbone of the theatre of those days.

In this respect television is following the pattern of the earlier radio days which relied heavily on adaptations of theatre plays, novels and "originals." Under the sponsorship of the United States Steel Corporation, the Theatre Guild of the Air produced hundreds of theatre plays which were broadcast throughout the country. Today the Theatre Guild produces the United States Steel Hour, which presents mostly original television plays by American authors. Other corporations, such as the du Pont Company with its *Play-of-the-Month,* and the Standard Oil Company of New Jersey with its *Play-of-the-Week,* continue the tradition of bringing plays before audiences of millions which, but for these programs, they would never experience. Television therefore provides a fertile field for the writer which will become increasingly important as the importance of this new medium is increasingly recognized by society, and the search continues to provide better plays and productions.

Before discussing the technical aspects of writing for television, I shall begin by differentiating between writing for this medium and the motion pictures and the theatre. Television may be said to be born of the earlier arts of radio, motion pictures and the theatre. Writing for the new medium interests me, however, not only as an art in itself, but also as a means of enriching the theatre in a way that motion pictures have never done. We have had over twenty years of silent pictures and over thirty years of talking pictures, and very few important writers or plays have come from the latter into the theatre. Instead of motion pictures enriching the theatre, the enrichment has usually been in the reverse direction.

There is a good reason for this. The motion picture is a director's medium rather than the writer's. This is because the directors of the silent pictures were in command of the medium when it began to use language. Given the basic story, which may be an adaptation from a novel or a play, or even an original, the writer tends to occupy a subordinate position, and his function began in supplying the director with such dialogue as he felt was necessary where visualization was not adequate to tell the story.

I remember once, when I was visiting Eugene O'Neill at Sea Island, he was receiving fabulous offers to come to Hollywood to write a picture, and each time he would send a telegram back refusing. One day he remarked, "Look, here is another telegram I have just received, and here is my answer to the offer." The answer was NO, NO, NO, NO, NO! This attitude toward the motion picture medium is common to the important writers of the world, very few of whom are interested in a medium where they are usually subordinated to the director, or to the codes with which I will deal later. In the case of Bernard Shaw, he told me that on several occasions he had refused to have pictures made of his plays, which were to be dialogued by a Hollywood nonentity. It was only when Gabriel Pascal, who had a genius for getting people to co-operate with him, came to see Shaw and in the same breath that he told him all the Hollywood people were "schwindlers" in his most charming Hungarian accent, he added, "Of course, Mr. Shaw, nobody should write the dialogue for *Pygmalion* except yourself." As a result, Shaw transformed his own play into one of the most brilliant of all motion pictures, and by adding a spectacular scene at a party, further enabled the play to form the basis of one of the world's most successful musical plays, *My Fair Lady*.

This tendency to subordinate the writer in Hollywood explains why so few authors in that medium ever achieve success in the theatre, unless they get out before it is too late. Recent examples in this connection are Dore Schary who, beginning as a writer and ending as a top-ranking executive, left Hollywood to write *Sunrise at Campobello*, and Leonard Spigelgass, whose comedy *A Majority of One* has delighted theatre audiences all over the world.

The deterioration of the new writer in Hollywood, according to Worthington Miner, usually comes about in the following manner. He has first written a successful Broadway play, usually after some years of penury. He is then invited to Hollywood to write an original screen play at a fabulous salary. Once this job is completed, no one is interested in his creative capacity. Another Broadway play is then bought by the Hollywood producer. The new writer may be asked to make the adaptation for the mass picture audiences of this other Broadway play, and the process may be repeated. If successful, the writer may end up as a Hollywood writer at a salary of $1,500 to $3,000 a week, according to his ability to serve the highly successful director with whom he is working. He thus loses the creativity of the theatre, with all its hazards, for the certainty of Hollywood. Yet all this may change in the next few years, now that "independent" picture-making is taking the place of the old studio productions.

The motion picture medium has heretofore existed by subordinating its authors. On the other hand, the television medium operates as a writer's medium, despite the great importance of the director in production, and writers should make every effort to insure that this shall continue.

The reader will undoubtedly be familiar with the various types of plays now current in television, which include the half-hour comedy, Westerns, crime and domestic serials, the one-hour dramatic plays or comedies, as well as the plays which run to an hour and a half in time. The time classification which is imposed on us in the United States does not exist in England, but it is a fact that even in that country, plays which run much longer than two hours are not practical. I shall deal here mainly with the technique of writing the one-hour, or one-hour-and-a-half, play which comes closest to that of the theatre, and will pass over the half-hour series, except as they may be included in what is said in regard to the longer form of plays.

Television differs from the theatre in a number of aspects which affect the writer. Most of these are due to the physical limitations of the small screen, which, however, provides some advantages over the physical limitations of the theatre stage and scenery. The advantages and disadvantages of the television screen may be enumerated as follows.

There is a tendency for the screen to become crowded when too many characters are used, and it is difficult to make the principals stand out in contrast against crowds. This is sometimes helped by the use of contrasting colors of clothing, as in color television.

It is not easy in the short time space of the television play to deal with as many characters as can be used in a stage play.

The effect of the small screen is to encourage the director to pump an emotional quality into the production which is not usually quite so necessary in the theatre. The purpose of this is usually to create some extra excitement in the television play which will be communicated *via* the small screen to the viewers. However this may sometimes be overdone, and the result may be to make the play unbelievable, or the actors appear to be overacting or "hamming."

The television medium is not as effective as the theatre in connection with comedies. A reason for this is that the comedy is not helped by the laughter of the audiences, as is the case with a play in the theatre. Laughter is contagious, and a comedy is always better when it is accompanied by the laughter of the audience. This condition does not exist with television comedy or farce, which is viewed in a home with a handful of people watching it. As the result of attending many hundreds of rehearsals and dress rehearsals of comedies in empty theatres, I can testify to the fact that not only do the comedies seem far less amusing, but the actors are unaware of when and where the laughs will come, and very often the first time the play is presented before an audience they will "step on the laughs"—that is to say, interrupt the audience laughter by continuing to speak while the audience is still laughing. In order to remedy this defect, it is usual in certain half-hour television comedies, or sometimes even in longer plays, to have a studio audience present which will laugh—or even to feed in artificial laughter from a recorded tape in order to reinforce the laughter of the small studio audience. This helps to remedy the situation, but even then the tendency is for the audience seated in the home to wonder why the audience in the studio laughs so easily, when what they are viewing does not seem to be very funny.

This difficulty of the medium as regards comedies throws some light on why both comedy writing and comedy playing are not nearly as prevalent in the longer television plays as might seem desirable. The physical make-up of most studios which deal with longer plays with a large amount of scenic changes is not such as to enable a studio audience of substantial size to witness the entire play. This, however, is far more possible with a shorter play in which less scenery is used, and this scenery set up in such a way that the studio audience is able to see all the sets and register its laughs as the acting takes place. Serious plays, or serious plays interlarded with comedy, are therefore the best for the television medium. But this does not mean that the plays of a lighter character are not effective. It does mean that those comedies which are dependent upon laughter to lubricate their most effective reception are handicapped in television.

Another handicap of the medium which is not generally recognized is the fact that the same television screen which is used for a work of fiction may have been used a few minutes before to tell an extremely realistic news story. There is, therefore, always the problem that the viewing audience tends to clothe the television play with more reality than is the case in the theatre, where all the surroundings of the play, including the audience, testify to its make-believe qualities. As a result, the television play which departs from realism is handicapped by the very nature of the medium. This does not mean that unrealistic plays or unrealistic productions are not capable of good television projection and reception. It merely means that in all plays which depart from realism, special precautions must be taken in order to make the medium effective. However, when the medium is used for fantasy, it can be far more effective than the theatre, for ghosts can appear and disappear, or the human figure can be enlarged or reduced, or scenes changed as if by magic, in ways not possible at all in the theatre.

On the positive side, the television screen offers an advantage over the theatre in the use of the "close-up," which enables the actor to indicate his feelings without words and by the enlarged expression of his face, so that the visual side of the medium helps the drama. When the stage play *A Trip to Bountiful* was produced by the Theatre Guild and Fred Coe in an adaptation from a television play, it was found that a "curtain" which effectively ended in a close-up in the television play could be seen only in the first few rows of the theatre and was quite ineffective in the rest of the house. As a result, the author and director had to employ much stronger visual effects along with the use of words, in order to create effective curtains.

Another advantage of television over the theatre lies in the clarity and subtleties of speech which are possible over the microphone but cannot be conveyed in the theatre, where the voice has to be projected into a large chamber or space. It must be realized that when we are viewing television, the voice of the actor is the major component of the production. It is under our control at home and we can increase the volume of the voice so that it is much louder than in actual life. On the other hand, we cannot control the size of the picture. This is arbitrarily fixed by the size of the screen, and while a head in close-up may be somewhat larger than the human head or the head of the actor, yet whenever there are two or more persons on the screen, they are nearly always smaller than life-size. As a result, we view a television play with smaller than life-size actors, but often with voices louder than they would normally use. Because of this, while we suffer visually from the diminished size of the actor (except in close-ups) as compared with the theatre, we do not suffer audibly as we do so often in the theatre when an actor sometimes cannot be heard beyond the first five rows without seeming to be shouting.

We know from the technique of producing radio plays, that it is not necessary to see the actors at all in order to tell a good story over the radio. By skillful writing, the audience is able to tell exactly where the action is taking place, and this is helped by sound effects and other devices, such as musical "bridges." A good writer for television will remember that the audio side is better than the visual, and that where there is any doubt as to whether the actor will convey what is intended visually, words or music or both should be added to carry the meaning from the small television screen out into the room where viewing is taking place.

The television medium, unlike the theatre, can make possible swift changes of scenery. The amount of realistic scenery presently used in television studios seems to me to be quite unnecessary and often wasteful. This could be avoided to a considerable extent were the authors to write some of their scenes in "limbo"; that is to say, in areas where scenery is omitted.

As has already been stated in Chapter IV in connection with exposition in the theatre, there is little or no room or time for exposition in the television play. Moreover, television is faced with an immediate problem which, springing from an inartistic source, has been elevated from an inartistic defect into an artistic advantage. I refer to the so-called "teaser," or opening, which has become a usual part of the television technique. The purpose of the teaser is to attract as many viewers as possible to the oncoming play, and its effect is very often most valuable in creating an immediate tension in the listener and a suspense interest in the play itself. The best teaser is usually one which excites the interest of the audience by beginning with a dramatic moment which rivets attention, or by introducing a beloved acting personality, or by otherwise arousing the curiosity of the viewers. In every instance the purpose is to attract and hold the immediate interest of an audience before starting to tell the story, and this is usually done before the name of the play and the name of the author, and so forth, are flashed on the screen. Having accomplished its purpose, the writer must then be sure not to let the interest drop in the next few minutes, for even if the viewer has decided to watch the play as a result of the effect of the teaser, his interest can rapidly drop off if the play becomes dull soon thereafter.

Various rules of playwriting for the theatre which have been set forth in earlier chapters, do not vary to a very great extent in television as compared with the theatre, but there are some generalizations which will be found useful in writing a play for television as compared with the theatre. The story is usually of greater importance than characterization, or the development of character. This is due to the time limitation as compared with the theater, where we have plenty of time for the characters to develop. However, we must again warn against the literal application of a rule. Cardboard figures, stereotyped figures, stock figures, have no more place in television than they have in the theatre, but lack of time is a more potent reason for using stock figures in television for the minor characters.

The best television stories or plots are those which do not use too many characters, not merely for reasons of economy, but because the medium does not lend itself to the telling of a large number of different stories about different characters which are entwined in the plot and progress along with the play. The medium is at its best today in telling relatively simple stories of a few people in whose lives we can become deeply involved, rather than painting on a very large canvas involving great numbers of people. This can be far better achieved in motion pictures than in television. A rather striking and unhappy experience of this character was encountered when Sir Laurence Olivier's motion picture of *Richard III* was shown on television at the same time it appeared on motion picture screens in theatres throughout the country. As a television play, the film was so crowded with large numbers of people and spectacular scenes that it failed to interest its viewing audience, and this in turn reacted against the success of *Richard III* in motion picture houses, where it was effective on the large screen.

Generally speaking, remarks which apply to the subject or theme chosen for the theatre play also apply to the television play, but of course with the warning that there are certain areas of controversy in which a television play may encounter difficulties in finding an outlet. This should not deter the writer, however, if he has a compulsive desire to write the play. The writer should use the same judgment that he uses in the theatre, but of course he should not carry this to the point of absurdity. For example, he might have no trouble in finding a producer for a play advocating birth control in the theatre, but he is unlikely to find an outlet for such a subject in television at the present time.

In my opinion, the theme is just as important in television as it is in the theatre, provided that it is not delivered in the form of a message or preachment. Again, the question of controversial themes will arise, and it may also be stated as a general truth that the better the writing of the play, and the more it appeals to the common sense of the audience by its artistry, the more the theme will be acceptable. This is because if the play is written on a high plane, it is hardly likely to arouse the kind of adverse audience response which may be accorded a lesser effort.

The construction of the three-act television play, whether it be for a one-hour showing or the longer hour-and-a-half showing, also follows the general rules of suspense which exist in the theatre. Moreover, the carry-over of scenes of suspense which exist at the end of each act should be quite as great as that which is usually required in the theatre.

It may come as a surprise to the television writer that his play is actually in competition with the commercial messages. The sponsor and advertising agency make every effort and spend a large amount of money to make the commercial attention-catching, and take the minds of the listening audience away from the play and onto their product. Because of this competition, in which the author seems to have all the advantages, it is never safe to relax. Generally speaking, the beginning of each act following each commercial should rivet the attention of the listening audience as much as possible, in order to divert their minds from the interruption back to the body of the play itself. For this same reason a good strong curtain to the first act, and an even stronger curtain to the second act, is very desirable, even though it may make it a little more difficult for the sponsor to communicate his commercial message.

The nature of the screen itself makes it desirable to avoid scenes of conversation which last too long, since such scenes tend to become static and slow the pace of the play. Variations in conversational scenes can be effected, as in motion pictures, by moving from the scene itself into and out of close-ups, so that the visual effect is moving even if the actors are stationary. Again, rapid jumps to different scenes tend to increase the pace in a way which is not possible in the theatre. Crowd scenes early in the play before we know the characters, are to be avoided as they create a sense of confusion. The introduction of characters by means of close-ups is also often desirable, so as to enable us to identify them easily.

The technique of the close-up permits the use of narration, either by a special narrator or by actors themselves who can speak out their thoughts to an audience in a soliloquy in a way which is difficult to achieve in the medium of the theatre. This technique may be said to be borrowed in part from Eugene O'Neill's *Strange Interlude,* in which the actors from time to time spoke their thoughts to the audience while the action on stage stopped. The use of narration or soliloquy, stylistically, usually calls for it to take place at predetermined parts of the play, as at the beginning of each act, so that it becomes part of the style of the play and does not seem to be accidentally thrown in at an arbitrary point. However, narration or soliloquy is not limited to any fixed position in the television play.

The problem of the three-act play in television is, as it is in the theatre, to hold the attention of the audience, but it is even harder to do this in television than in the theatre. One reason for this is because it is much easier for a member of the viewing audience to turn off his machine and go to bed, as compared with the members of the audience who have to leave the theatre after having paid for their tickets, and who must brave the outside elements in order to go home. Suspense interest therefore becomes a very important part of television writing and partly explains why so many crime programs seem to survive over the years. Certainly there is no easier way to provoke suspense interest than to witness the discovery of a murder, and then to embark on a manhunt to ascertain who committed the crime.

The television play has to solve all the same problems of suspense for the first, second and third acts as the stage play. However, in the hour-and-a-half play there are additional factors which make it difficult to hold the attention of the audience. The first of these is the tendency of the eyes to become tired watching the television set for too long a period. Despite all of the improvements which have been made in this field, it is nevertheless a tiring medium to watch as compared with the theatre. Our eyes are somewhat relieved in watching color television, but the ordinary black-and-white television tends to become monotonous after viewing it for a certain length of time, which in turn forces the viewer to be less receptive to the play as it progresses into the third act. For these reasons, the hour-and-a-half television play seems to suffer from almost a chronic disease in that it tends to lose much of its listening audience in the third act. Because of this, it is not desirable in television to relax the tension of the play after the second act in a way which is common in the theatre. For instance, taking the old rule of getting your character up a tree in Act One, throwing stones at him in Act Two, and getting him down again in Act Three, we should modify this rule in television as regards Act Three by saying, "And keep on throwing stones at him all through Act Three and do not bring him down until the end of the play, if possible."

The question of the ending of the play is also very important in the television medium. When the Theatre Guild produced the first six one-hour plays on the National Broadcasting Company's network after World War II, we followed very carefully the old rule of the theatre that a play should have a beginning, a middle and an end. When we returned to the medium several years later, we found that another formula was highly popular in the studios. It was that while a play should have a beginning and a middle, it is not at all necessary that it should have an end. Indeed, the tendency was to leave the end to the imagination of the audience. In most instances, this left the audience with a feeling of bewilderment, followed by disappointment at having spent an hour viewing the story without reaching any conclusion. This practice, while generally discarded today, can be used again with success where occasion calls for it, as where the end of the play can be safely left to the imagination of the audience, or where it might be censorable if fully disclosed!

After having written the first draft of his television play, the writer will do well to consider: Is the end of the play too easy to prognosticate, and if so, can he remedy this in some way, as by some sort of twist in the story? Is the act spacing correct? This is to say, does the play divide fairly evenly into the necessary three acts? Can the leading characters be developed so that they will be attractive for stars to play? This is because in television, even more than in the theatre, parts for stars are desirable. Actors and actresses with reputations now tend to be more "choosy" in this field than was formerly the case, and the question of whether they will or will not appear in a television play usually depends upon whether the role is important enough to tempt them. If the writer is attempting to say something beyond the story itself, has he made his point abundantly clear without writing in special speeches or messages at the end of the play? If not, ascertain if he cannot achieve the same purpose by dwelling on the theme from place to place throughout the play so that by the time we come to the end, we have absorbed it painlessly.

The writer should not be discouraged if he finds that the editor attached to the staff of the producer calls for some changes in his play. The editor is usually the first to read the play, and if, as is often the case, he is a creative editor, he can be of great help in assisting the author in overcoming any shortcomings in his work. The same may be true of the director selected.

Part of the work of the television writer consists of adapting theatre plays, motion pictures and novels for television. The adaptation of theatre plays looks, on the surface, an easy undertaking. In actual fact it bristles with difficulties. Take for instance the simple attempt to cut down the stage play from a time period of two and a half hours in the theatre to one hour on television. In theory all the author has to do is to cut out the extraneous characters and leave the main story. In practice this will usually not work. I remember that in our first television play, in the year of television innocence 1947, done in partnership with NBC, we applied this method to *John Ferguson*, leaving in all the so-called "big" scenes and cutting the connecting material. The result was that we turned a fine drama into a melodrama with a series of climactic scenes all piled on top of one another. The adapting of a stage play not only requires the use of considerably more scenery (especially where the stage play is in one set) but it also requires a re-creation of the play in terms of the television medium, which shuns long static scenes and calls for physical as well as mental action. While it is usually possible to use the best or most striking scenes of a stage play in the adaptation, the adapter must deal with the story as a whole, as though he were writing a totally new play. Most of Shakespeare's plays need special television treatment in the identification of characters by the viewers, and are often unsuccessful because they do not receive it.

What has been said about adapting novels and motion pictures for the theatre applies in general terms to television, except of course that motion pictures are more suited for adaptation to this medium than to the theatre.

I have always felt that one of the advantages of live television, as compared with film or motion pictures, was the lack of complete perfection, which is an accompaniment to a television play acted by live actors rather than depicted on a film. Every television viewer knows that life is full of errors, for he sees this every day in news pictures on his screen. Real people make mistakes, hesitate over words, say a line and correct it, and this goes on day after day, and is associated with a sense of reality. Why do our television producers believe that every actor must be absolutely word perfect and never correct himself in the play as he would actually do in life? It has become one of the conventions of the medium that there must be no hesitation or, as it is called, "fluffing"; and hundreds of dollars are spent in the remaking of films in order to correct mistakes made by the actor, so that the film is finally made with what I call "the imperfection of perfection." With the introduction of magnetic tape, which is now revolutionizing the television medium, there is a tendency to repeat the error of the motion pictures and television films, and to demand a perfection in the final product which is not consistent with life itself. I hope this will not prevail with tape recording, for it will ultimately result in the same difficulty we now have in television plays recorded on films.

One of the advantages of so-called live television is that the actor has to learn the entire role and play it in one performance, so that his emotions grow with the progression of the play, and the development of his performance reaches a peak either in the dress rehearsal or in the performance on the air. The great value of the tape recording is that it preserves this acting performance so that what we see on the television screen is the actual final performance of the play as rendered by the actors. Quite different is the case with the motion picture film, whether used on the screen or in television. Here the work of the actors and actresses is performed in a short scene at a time, and the pieces put together in the cutting room. No matter how good the performance is, there is usually something synthetic in the final result. This should not be imported into tape recording.

Many writers disdain writing for television because of the restraints put upon the subject matter by the sponsors and advertising agencies. I believe it has sometimes been lucky for the world that we have had such restraints in the past. Some of the greatest writers in the theatre, and certainly one of them the greatest writer of all time, William Shakespeare, were always under the severe restraint of not being able to criticize their particular form of government. Shakespeare could not write a play attacking Queen Elizabeth, or even her father, King Henry VIII, or the social and economic conditions of the peasants and working classes in England, or the divine right of kings, or the Church of England, or whatever happened to be a treasonable question of the day. The same was true of Molière. The result is that Shakespeare's and Molière's plays are still alive in the theatre of today. Had Shakespeare written what are called "socially conscious plays" he might have languished in prison instead of writing over thirty noncontroversial masterpieces. This shows that there are plenty of important subjects to write about without entering into the realm of political or economic controversy. I do not mean by this to suggest that censorship is desirable, only that great works of art can be written in spite of it in some of its forms.

Many of us remember the depression of the thirties, and what we were in the habit of calling the "socially conscious plays." They were written almost entirely about the economic problems of that time, and with the improvements in our economic system which took place later, the targets against which these plays were aimed have largely disappeared. As a result, the plays are usually obsolete and will not be of much interest unless these economic conditions return.

Television and motion pictures both are governed by codes which represent attempts to draw up a "book of rules" on what writers may or may not deal with in their plays—what they can write and what they cannot write.

The Motion Picture Production Code was drawn up in 1930 by the Motion Picture Association of America, Inc., an organization made up of picture manufacturers, and while it has been modified somewhat in the last few years, the original prohibitions are still in existence, although not as strictly enforced as was formerly the case. The National Association of Radio and Television Broadcasters prepared in 1950 a code which was largely a copy of the motion picture code, although in some respects it was more drastic, since it was based on the fact that television is brought into the living room of the home.

It is ironic that the American mass entertainment media, which includes motion pictures, radio and television, have the strongest moral codes of any country in the world. If it were possible to influence national morality by the enforcement of codes in the mass entertainment fields, we should as a consequence be the most moral nation in the world. However, so far from this being the case, our crime and divorce rates are higher than those of any other country and indicate clearly that there is very little relationship between morality as enforced by codes in the mass entertainment media, and morality as practiced in the real world. It is quite possible that the existence of these codes in the mass entertainment media are to some extent responsible for the discrepancy between the morality of our codes and the morality of our people. The mores of the country are greatly influenced by the great masters of literature who propound their ethics through the medium of important books and plays. Because of the necessity of the writer to create works of art which fit into the limitations of these codes, the writing of such plays is usually done by authors who sugar-coat their stories and create an unreal world which does not in any way fool the listener, who reads the newspapers and knows quite well what goes on in the world of reality. However, in this respect conditions are constantly improving.

There are other provisions in the so-called television code which should be brought to the attention of the writer. One of the most important is that in regard to crime. The criminal must always be punished before the picture is over, or he must be on his way to punishment. The reason this seems to be so absurd is because the intention is to show that crime does not pay. As a result of this time-worn excuse, we fill the home television screens with an avalanche of crime stories, all of which end up with the above cliché. Actually, the very pictures themselves belie the idea that crime does not pay, for it has certainly paid the purveyors of crime series, otherwise they would not be using them to sell their goods to the public. The exploitation of crime under this hypocritical excuse for commercial purposes is obviously having a bad effect on the youth of the country as a whole. Thus television, which should enable the best of the theatre, literature and education to be brought into the home, is often misused in this way to spread crime, corruption and juvenile delinquency. However, it is not possible to fool the American public for long. They will ultimately call a halt to the debasement of the medium. The public knows that it is being fooled when it watches these pictures where the code is strictly enforced, and in which every species of brutality can be exploited so long as the criminal is punished. It is equally being fooled by stories in which every marriage ends happily. The audience has been fed so much nonsense in the past that, with certain exceptions, it regards the world of television plays and motion pictures as a sort of Never-Never Land, to which we listen in the same way that we listen to fairy tales.

We as a people have a great desire to better ourselves, and the motion pictures and television should be a source of inspiration in guiding us. It is obvious that these media are susceptible of great improvement and will not long continue to operate under conditions which prevent them from being used by first-class writers. Indeed, a notable improvement is already taking place and may be expected to continue.

Fortunately, we do not stand still in America. Ideas change. We are becoming more broad-minded. As the public tires of stereotyped writing and bad productions, the good writer will be more and more in demand for the television medium. In this respect, the public taste is like a pendulum and keeps swinging back and forth. I am a firm believer in the fact that there is nothing we can produce in the theatre, motion pictures, or television which is too good for the public. If the public is not interested in works of a high standard, it is because the authors and producers have failed in making them interesting. And because of this fact, because we have perhaps the most intelligent audience in the world, an audience which is growing in its demands, our mass media will keep improving to meet the public taste and will attract more and more fine writers to devote their efforts to this end.

There are also many good reasons why a writer whose main interest is in writing plays for the theatre, should use the television medium in order to gain experience which will be helpful to him later in the theatre. A writer in television should give as much time in his beginning efforts as he can spare, and do his best to write the finest television play of which he is capable. He will surely find, with the great competition which exists among programs today, that if he has put his heart and soul into the television play, it will find a response among some of the better programs. Not only will he have the experience of trying to do his best writing, but if the television play is accepted and produced, it is always possible that it will arouse attention and serve as a basis for a theatre play or a motion picture. Therefore, the new writer for television should regard it not as a secondary medium, but as a steppingstone to the more extensive and lucrative media of motion pictures and theatre. Examples of successful plays and motion pictures which have stemmed from television plays are almost too numerous to quote, but I give the following as examples: Paddy Chayefsky's *Middle of the Night,* Ira Levin's *No Time for Sergeants,* Arnold Schulman's *A Hole in the Head,* N. Richard Nash's *The Rainmaker,* Horton Foote's *A Trip to Bountiful,* and Frederick Knott's *Dial "M" for Murder.* The two plays which I have liked best in the season of 1959–60 are *The Miracle Worker* by William Gibson and *The Tenth Man* by Paddy Chayefsky, both of them formerly television writers.

Other television plays have been made directly into motion pictures, such as Reginald Rose's *Twelve Angry Men.* An amusing example of the metamorphosis of a play is found in Arnold Schulman's *My Fiddle Has Three Strings,* first produced by us at the Westport Country Playhouse. Then the author rewrote it as a successful television play, *My Heart Is a Forgotten Hotel.* Then he rewrote it as an unsuccessful play *Hole in the Head* which finally became a most successful motion picture!

My final advice for the writer for television is to disregard all advice, including my own, which tends to make the medium one which calls for the following of rules. The only rules which actually will always prevail in television are those which are due to the physical limitations of the screen. For the rest, television is a new medium and susceptible to the freest usage. The author, like Caesar, should look for new worlds to conquer. The opportunities are there for him to find.

CHAPTER XI

Conclusions

THROUGHOUT these chapters, I have endeavored to emphasize the fact that the work of the playwright is of the highest importance and that probably more than in any other field he can influence his own times, as well as the future, by the inspiration of his vision and its effect on his audiences.

Of far greater importance to the playwright than any books or courses on playwriting is the general rule that no matter how competent he becomes in the art of playwriting, what he garners from life itself is the best education for the writing of plays. Probably a more banal statement could not be made, yet it is often misunderstood. Indeed, many writers and teachers are of the opinion that the playwright learns most by working in the theatre itself. I disagree.

One of the curses of our age is that we live in an era of specialization, as a result of which the playwright, believing that his specialty is the theatre, tends to live in the theatre more than he does in the outside world, and to become corrupted by its influences. Actually there is often no greater ignoramus than the specialist who knows practically everything about his own subject and almost nothing about anything else. When we state that the playwright learns more from life itself than he can in any other way, we also add that he should avoid specialization, and even that specialization which is involved in the writing of plays. Shakespeare, generally remembered as a specialized writer of plays, might equally have regarded the writing of poetry as his second career. Indeed, had he never written a play at all, his poems would have entitled him to a high position in English literature. I further believe that if novels had been current at the time, he might also have written many of these after his retirement from active life in the theatre.

Shaw's plays are greatly enhanced by his vast political, social and economic knowledge. He was also familiar with many aspects of business practices, some of which were gained in actual business life. Robert Sherwood spent many years in the newspaper world and in government work, assisting Harry Hopkins and F. D. Roosevelt. Maxwell Anderson was a newspaperman before he became a playwright. Eugene O'Neill spent several years before the mast before he became a playwright and much of his later writing is based on what he learned in his early life. If anything, O'Neill's later insulated way of living was not too valuable for him as an artist, and resulted in his relying heavily in his later plays on memories of his younger days.

Because we live in a period which overvalues specialization, we tend to forget that the best-educated man is often one who has learned enough of all the specialized fields to have broadened his own views in his own particular field. It was once generally believed, as part of our modern education, that while a general knowledge of the humanities is valuable, a man should specialize only in one field. The fallacy of this was exposed by the late Charles F. Kettering, who constantly asserted that specialization, despite all the values which were derived from it, could become disastrous if too rigidly adhered to. I remember on one occasion he spoke of the fallacy which existed not so long ago, of dividing all chemists into organic and inorganic chemists. Kettering pointed out that while a man might specialize in one field or the other, he was not really a good chemist unless he understood the field in which he did not specialize, and furthermore was also a physicist, a metallurgist, and an engineer—in other words, a complete scientist. He likened specialization to the threads which form the warp in the fabric of knowledge—that is to say, the specialist follows his line of specialization through the length of the fabric. But he pointed out that the cross threads pass over every one of the threads of specialization, and it was in this realm that he felt the broadest education was secured.

In my opinion, the successful writer today, whether he chooses to write for the theater, the novel, motion pictures, or television, must familiarize himself so far as possible with every aspect of life, with all its specializations. He will not be any the worse for knowing something of atomic science, of the economics of large and small nations, of the operation of large businesses as well as grocery stores, and whatever knowledge exists of the conscious or subconscious of the human psyche. He should be as familiar with the religions of peoples as he is with the effects produced by lack of religion. He should be equally at home among the strait-laced and the drinkers, the suburbanites and the city dwellers, and the sophisticates and the rural population. However, he will find that he will often do his best work in dealing with the people and situations in which he has his own roots. But this should be no limitation, for while he is doing this, he will also deal with situations which have come to interest him later in life, and may even employ incidents from his early life illuminated by viewpoints acquired later, as O'Neill did in *The Iceman Cometh*.

That the active creative mind is not limited to the exercise of a single profession is well illustrated by the versatility of many of the greatest painters of the Renaissance. For example, Leonardo da Vinci was not only one of the most magnificent painters of his era, but he was also a skilled scientist and inventor, having invented among other devices, the general principles of the helicopter. He was also an important architect, and developed many substantial engineering projects for the reigning Duke of Milan. Michelangelo, who was a great painter, a magnificent sculptor and an architect, also supervised the building of the walls of Florence near San Miniato. Other Florentine sculptor-architects, such as Brunelleschi, made important contributions to the arts of building and civil engineering. Thus those painters were not only artists, but were also what we call scientists today, indicating that the techniques of art and of science are not incompatible.

Indeed, scientific knowledge is likely to be of special value to the playwrights of today and tomorrow, for as we move more and more into a scientific era, it becomes impossible for the best minds to shut out the developments of science and to treat them as though they did not exist. The average man, schooled in the humanities, tends to be intimidated by the idea of possessing some scientific knowledge. Actually the fact that children can be taught to understand basic science during their high school periods is an indication that any writer of ability can master the basic principles of science without having to specialize in it. Armed with an elementary knowledge of the basic underlying principles of chemistry and physics, if a writer wishes to become more proficient in any particular branch in order to write a play on a subject which includes a background of science or a knowledge of scientific material, he can always secure this additional information from the expert, and be able to understand it.

Among playwrights and novelists who have had scientific experience may be mentioned the famous Austrian, Dr. Arthur Schnitzler, who practiced medicine throughout his life, and was one of the finest playwrights of his day. The same is true of Dr. James Bridie of Glasgow, who wrote many fine plays and was also an honored medical practitioner. His best plays, *The Sleeping Clergyman* and *The Anatomist*, might not have been written but for his medical knowledge. And Anton Chekhov might not have written with such delicate perception about humanity but for his scientific education as a medical man which added to his artistic vision. Dr. A. J. Cronin, one of the best British novelists, was also a medical doctor. Dr. William Carlos Williams, one of America's best poets, is a practicing medical man, while Dr. Merrill Moore, author of many fine sonnets, was a recognized psychiatrist attached to the Massachusetts General Hospital.

Living is a process of education which has nothing necessarily to do with the places in which one is educated. Bernard Shaw had the sketchiest of high school educations; Eugene O'Neill never made a university degree, having been expelled from Princeton and having spent but a short period at Harvard. Shakespeare's lack of formal education beyond a little Latin and less Greek is well known. Indeed the fact that so many men have achieved fame in literature and in the theatre without a formal education is a tribute to the fact that they have taken their education where they have found it, in life itself, in their joys and sorrows, in their surroundings, and from reading. I have found that most of the good writers for the theatre of today are well-read men, and the best of them have learned the technique of living in an atmosphere in which they live only vicariously in the theatre. Such writers have had to stretch their imaginations and realize that there are no limits to what the human mind can accomplish in the pursuit of knowledge. The adding up of this knowledge in the light of experience becomes wisdom, and in the long run, wisdom is what we demand as a major commodity from our major playwrights.

One of the surest ways of acquiring elasticity of mind is by breaking away from the idea that we are limited to working in one field in order to master it. This conclusion is not only valuable for the theatre, but for all occupations. I remember when I was quite young, hearing a lecture by Lord Roseberry on the subject of the Englishman of the nineties. He stressed quite forcibly the fact that most Englishmen not only worked in a business or profession, but also had a hobby which prevented them from being lopsided as a result of too specialized an immersion in their daily work. In my knowledge of many Englishmen throughout my life, I have observed how true this has been, and how many of my British friends are not only expert in their businesses but also in other fields. I remember Dr. William Martin, one of the principal authorities on patent law, was also an authority on Shakespeare. A man I knew who worked in a patent agent's office was not only a good technical assistant, but had written an encyclopedia of music. The very diversification of their interests made them broader and more interesting men, and from their avocations they brought to their vocations a point of view which freshened their interest in their daily work.

At this point I cannot stress too strongly to the young writer the necessity for dealing in important or serious subjects if he intends to make a career in the theatre. The fact that the present-day theatre seems to deal more favorably with escapist plays on trivial subjects should not deter him. Nothing ultimately becomes more boring than frivolity, and while it may seem at times that the public taste demands that serious subjects be avoided in the theatre, this is a temporary condition which may cease today or tomorrow, at the moment when a contemporary playwright deals with an important subject in terms of sufficient theatrical excitement.

The mounting high costs of producing serious plays in the American and English theatres, resulting in the continuous raising of theatre-ticket prices, is one of the reasons why authors, even when dealing with serious subjects, so often resort to sensationalism in an effort to obtain box-office success. One of the greatest contributors to these costs is the scenic brotherhood in all departments, few of whom are ready to assume responsibility for the harm they are doing to the theatre. Indeed, the tendency of many of them is to blame the producers and directors for their own shortcomings. Producers, writers and directors should remember that two of the greatest periods of the theatre, the Greek and the Elizabethan, flourished without scenery at all in the modern sense of the word. Moreover, millions of Chinese, Japanese and other Asian audiences have supported the theatre for hundreds of years without scenery, relying on the imaginations of the audiences to supply this. Are our audiences less intelligent and less imaginative? I doubt it. If, as is happening now, the total scenic costs—which often amount to over one-third and sometimes one-half of the cost of producing and operating plays—are driving good plays out of the theatre, then we should as soon as possible drive extravagant realistic scenery out of the theatre.

The playwright of today is the living link between the theatre of the past and the theatre of tomorrow. If he does not regard himself as a custodian of the best traditions of the past as well as the creator of innovations of the present and the future, we shall make little progress in the theatre and will pass but little on to posterity. The play which deals successfully in the artistic sense with a subject of importance tends to live on as long as the subject is of human interest. In this connection, tragedy seems to live longer than comedy. If we will examine the reputations made in the theatre by the world's greatest writers over the past twenty-five hundred years, we will find that with few exceptions these writers did not deal with the frivolities of the day. (One of the notable exceptions is the theatre of the English Restoration, much of which has survived because of the satiric viewpoint of its playwrights, and the wit with which they dealt with the follies of their day.)

What do I mean when I refer to important or serious subjects? Euripides dealt with family relations (*Oedipus*) and war (*The Trojan Women*); Aristophanes with social subjects such as government and war; Shakespeare with important historical characters in action, and such subjects as jealousy in *Othello,* vengeance in *The Merchant of Venice,* family feuds in *Romeo and Juliet,* and hypocrisy in *Measure for Measure.* Molière wrote a gallery of portraits exemplifying human traits, and especially human follies. The modern writers who made their greatest reputation, such as Shaw, Sherwood, Maxwell Anderson, Behrman, O'Neill and so forth, dealt importantly with important subjects of their day.

A recent examination of the new plays being written by some of the young playwrights of England and France leads me to believe that there is a lack of interest in spiritual or intellectual values on the part of these writers which bodes ill for the future of their theatres. It is quite understandable that in an era of changing values, the ridiculing of old forms and traditions should be the order of the day. This is equally true of many of the young writers of this country, who, following in the new tradition of decadence, seem to have banished intellectual content from their plays and replaced it with pictures of degenerate characters in futile action.

Those who criticize these writers for their lack of form and intellectual content should remember that from a free theatre which breaks with the traditions of the past, there may well arise an important theatre of the future. Certainly the young *avant-garde* theatres of the democracies are to be preferred to the absurd plays of "socialist realism" which are now the pampered darlings of the subsidized Soviet theatres. In general, these plays of socialist realism present about as much "realism" as a fairy tale, being generally dedicated to the proposition that the Soviet system is producing industrial heroes and cultural heroes of Communism who, like Saint George, are destroying the dragons of distrust or skepticism for the ultimate success of Communism. Surely the naïve Horatio Alger-like qualities of these plays cannot deceive even the most receptive audiences. On the other hand, we must be equally critical of the sex-ridden plays of our own *avant-garde* writers. They too are as deficient in one way as the Soviet plays are in another. One of their English apologists (and erstwhile perpetrators), Wolf Mankowitz, was recently quoted in *Newsweek* magazine apropos of English playwrights of today to the effect that "The satirist doesn't know any solutions. The assumption of these socially conscious midgets that they can stand up, hurl a few thunderbolts and change anything, is absurd." When England possessed giants who were writing plays, instead of midgets, these giants such as Bernard Shaw, John Galsworthy and others, did stand up and hurl thunderbolts, and changed the thinking of the Western world. The English theatre, like our own, obviously needs more giants and fewer midgets.

In my opinion, there has never been a time in the history

of the world theatre when plays with spiritual values were more needed than at present. We particularly need plays in our theatres which will give leadership to Western ideals which are in jeopardy from a new civilization which inhibits free writing and independent thinking on the part of its writers. Never did a task need more doing—and who is doing it? When fascism was a threat to the world, Robert Sherwood, Maxwell Anderson, Sidney Howard, S. N. Behrman, Lillian Hellman and a dozen others wrote plays burning with conviction on the subject. Playwrights who are not midgets had better take up their pens and deal with the problems of the present-day world, or sooner than they think their pens may be taken from them.

The critics of our day share an equal responsibility with our writers in influencing the public taste. In the past few years, too many of them have been guilty of condoning plays steeped in sexual decadence and moral corruption, merely because they have been disguised under the mask of poetry or written with strong dramatic power by some of our most successful American playwrights. In the best period of the American theatre of thirty years ago, the critics were the eager supporters of the most serious writers. The student of drama will experience a thrill of excitement if he will read the magnificently written notices of the drama critics on the first viewing of Eugene O'Neill's masterpieces, *Strange Interlude* and *Mourning Becomes Electra*. (These can be found in the press books of the Theatre Guild collection in the Yale Sterling Library.)

The following excerpt from Brooks Atkinson's review of *Mourning Becomes Electra* in *The New York Times* of October 27, 1931, will illustrate:

> ... Using a Greek legend as his model, Eugene O'Neill has reared up a universal tragedy of tremendous stature—deep,

dark, solid, uncompromising and grim. It is heroically thought out and magnificently wrought in style and structure, and it is played by Alice Brady and Mme. Nazimova with consummate artistry and passion. Mr. O'Neill has written overwhelming dramas in the past. In *Strange Interlude* he wrote one almost as long as this trilogy. But he has never before fulfilled himself so completely; he has never commanded his theme in all its variety and adumbrations with such superb strength, coolness and coherence. To this department, which ordinarily reserves its praise for the dead, *Mourning Becomes Electra* is Mr. O'Neill's masterpiece.

Our present-day critics are capable of equal efforts could they but encounter genuine masterpieces in the modern theatre. However, when serious plays are produced today there is too often a tendency for the critics to appraise them in terms of technical playwriting rather than in terms of their content. That such plays will not appeal to the "expense account" box office addict is a foregone conclusion, but among the millions of theatregoers in this country there are enough to support the play of serious intent even if it falls short of being a masterpiece. Indeed, unless an atmosphere of appreciation for serious work is nurtured by the critics, there will neither be masterpieces nor any other kind of serious plays on serious subjects in our theatre. One of the first steps in creating such an atmosphere is already in existence, the almost perennial deploring by the serious critics that our theatre is not dealing with important issues. The second step, the judging of such plays by the same standards with which the rest of the theatre is judged, is yet to come —for the amazing condition exists that the defects in the trivial unimportant play, so long as it provides good entertainment, are often overlooked, while the defects of the play on an important subject are usually highlighted. William

Inge, speaking of the treatment his least successful play, *A Loss of Roses,* received from the New York critics, is quoted as saying, "It amazes me how violent critics get when a play is not a hit. They act as though it were a personal affront to them that such a presentation should be made. Everyone realizes that the theatre is in a bad condition. But you don't treat a sick child by beating her. I think a playwright who has set out to write a serious piece of work for the theatre ought to be able to expect respect. Instead, I was treated as if I had spit on the floor."

The young playwrights, confronted with this condition, should remember that fashions exist in dramatic criticism as they do in any other branch of the theatre and of life. Once a playwright appears who again deals with serious subjects in terms of such theatrical excitement that he can overcome the objections of the critics, they will be the first to hail him. Shaw did it fifty years ago—new writers can do it today.

It is interesting at this point to speculate on what will be the effect of the many grants to playwrights now being made by the Ford Foundation, which seems to presuppose that the playwright will do better work if he is attached or associated with a theatre which is one of a group of regional theatres located in provincial cities. It is too early yet to ascertain the value of such grants given under these conditions. It would seem that some of these theatres have given unusual opportunities to young playwrights which have produced good results, and that the giving of such grants may well help them in learning their craft.

The value of combining the grant to the playwright with a grant to a director or to a little theatre will ultimately depend upon the professional ability of the latter to help the young playwright by making a production worth while. The purpose of these grants is to help simultaneously both the new writers as well as the directors and the little theatre groups in the various cities. Whether the desire to help the little theatre groups may not in turn act as a deterrent to the young American playwright is yet to be learned. I have recently run across at least three young playwrights who are desperately in need of grants in order that they may live while they are writing new plays, and none of them will apply for grants which, in their opinion, carry with them not only banishment to cities in which there is very little interest in the theatre, but also condemn their work to be put on by nonprofessional producers, inexperienced directors, and partly amateur actors.

There are of course many regional theatres throughout the country to which the above remarks do not apply. It is desirable that such theatres should be directly subsidized, so that having first achieved the necessary level of professionalism, and having developed good audiences for experimental or new plays, they can then produce successfully the plays of novices under the practiced hands of thoroughly experienced directors and actors. Where the regional theatres have already reached professional competence, the grants for trying out new plays will of course be of considerable value in aiding the theatres to continue in existence.

The granting of subsidies by the Ford Foundation to young poets in order to enable them to devote time to the writing of plays seems to me to be a forward-looking step in the right direction. If successful, it may well result in bringing our poets back to the theatre, from which they have been absent far too long.

My final conclusions take me back to my first chapter. Above and beyond all that can be accomplished by teaching, there remain as the prime considerations the aims and aspirations of the playwright. The theatre offers him companionship with the great playwrights and poets down the ages. The writer alone is the custodian of his talent, which is God-given. Whether he aims to achieve in the highest echelon, or on a lower level, he has but to be true to the best of himself, and he will be true to the best of the theatre. To quote James Russell Lowell:

> Greatly begin!
> Though thou have time
> But for a line,
> Be that sublime.
> Not failure, but low aim,
> Is crime!

INDEX

Abbott, George, 24
Abe Lincoln in Illinois, 194
Abnormal psychology, 44
Ackerly, J. R., 44
Actors, selection, 153-55
Actor's point of view, 95-96
Adaptions, 167-72
Adding Machine, The, 63, 116, 145
Affairs of Anatol, The, 36
Agent, play, 153
Aguglia, Mimi, 201
Ah, Wilderness!, 60, 141, 183
American Dramatists Guild, 153
American Dream, 179
Anastasia, 124, 192
Anatomist, The, 240
Anderson, Maxwell, 39, 55, 57, 89,
   90-91, 96, 194, 203, 237, 243, 245
Andersonville Trial, The, 186
Andreyev, 27
Anna and the King of Siam, 172
Anna Christie, 124
Archer, William, 73
Archibald, William, 103
Aristophanes, 19, 51, 190, 243
Aristotle, 38
Arms and the Man, 71, 192
Artificial comedy, 181-82
"Aside" in the theatre, 79-80
Aspern Papers, The, 170
As You Like It, 146
Atkinson, Brooks, 24, 245-46
Auprès de ma Blonde, 95
Avant-garde plays, 116-17, 208-09,
   244

Back to Methuselah, 185
Bacon, Roger, 83
Bagnold, Enid, 65
Baker, George Prince, 23, 91, 124,
   150
Baltimore, 90, 138
Barrie, James M., 199
Barry, Philip, 23, 27, 57, 98, 121,
   180, 185
Bartholomae, Philip, 173
Bayreuth Festival, 16
Beaumont, 172
Beckett, Samuel, 37
Behan, Brendan, 89, 116
Behrman, S. N., 39, 47, 55, 57, 60,
   92, 95, 99, 104, 105, 135-36, 181,
   182, 243, 245
Belasco, David, 160, 187
Bells Are Ringing, 127
Bennett, Arnold, 30
Bennett, Richard, 108
Berlin, Irving, 173
Bittersweet, 173
Blackmer, Sidney, 63
Blue Bird, The, 199
Bolshoi Ballet, 16
Bolton, Guy, 124-25, 173, 192
Booth, Shirley, 63
Booth Theatre, 139
Born Yesterday, 40, 190
Boston, 92, 105, 108
Boy Meets Girl, 40, 173
Brady, Alice, 246
Brand, Dorothea, 98
Brecht, Berthold, 39

251

Earth Spirit, 45, 211
Eaton, Walter Prichard, 24
Edinburgh Festival, 16
Effects, scenic, 159
Eliot, T. S., 27
Elizabethan theatre, 36
Elizabeth the Queen, 90, 194
Emperor Jones, The, 61
Empire Theatre, 111
Endgame, 37
End of Summer, 47
Enemy of the People, An, 52
English 47 Workshop, 23-24
Entertainment field, plays about, 195-96
Epilogue, 146-47
Episode, the, 36
Ervine, St. John, 30, 85, 144
Euripides, 19, 51, 122, 243
Everyman, 184
Expressionist plays, 208-09

Fairy tale, the, 199-200
Family life comedies and dramas, 183
Fanny's First Play, 129
Farce and farce comedy, 208
Father, The, 73
Faust, 76
Ferber, Edna, 195
Festivals, 16
Fields, Joseph, 128, 179
First act, the, 133-35
First Man, The, 150
Fledermaus, 174
Fletcher, 172
Flying Dutchman, The, 117
Folk comedy, drama, or legend, 200-01
Fontanne, Lynn, 90, 95-96, 105, 136
Ford Foundation, 24, 163, 247, 248
Ford's Theatre, 90
Foote, Horton, 234
Form, 121
Formula play, 150-51
Fosse, Robert, 174
Foul language, 107-09
Four-act play, 131-32
Franken, Rose, 29
Freedman, Harold, 47
From Morn Till Midnight, 115

Frost, Robert, 27
Fry, Christopher, 27

Galsworthy, John, 30, 42, 55, 244
Garrick Gaieties, 99
Gauguin, Paul, 20
Geisha, The, 176
Gestation period, 82
Getting Married, 51, 204
Ghosts, 211
Gibson, Will, 234
Gielgud, John, 158
Gilbert, William S., 172
Gilroy, Frank, 188
Giraudoux, 39
Girl of the Golden West, The, 187
Glaspell, Susan, 111
Glass Menagerie, The, 73, 80
Goethe, 77
Gogol, 191
Gold, 61
Goodrich, Frances, 37
Gozzi, 121
Great Big Doorstep, The, 172-73
Great God Brown, The, 50, 79
Green, Adolph, 127, 174
Greene, Patterson, 74
Green Grow the Lilacs, 27, 188
Green Pastures, 200
Guiterman, Arthur II, 111, 128
Gwyn, Nell, 147

Hackett, Frances and Albert, 37, 171, 172
Haggott, John, 158
Hairy Ape, The, 61
Hamlet, 140
Hammerstein, Oscar II, 27, 168, 173, 175, 176
Hart, Moss, 40, 64, 99, 179, 191
Harvey, 197, 200
Hayes, Helen, 96
Heartbreak House, 92, 116, 149
Hedda Gabler, 122
Heflin, Van, 47
Heiress, The, 170
Helburn, Theresa, 24, 139
Hellman, Lillian, 29, 111, 129, 245
Hepburn, Katharine, 97, 98
He Who Gets Slapped, 27

DATE DUE

DATE DUE			
MAY 1 4 1985			
GAYLORD			PRINTED IN U.S.A.